A Guided Reader to Early Years and Primary English

A Guided Reader to Early Years and Primary English draws on extracts from the published work of some of the most influential education writers to provide insight, guidance and clarity about key issues affecting the Early Years and primary English curriculum.

The book brings together key extracts from classic and contemporary writing and contextualises these in both theoretical and practical terms. The extracts are accompanied by a summary of the key ideas and issues raised, questions to promote discussion and reflective practice, and annotated further reading lists to extend thinking.

Taking a thematic approach and including a short introduction to each theme, the chapters cover:

- models of and approaches to Early Years and primary English;
- speaking and listening in English lessons: story-telling, drama, booktalk and debate;
- reading and responding to texts in English lessons;
- writing in English lessons: finding a voice;
- knowledge about language: grammar, spelling, punctuation and handwriting;
- the rich landscape of children's literature;
- non-fiction literature in English lessons;
- planning, assessing and recording progress in English: the learning cycle.

Aimed at trainee and newly qualified teachers, those working towards Masters level qualifications and all those involved in the teaching of Early Years and primary English, this accessible but critically provocative text will be an essential resource for those wishing to deepen their understanding of Early Years and primary English education.

Margaret Mallett taught in Primary schools in Northumberland and Kent following an academic career as Lecturer and then Senior Lecturer in Language and Education at Goldsmiths College, University of London. She is a member of the editorial team of The English Association's primary journal *English 4–11*, and reviewer of professional and children's books for *Books for Keeps* online and *The School Librarian* journal.

A Guided Reader to Early Years and Primary English

Creativity, principles and practice

Margaret Mallett

Routledge
Taylor & Francis Group

LONDON AND NEW YORK

First published 2016
by Routledge
2 Park Square, Milton Park, Abingdon, Oxon OX14 4RN

and by Routledge
711 Third Avenue, New York, NY 10017

Routledge is an imprint of the Taylor & Francis Group, an informa business

British Library Cataloguing in Publication Data
A catalogue record for this book is available from the British Library

Library of Congress Cataloging in Publication Data
Mallett, Margaret, author.
A guided reader to early years and primary English : creativity,
principles and practice / Margaret Mallett.
pages cm
Includes bibliographical references.
1. Language arts (Primary) 2. Content area reading. 3. English
language—Study and teaching (Primary)—Foreign speakers. I. Title.
LB1528.M287 2016
372.6—dc23
2015020119

ISBN: 978-0-415-66196-6 (hbk)
ISBN: 978-0-415-66197-3 (pbk)
ISBN: 978-1-315-69787-1 (ebk)

Typeset in Helvetica and Bembo
by Swales & Willis Ltd, Exeter, Devon, UK

MIX
Paper from
responsible sources
FSC® C013056
www.fsc.org

Printed and bound in Great Britain by
TJ International Ltd, Padstow, Cornwall

Contents

Figures

Acknowledgements

The author is grateful to all those who have given permission to reproduce the extracts listed below. While every effort has been made to trace and acknowledge ownership of copyright material used in this volume, the publishers will be glad to make suitable arrangements with any copyright holders whom it has not been possible to contact. As always, I thank David for his generous help and advice.

Chapter 1: Models of and approaches to Early Years and primary English

Extract 1

Dixon, J. (1975, 3rd edn) *Growth Through English: Set in the Perspective of the Seventies*. Oxford: Oxford University Press for the National Association for the Teaching of English, 3–4, 7, 13.

Extract 2

Britton, J.N. (1971) The role of fantasy. *English in Education*, 5 (3), 42–3, 44.

Extract 3

Britton, J.N. and Newsome, B. (1968) What is learnt in English lessons? *Journal of Curriculum Studies*, 1 (1), 71–3.

Extract 4

Whitehead, M.R. (2004, 3rd edn) Playful encounters. In *Language and Literacy in the Early Years*. London: Sage Publications, 133–4.

Extract 5

Cremin, T., Reedy, D., Bearne, E. and Dombey, H. (2015, 2nd edn) *Teaching English Creatively*. Abingdon: Routledge, 1–4.

Chapter 2: Speaking and listening in English lessons: story-telling, drama, booktalk and debate

Extract 6

Medlicott, M. (2004, 2nd edn) Storytelling. In P. Hunt (ed.) *International Companion Encyclopedia of Children's Literature*, vol. 1. Abingdon and New York: Routledge, 619–21.

Extract 7

Clark, L. (2001) Foundations for talk – speaking and listening in the early years classroom. In P. Goodwin (ed.) *The Articulate Classroom: Talking and Learning in the Primary School*. London: David Fulton, 87–8.

Extract 8

Chambers, A. (2011 edn) The three sharings. In *Tell Me: Children, Reading and Talk* (published in this edition with the companion book *The Reading Environment: How Adults Help Children Enjoy Books*). Stroud: Thimble Press, 103–7.

Extract 9

Mallett, M. (1997) 'Can you say a little more about that?' Helping children to make their response to fiction explicit. *Education 3–13*, 25 (1), 11–17.

Extract 10

Nicholson, C. (2011, 3rd edn) Reading the pictures: Children's responses to *Rose Blanche*. In P. Goodwin (ed.) *The Literate Classroom*. London and New York: Routledge, 108–10.

Extract 11

Mallett, M. and Newsome, B. (1977a) The life of St. Patrick. In *Talking, Writing and Learning, 8–13*. London: Evans/Methuen for the Schools Council, 153–4.

Extract 12

Mallett, M. and Newsome, B. (1977b) Evaluating drama: The Three Wise Men. In *Talking, Writing and Learning, 8–13*. London: Evans/Methuen for the Schools Council, 157–8.

Extract 13

Rooke, J. (2013) Teachers created dialogic spaces for children to collaboratively talk about and assess their writing. In *Transforming Writing: Final Evaluation Report*. London: National Literacy Trust, 50–1.

Chapter 3: Reading and responding to texts in English lessons

Extract 14

Perkins, M. (2011, 3rd edn) Making space for reading: Teaching reading in the early years. In P. Goodwin (ed.) *The Literate Classroom*. London and New York: Routledge, 21–3.

Extract 15

Meek, M. (1988) *How Texts Teach What Readers Learn*. Stroud: Thimble Press, 30–1.

Extract 16

Gamble, N. (2004, 2nd edn) Teaching fiction. In P. Hunt (ed.) *International Companion Encyclopedia of Children's Literature*, vol. 2. Abingdon and New York: Routledge, 755–9.

Extract 17

Mills, C. and Webb, J. (2004, 2nd edn) Selecting books for younger readers. In P. Hunt (ed.) *International Companion Encyclopedia of Children's Literature*, vol. 1. Abingdon and New York: Routledge, (a) 771–2, (b) 774, (c) 775–7.

Extract 18

Stafford, T. (2011, 2nd edn) Reading visuals. In *Teaching Visual Literacy in the Primary Classroom*. London and New York: Routledge, (a) 9–11, (b) 57–9.

Extract 19

Horner, C. and Ryf, V. (2007) *Creative Teaching in English*. Abingdon and New York: Routledge, (a) 155–6, (b) 173–5.

Extract 20

Bearne, E., Clark, C., Johnson, A., Manford, P., Mottram, M. and Wolstencroft, H. with Anderson, R., Gamble, N. and Overall, K. (2007) *Reading on Screen*. Leicester: United Kingdom Literacy Assocation (UKLA), p. 24 from 'the ability to design' to 'an important contribution'.

Chapter 4: Writing in English lessons: finding a voice

Extract 21

Dombey, H. with Barrs, M., Bearne, E., Chamberlain, L., Cremin, T., Ellis, S., Goodwin, P., Lambirth, A., Mottram, M., Myhill, D. and Rosen, M. (2013) What writing is and how we go about it. In *Teaching Writing: What the Evidence Says*. Leicester: United Kingdom Literacy Association (UKLA), 2–3.

Extract 22

Mallett, M. (2003) Ways of representing experience. In *Early Years Non-Fiction*. London and New York: Routledge Falmer, 6–7, 72–3.

Extract 23

Marshall, S. (1963) The writing books. In *An Experiment in Education*. Cambridge: Cambridge University Press, 110, 112.

Extract 24

Barrs, M. and Cork, V. (2001) *The Reader in the Writer*. London: Centre for Literacy in Primary Education, 73–4.

Extract 25

Horner, C. and Ryf, V. (2007) Writing fiction: A creative approach. In *Creative Teaching: English in the Early Years and Primary Classroom*. Abingdon and New York: Routledge, 94–7.

Extract 26

Hughes, T. (2008, 2nd edn) *Poetry in the Making: A Handbook for Writing and Teaching*. London: Faber & Faber, p. 124 'Words and Experience'; p. 23 Note to chapter 1, 'Capturing Animals'.

Extract 27

Wyse, D., Jones, R., Bradford, H. and Wolpert, M.A. (2013, 3rd edn) Poetry. In *Teaching English, Language and Literacy*. Abingdon and New York: Routledge, 52–3.

Extract 28

Mallett, M. (2012, 4th edn) Persuasive genre. In *The Primary English Encyclopedia*. London and New York: Routledge, 315–16.

Extract 29

Wilson, A. and Scanlon, J. (2011, 4th edn) Writing frames. In *Language Knowledge for Primary Teachers*. Abingdon and New York: Routledge, 39.

Extract 30

Safford, K. (2010, 3rd edn) Multilingual writers. In J. Graham and A. Kelly (eds) *Writing Under Control*. London and New York: Routledge, 36–8.

Extract 31

Graham, J. (2010, 3rd edn) Children who claim that they hate writing ... In J. Graham and A. Kelly (eds) *Writing Under Control*. London and New York: Routledge, 206–9.

Extract 32

Cigman, J. (2014) Introduction. In *Supporting Boys' Writing in the Early Years: Becoming a Writer in Leaps and Bounds*. Abingdon and New York: Routledge, xxi–xxii.

Extract 33

Safford, K., O'Sullivan, O. and Barrs, M. (2005) *Boys on the Margin: Promoting Literacy at Key Stage 2*. London: Centre for Literacy in Primary Education, (a) 2, (b) 105–6.

Extract 34

Bearne, E. (2004) Multimodal texts: What they are and how children use them. In J. Evans (ed.) *Literacy Moves On*. London: David Fulton, 27–8 from 'In rethinking literacy' to 'ideas in each mode or medium'.

Extract 35

Dunn, J., Niens, U. and McMillan, D. (2014) 'Cos he's my favourite character!' A children's rights approach to the use of popular culture in teaching literacy. *Literacy*, 48 (1), 27.

Chapter 5: Knowledge about language: grammar, spelling, punctuation and handwriting

Extract 36

Wilson, A. and Scanlon, J. (2011, 4th edn) Language as process; language as product. In *Language Knowledge for Primary Teachers*. London and New York: Routledge, (a) 3, (b) 6–7.

Extract 37

Hendy, M. (2013) Improving writing through teaching grammar in context: A silver lining to every cloud! *English 4–11*, 49 (autumn 2013), 11–13.

Extract 38

Kelly, A. (2009) Transcription: Spelling, punctuation and handwriting. In J. Graham and A. Kelly (eds) *Writing Under Control*. Abingdon: David Fulton, (a) 132, (b) 138–41.

Extract 39

Peters, M.L. (1985) Attention and perception. In *Spelling: Caught or Taught: A new look*. London: Routledge & Kegan Paul, 25–6.

Extract 40

O'Sullivan, O. (2011) Teaching and learning spelling. In P. Goodwin (ed.) *The Literate Classroom*. London and New York: Routledge, 60.

Extract 41

Truss, L. (2003) *Eats, Shoots & Leaves: The Zero Tolerance Approach to Punctuation*. London: Profile Books, 26–7.

Extract 42

Dombey, H. (2013) *Teaching Writing: What the evidence says*. Leicester: United Kingdom Literacy Association (UKLA), 29, section 6.20.

Extract 43

Wyse, D., Jones, R., Bradford, H. and Wolpert, M.A. (2013, 3rd edn) Handwriting. In *Teaching English, Language and Literacy*. Abingdon: Routledge, 245–8.

Extract 44

Medwell, J. and Wray, D. (2014) Handwriting automaticity: The search for performance thresholds. *Language and Education*, 28 (1), 34–51.

Chapter 6: The rich landscape of children's literature

Extract 45

Styles, M. (2004, 2nd edn) Poetry. In P. Hunt (ed.) *International Companion Encyclopedia of Children's Literature*, vol. 1. London and New York: Routledge, 396–9.

Extract 46

Lewis, D. (2001) Describing the interaction between word and image. In *Reading Contemporary Picturebooks: Picturing text*. London and New York: Routledge, 31–3.

Extract 47

Cook, E. (1971) Myths, legends and fairy tales in the lives of children. In *The Ordinary and the Fabulous*. Cambridge: Cambridge University Press, 1–2, 6–9.

Extract 48

Bearne, E. (4 October 2004) *Short Stories for Children*. Unpublished paper presented to students on the Children's Literature M.Ed. course, University of Cambridge Faculty of Education.

Extract 49

Mallett, M. (2010) Genre features of longer stories and novels. In M. Mallett (ed.) *Choosing and Using Fiction and Non-Fiction 3–11*. Abingdon and New York: Routledge, 99–100.

Extract 50

Bearne, E. (2013) Seeing and hearing Dickens. In E. Bearne (ed.) *Teaching Dickens in the Primary School*. Leicester: English Association Issues in English, No. 10, 22–25.

Extract 51

Pizzi, K. (2004, 2nd edn) Contemporary comics. In P. Hunt (ed.) *International Companion Encyclopedia of Children's Literature*, vol. 1. Abingdon and New York: Routledge, (a) 385–6, (b) 393–4.

Extract 52

Sackett, H. (2013) Children's comics for a new generation of readers. *Books for Keeps*, 207 (2), 12–14.

Chapter 7: Non-fiction literature in English lessons

Extract 53

Mallett, M. (2010) Logbooks, diaries, letters, autobiography and biography. In M. Mallett (ed.) *Choosing and Using Fiction and Non-Fiction 3–11*. London and New York: Routledge, 255–6.

Extract 54

Unstead, S. (2012) Review of 'Fantastic Mr Dahl' by Michal Rosen and Quentin Blake (illustrator). *Books for Keeps*, 198 (2), 25.

Extract 55

Mallett, M. (2008) *The Lyrical Voice in Non-Fiction: 'Think of an Eel' by Karen Wallace and Mike Bostock*. English Association Bookmark 3. Leicester: English Association, 3–6.

Extract 56

Sanderson, R. and Bowers, J. (2013) It's not always about books. *English 4–11*, 49 (autumn 2013), 2–4.

Chapter 8: Planning, assessing and recording progress in English: the learning cycle

Extract 57

Wyse, D., Jones, R., Bradford, H. and Wolpert, M.A. (2013, 3rd edn) Planning. In *Teaching English, Language and Literacy*. Abingdon and New York: Routledge, (a) 275–6, (b) 278–9.

Extract 58

Drummond, M.J. (2012, classic edn) 'Learning Stories' and 'Returning to Jason'. In *Assessing Children's Learning*. London: David Fulton, (a) 163–4, (b) 171–2.

Extract 59

Rooke, J. (2013) Teachers used a variety of marking techniques to engage children in assessment. In *Transforming Writing: Final Evaluation Report*, Appendix 2. London: National Literacy Trust, 46–8.

Extract 60

Godwin, D. and Perkins, M. (2002, 2nd edn) Planning, assessment and recording. In *Teaching Language and Literacy in the Early Years*. London: David Fulton, 126–7.

Introduction

Aims, scope and themes in the book

It has been an enjoyable task to gather together these extracts taken from some of the most helpful, and in some cases most inspirational writing, about teaching and learning in English lessons for the under-elevens. Some extracts bring voices from the past while others are drawn from the work of teachers and scholars who are still active. The wisdom in the extracts helps meet the three main aims of the book. First, they help establish some principles to take to planning, teaching and assessing English and they equip the reader to contribute to debates about important issues that affect the English curriculum. It is certain that you will find these issues being fought over by politicians and professionals throughout your career. Here I am thinking, for example, of the 'simmering volcano', the debate about how and when to teach knowledge about language and the passionate feelings about the best ways to teach children to read and to become critical and sensitive readers enjoying the even richer treasure store of children's literature now available. Other ever-present debates are to do with nurturing children's talk and drama and helping them find a 'voice' for their writing. Second, an understanding of key principles enriches and energises classroom practice. This leads directly to the third aim, which is to encourage practitioners to value and support creativity not only in the children's activities and approaches to their work, but also as important in their own daily practice and in their reflection on their teaching and planning. To help here, each extract is followed by some comment and by suggestions for discussion with colleagues. Yes – this collaboration helps make teaching fruitful and involving. Some of the suggestions for action research – small-scale classroom projects – also are often best carried out collaboratively. The annotated 'Further reading' lists at the end of most chapters are intended to broaden and extend knowledge and understanding.

The English curriculum in the Early and Primary Years

Although there is quite a lot of agreement about the main elements of the Early Years and primary English curriculum, there continues to be much debate about how they should be taught, about their relative importance and about the amount of time that needs to be spent in the classroom on each element. In a nutshell, some approaches give highest priority to the acquisition of reading and writing skills and the more traditional kinds of teaching of language knowledge. Other approaches, while acknowledging the crucial importance of acquiring these skills, place at the heart of things the creativity and response of the child to all kinds of experience, whether in the real world or in the inner world of the imagination. Here, English is seen as a process subject where children are active, participative learners becoming ever more able to talk and write about their experiences, ideas and about texts, to read reflectively and find a writing 'voice'. Of course in practice many teachers weave together a combination of these approaches while keeping an eye on the statutory requirements in place at the time. This reader explores many of the issues that affect practice. But perhaps I should share with you first what I believe to be at the heart of English teaching whatever the age of the class. It is, I think, fiction – the fiction children read, that they have read to them, that they talk about and the stories and poems they write themselves – what James Britton called 'language in the spectator role'. But in this rich subject we call English I also believe there is a vital place for the language of the real world of practical activity. This kind of language has been termed by James Britton 'language in the participant role' (Britton, 1970: 97–125). Such language is important in subjects across the curriculum. In English lessons we use 'participant' language when we discuss topics of interest, topics which are sometimes excitingly controversial and when we talk about what is happening in the world around us and how this is reported to us by the media. We must remember that becoming a critical reader is to do with increasing awareness of the perspectives and views of those who make the news or write about it. Children also need help in developing their critical intelligence to understand the motivations and manipulations of advertisers and others trying to persuade them. The primary school is where children can start to develop the abilities needed to look at the world critically.

Next, then, I set out what is in each of *A Guided Reader*'s eight chapters, which together aim to cover all those aspects of the English curriculum that I believe to be of importance.

- Chapter 1 presents some different models of and approaches to English teaching and recognises play as the forerunner to cultural activity before moving towards an integrating 'creativity' model.
- Chapter 2 focuses on the power of speaking and listening to develop thinking, feeling and imagining. There are extracts about: story-telling, role play and improvised drama – powerful contexts for important and interesting uses of language; about 'booktalk' and talk by children about their own writing.
- Chapter 3 turns to the teaching of reading, the reading environment and some different views about the development of critical reading. The range of texts is wider

than ever: as well as reading print, children read on screen – encountering both print and digital texts and multimodal and multimedia texts (see also Chapter 6).

- Chapter 4 homes in on writing in English lessons and on helping children find a 'voice', particularly for personal writing, stories, poems and play scripts in multi-modal, multimedia and print forms.

- Chapter 5 delves into the kind of language knowledge teachers help children acquire by age eleven; and so the extracts give views on teaching and learning about parts of speech, grammar and the secretarial aspects of writing – spelling, punctuation and handwriting.

- Chapter 6 is concerned with children's literature – with fiction of all kinds in print and electronic media: poetry, picturebooks, traditional tales, short stories, longer stories and novels and multimodal and 'popular culture' texts.

- Chapter 7 turns to literary kinds of non-fiction – including autobiography and biography – and to children's magazines and texts to support debate.

- Chapter 8 presents the views of those who have thought deeply about the best ways of planning, assessing and recording children's progress in talking, listening, reading and writing.

The reader covers English activities from the earliest years – even before schooling begins children enjoy stories and rhymes – to the age of eleven. Where appropriate, I suggest how an issue or topic relates to children at different stages. The age categories set out in UK documents change when new governments are appointed and they nearly always revise the national curriculum, what is required at each stage and sometimes the organisation of age phases. I believe that while intending teachers specialise in an age range, for example in parts of the United Kingdom, within the Early Years/Foundation, Key Stage 1 and Key Stage 2 phases, it is important to understand what is good practice at each stage up to eleven years. So a teacher of the very youngest children will benefit from being aware of what follows in the later stages, and teachers of the older primary age groups will want to build on best practice and on what has already been achieved in the Nursery years and Reception class. This free-flowing exchange of understanding and insight between teachers of different age groups is something enthusiastically supported in this *Guided Reader*.

Children aged 0–5: the roots of 'English'

Babies and young children have a playful, explorative approach to the world and respond with delight to nursery rhymes, songs, picturebooks and stories from their earliest months. James Britton makes a link between early play and later cultural enjoyments, including those that happen in English lessons in primary school (see Whitehead 2002). The best-informed Nursery practitioners and playgroup teams recognise the fluidity of a young child's activities and do not think in terms of 'subjects'. A vignette of everyday good practice shows this fluidity. A student teacher took a class of five-year-olds on a nature walk to introduce these young scientists to skilful observation and recording. Back in the classroom they found out more about the creatures and plants they had seen from early fact books and DVDs. But then the emphasis changed and the children listened to stories and poems about woods, insects and frogs. The spirit of 'English' weaves through children's days not only through the stories and poems they hear, but also in the conversations they have about their experiences, preoccupations and feelings. Nowhere is an 'English focus' more rewarding for these very young children than when they explore their own world and their feelings about it in role play. This is the activity that helps integrate experiences in the real world with experiences in the inner world of the imagination. And role play is also a hugely important context for language exploration and development.

Is it appropriate to talk about language knowledge and language study with very young children? Some different views on this will emerge from the extracts in the relevant chapters. Early Years educators mostly believe the answer is – yes, but such teaching needs to be tailored carefully round children's questions, experience and interest (Whitehead, 2010: 84–5). As soon as children begin to show interest in books a metalingual vocabulary can be built as they encounter words like 'letter', 'word' and 'sound'. Again, supporting and encouraging children's questions and comments about stories is a rich context for acquiring a language with which to talk about books. The role of the adult, in helping children to tune into all this new knowledge and understanding, involves having real conversations with these very young learners.

Children aged 5–7: becoming able to read, enjoy and talk about an increasingly wide range of literature and to make progress in writing

During this age phase, termed Key Stage 1 in the National Curriculum for England, children become more capable of collaborating with their peers in discussion – able to 'turn take' and to listen and respond to what others say. Children so much enjoy and continue to learn from drama and role play that many teachers follow 'Early Years' practice by having a role play corner with a theme – a space ship, the Gruffalo's den or a chocolate factory. This can lead to lively drama and sometimes to writing.

The world of children's literature opens up in these years. Reading a story out loud to the whole class helps develop a community spirit and also helps less confident readers to experience more advanced language and more subtle stories and characterisations. When it comes to children's individual reading there is an ever richer and more exciting set of choices to open up a child's imagination. As well as print storybooks and poems there are multimodal and multimedia texts to enjoy. This is the time when 'bridging books', chapter books where text as well as pictures tell the story, come to the fore. Children are entitled to have 'popular culture' texts as part of the classroom collection. Superheroes and comic and cartoon are particularly well liked by this age group. Perhaps the biggest challenge is to harness children's exuberance and energy to writing tasks. The role play corner, as mentioned above, can inspire here, and many children like to put their thoughts, observations and feelings about family visits and holidays and about school outings into writing. This is the age at which children are becoming more aware of the importance of having a purpose and an audience for their stories and first-person accounts. At the same time, of course, there are routines to fit into each day, including work on handwriting and learning about aspects of language knowledge.

Children aged 7–11: expanding and refining talking and debating, reading and writing in all genres, particularly fiction

These years fall within the 'Key Stage 2' phase in the National Curriculum for England. Children are very much more mature at age eleven than they were at age seven, and Key Stage 2 can be seen in two parts with Years 3 and 4 termed lower Key Stage 2 and Years 5 and 6 upper Key Stage 2. Subjects become more differentiated as children move through the Primary Years. However, language and literacy learning continue to be cross-curricular: indeed some of the most interesting contexts for speaking, listening, reading and writing are in history, geography and science lessons. It is also the case that fiction – the stories and poems that are at the heart of English – can bring a personal foothold to learning in other lessons. A powerful poem or first-person account about a volcanic eruption can enrich a geography lesson and a story involving the life of a Victorian child a history lesson. The natural link between English and the other arts subjects – music, art and craft and drama – continues. But it is above all in English lessons that fiction in its rich variety finds its home and it is here that children can build on what they have achieved earlier on, increase their reading range of both print and digital texts and meet the challenge of more demanding poems and stories. Literature supports children's expanding ability to think and feel. It is by encouraging both individual and collaborative efforts to find the deep meanings in texts that progress is made and sensitive and critical reading is developed. Here I am thinking of Aidan Chambers' 'booktalk', which provides a framework for deep discussion of texts (see Extract 8, Chapter 2). To keep young readers and writers motivated and inspired, it is important to take account of their choices by including some 'popular culture' texts alongside more traditional fiction.

Children's talk becomes an increasingly useful tool for analysis and thinking about non-fiction texts in different modes and media. The debates about all kinds of issues that are such a strong feature of English work in the later primary schools years – about advertising, the environment and news stories – help the development of critical reading and writing. Role play and drama continue to be a most fruitful context for examining issues as well as being highly enjoyable. Children's progress in writing their own stories, poems and personal accounts is partly evident by the range of genres they can control and the depth of their ability within each particular kind of writing. The late primary school stage is the time for teachers to help children expand and refine their knowledge about language. In Chapter 5, 'Knowledge about language' the extracts show some very different perspectives on this. But most of the well informed would agree that we need more than just the 'naming of parts'.

The social and cultural context of learning

Children have their being and develop in a social and cultural context and acquire understandings and values within this context. The relationships which children experience, the way the people that surround them at home have communicated ideas and feelings, have a great impact on the way children learn in school. It is in English lessons in particular that individual perspectives on all those things to do with being human are valued and explored. Feelings as well as ideas and thoughts come into play. So in responding to the needs of the children in their care, from whichever group within our constantly changing society they belong, reflective teachers do all they can to provide interesting and effective lessons. Encouragement to talk about their own experiences and thoughts, to write about them and to discuss their reading underpins good English work. An important part of the teacher's role is to select a wide and interesting range of resources including fiction and non-fiction and both print and screen-based texts. An informed collection includes quality books, taking in fiction from different parts of the world and from those places where the children have their roots. Children deserve involving texts and need some which connect with their preoccupations and experiences. Annotated lists of children's books and resources are a strong feature of Chapters 5 and 6 on children's literature.

The presence of children in our schools who are bilingual or multilingual and who are learning English as a new language has had a considerable impact on how we understand language and intellectual development. Some of these issues are explored in Eve Gregory's book on learning to read in a new language in which she emphasises the role of the teacher in co-ordinating formal and informal learning (Gregory, 2008: 110). Of considerable interest also is Clare Kelly's account of her research into Nursery-aged children's literacy learning in which she explains through a case study approach how children from different communities draw on both home experience and adult support to make a link with the new world of literacy (Kelly, 2010).

When it comes to reading we need to see this in a social context, taking account of what Aidan Chambers calls 'the reading environment' (Chambers, 2011: 15–21). Aspects of the reading environment include where reading takes place, the reading materials, reasons for reading and our general attitude to it. (This applies to children's writing, too.) One important way in which the school culture has been changing is the response to the arrival of the digital world and the expanding range of texts, many of them now read on screen. Teachers will be helped by the emphasis of the work of the Centre for Children's Literature at Cambridge University. These researchers approach children's television programmes, video games and films as texts in their own right. Their work also covers innovative print texts – graphic stories and novels as well as cherishing traditional tales and classic stories. A greater awareness of the value of visual kinds of literacy has led to the multimodal texts children read – in innovative picturebooks for example – and those they write and draw themselves. These issues will be addressed in Chapter 6 of this *Guided Reader* 'The rich landscape of children's literature'.

Teacher as researcher

Principles and practice should link seamlessly. If we want teachers to be part of the way in which the curriculum develops and changes they need to be researchers. Classroom research confirms the status of teachers as professional and reflective practitioners. The kind of research known as 'action research' is particularly suited to studies undertaken in school. First of all the research is essentially teacher led. But involving others, including colleagues, students and college tutors, helps to reduce subjectivity. Second, it has immediacy because the questions investigated have nearly always come to mind in the course of practice. Third, action research, like teaching, is cyclical and can enrich practice as it goes forward. There is the formulation of a question or hypothesis, the planning, teaching and evaluating and then the fruits of the research are taken into the next round of planning and practice.

While it has much in common with the various tasks around everyday successful teaching, action research involves a more than usual amount of planning, evaluation and recording. Anyone starting out on classroom research into children's reading and writing development would find *Classroom Action Research in Literacy* by Eve Bearne and her colleagues a very helpful guide. This research team believe that well-planned action research can be as systematic as any other kind of research (Bearne *et al.*, 2007: 1–4). What kind of data need to be collected? They might include recordings of children's talk for transcription, examples of writing and careful notes of observations. These observations need to be dated and the social context of the learning, those present and time spent on particular activities recorded. When the research stage is completed the findings and conclusions need to be set out rigorously and clearly. A reference section helps situate the findings in the context of other relevant research and thinking. The effort involved in taking on this sort of project with all the other tasks a teacher has to complete must be recognised. Where two or more teachers are involved in something that truly interests them, the work can be shared. Sharing the fruits of research is the high point and can be satisfying and enjoyable, and sometimes an article on the research might be published in journals like *English 4–11* (the English Association) and *Teaching English* (the National Association for the Teaching of English). Projects undertaken by my students over the years have included: drama as a context for debate about an environmental issue; progress of groups of children in persuasive kinds of writing with and without the use of writing frames; the effect of teacher-led talk about a fairy tale on the stories told and written by seven-year-olds; the effectiveness of different strategies in improving the spelling of two ten-year-olds; the role of collaboration in screen-based script writing.

How to use *A Guided Reader*

The 'Comment' paragraphs and the 'Questions to discuss with colleagues' after each extract are intended to lead to further reflection. Questions and suggested activities can be used as a starting point for group discussion or for the preparation of a presentation or short essay. There are also, in most chapters, suggestions for carrying out small-scale 'action research' projects.

The exclusive use of the male pronoun by those writing some decades ago grates on modern ears. Just a very few extracts in *A Guided Reader* feature this usage.

References

Bearne, E., Graham, L. and Marsh, J. (2007) *Classroom Action Research in Literacy: A Guide to Practice*. Leicester: United Kingdom Literacy Association (UKLA).

Britton, J. (1970) *Language and Learning*. London: Allen Lane The Penguin Press.

Centre for Children's Literature, Cambridge University, Cambridge. Available at: www.educ. cam.ac.uk/centres/childrensliterature.

Chambers, A. (2011, 2nd edn) *Tell Me: Children, Reading and Talk* with *The Reading Environment*. Stroud: Thimble Press.

Gregory, E. (2008, 2nd edn) *Learning to Read in a New Language: Making Sense of Words and World*. London: Paul Chapman.

Kelly, C. (2010) *Hidden Worlds: Young Children Learning in Multicultural Contexts*. London: Trentham Books.

Whitehead, M.R. (2002) Introduction. In *Developing Language and Literacy with Young Children*, 0–8 series edited by Tina Bruce. London: Sage, xii.

Whitehead, M.R. (2010, 4th edn) *Language and Literacy in the Early Years*. London: Sage.

Models of and approaches to Early Years and primary English

Introduction

In this chapter I take the term 'model' to refer to a set of principles and beliefs which guide what we do day by day. Whenever teachers plan a lesson, that plan will be influenced by the principles and beliefs they carry with them. When we think about models of English teaching we can learn from what writers have said in the past. So this chapter starts in Section 1, Extract 1, with John Dixon's particularly clear and helpful analysis. His book *Growth Through English* has informed approaches to English lessons on both sides of the Atlantic since it was first published in 1967. It was one outcome of the lectures, talks and fruitful interactions between British and American delegates at a conference in America known as the Dartmouth Seminar, which had taken place the previous year. He identifies three models – a 'skills' model, a 'cultural heritage' model and a 'personal growth' model. Each model emphasises a different element of the English curriculum: the debate about how to combine these elements into a single coherent model continues.

But what about children's learning and experience in early childhood before they come to school? In Section 2, approaches valuing the important role of play in early childhood are considered. James Britton's inspirational article 'The role of fantasy', Extract 2, makes the important link between children's play in their earliest years and their later enjoyment of all things cultural including art, music and literature. Stories – those that children read, write for themselves or have read to them – as well as poems, plays and improvisations are near the centre of the English curriculum for all age groups. Britton's link between early play and this later learning and enjoyment is an important one for those who teach and those who learn in English lessons.

What is at the very heart of English? In Section 3, Extract 3, Britton and Newsome identify what they believe to be at the centre of English lessons for all age groups.

They begin by drawing attention to the inner representation of the world, or 'world picture', we all carry around with us. We can use this 'world picture' to operate as 'participants' in the real world; simple examples here would be getting from place to place on a journey or making a cake. This way of using our 'world picture' is crucial for managing everyday activities and is also important in most curriculum subjects. However, we can use this inner representation of the world in a different way as 'spectators' in activities involving reflecting, improvising and musing on this 'world picture'. These activities take place when we write, when we talk to others and when we read all kinds of literature. For Britton and Newsome, activities and their associated language in the 'spectator role' are the essence of English lessons. Still in Section 3, Extract 4, Marian Whitehead argues convincingly for the value to children of becoming 'spectators of fiction' and points to the likely cumulative benefits to the imagination of listening to and reading stories and rhymes. But, of course, the cultural context in which children live and learn is constantly changing and the range of media and texts to choose from is wider and richer than was the case when Dixon and Britton were writing; the inspiration innovative texts and new media encourage are very much part of Teresa Cremin's vision of creative English teaching explored in Extract 5 in Section 4. New texts and constantly developing media are a theme throughout the book and particularly in Chapter 6 'The rich landscape of children's literature'.

Few teachers or those writing about English teaching today would propose exclusively following one of Dixon's models – 'skills', ' cultural heritage' or even 'personal growth' – although they might lean towards one of them. Section 4 considers new approaches which are united by a belief that it is a child's creativity and urge to make sense and learn that should be nurtured and developed. For the age groups at the heart of this book, a 'creative' approach is desirable across the curriculum. Here, though, the extract I have chosen, from *Teaching English Creatively*, considers the implication of a 'creative' approach in English lessons. The editor and contributor to the book, Teresa Cremin, integrates what many would feel is the best from each of the Dixon models. She teases out those elements in the English curriculum that require the teaching and learning of skills, although for her the mastery of spelling, punctuation and grammar and the language knowledge this entails involves more than drills and mechanical learning. The emphasis she and other leading writers from this generation place on quality texts of all kinds and on the wider media gathers in the strengths of the 'cultural heritage' model. However, the newer version is richer and includes digital texts and quality books from across the world. Cremin's 'creativity' model with its emphasis on children's active exploring of ideas and their imaginative engagement with literature and their own talk and writing is perhaps closest to the 'personal growth' model. Without referring to Dixon's writing directly, it also helps us address some of the possible limitations of this model, limitations of which Dixon is himself aware.

The ideas and insights in the extracts in this chapter will, I believe, help teachers to reflect on current debates about the English curriculum, whether they work in an Early Years or a primary classroom.

Section 1: Models of English teaching

Extract 1

Source

Dixon, J. (1975, 3rd edn) *Growth Through English: Set in the Perspective of the Seventies*. Oxford: Oxford University Press for the National Association for the Teaching English, 3–4, 7, 13.

This extract is taken from the third edition of John Dixon's seminal work published in 1975. The first edition, published in 1967, was an outcome of a seminar held in Dartmouth, Alabama in the previous year. Here teachers and academics from Britain and North America worked to find a way of defining what is meant when we refer to 'English' as a classroom subject. John Dixon captures the complexity of this task: 'English is a quicksilver among metals – mobile, living and elusive. Its conflicting emphases challenge us today to look for a new coherent definition.' Three models were identified by the participants in the seminar. First, a 'skills' model, which emphasises the acquisition of all those things needed to read, write and spell. The problem here was to do with what a narrow interpretation left out. The second model, the 'cultural heritage' model, saw a main contribution of the English lesson as the passing on of a canon of great literature to successive generations, a canon which would provide models for children's own writing. Again, the main problem was with an over-emphasis on one aspect of English, as Dixon explains in the extract before homing in on the 'personal growth' model he favours.

> During the skills era this was stretched till the operations specific to the written system of language became the centre of English. The heritage era put 'skills' in their place as a means to an end. But it failed to reinterpret the concept of 'skills' and thus left an uneasy dualism in English teaching. Literature itself tended to be treated as a given, a ready made structure that we imitate and a content that is handed over to us. And this attitude infected composition and all work in language. There was a fatal inattention to the processes involved in such everyday activities as talking and thinking things over, writing a diary or a letter home, even enjoying a TV play. Discussion was virtually ignored, as we know to our cost today on both sides of the Atlantic. In other words, the part of the map that relates a man's language to his experience was largely unexplored. (Think of the trivial essay topics that still result from this ignorance.) The purposes and pressures that language serves tended to be reduced to a simple formula – a lump sum of inheritance …
>
> It was for this reason that members of the Seminar moved from an attempt to define '*What* English is' – a question that throws the emphasis on nouns like *skills*, and *proficiencies*, *set books*, and the *heritage* – to a definition by process, a description of the activities we engage in through language. How important these activities may be to us personally, how deeply they may affect our attitudes to experience, is suggested

by much of the best writing, drama and talk that goes on in English lessons. Here we see not only the intellectual organising of experience that goes on in other subjects, but also a parallel ordering of the feelings and attitudes with which pupils encounter life around them ...

Language is learnt in operation, not by dummy runs. In English, pupils meet to share their encounters with life, and to do this effectively they move freely between dialogue and monologue – between talk, drama and writing: and literature, by bringing new voices into the classroom, adds to the store of shared experience. Each pupil takes from the store what he can and what he needs. In doing so he learns to use language to build his own representational world and works to make this fit reality as he experiences it.

Comment

Dixon sets his three models of English in an historical dimension. By this I mean that he associates the models in their more rigorous form with particular historical and social contexts. The 'skills' model was taken up in the elementary schools established in significant numbers after the 1870 Education Reform Act where becoming literate was the priority and the approach tended to be mechanistic. Large classes sat formally at desks and carried out drills and tasks. The 'cultural heritage' model notably held sway in many of the state grammar schools established by the 1944 Education Act: a canon of what were thought to be the finest literary texts dominated English lessons. These two approaches limited children's experience in English lessons, in one case by over-emphasising skills and in the other by being restricted to a relatively narrow range of texts. Dixon favours a model, the 'personal growth' model, that puts children at the centre of their learning in English lessons. At the heart of this approach is the children's response to literature and the organisation of their thoughts, ideas and feelings in talk and writing. The model could inform teaching of all age phases and was very much in the progressive spirit of the Plowden Report (1967). Current approaches, in the UK at least, as we shall see later when considering Cremin's 'creative' approach to English, are often founded on the 'personal growth' model. But, as is nearly always the case with models and approaches, the 'personal growth' model has been criticised. Some, for example Gunther Kress and Theo van Leeuwen, have considered that Dixon, along with others sympathetic to what have been termed 'reader-response theories', moved too far in accepting the validity of children's subjective understanding of texts, even when these understandings were not compatible with the author's intentions (Kress and van Leeuwen, 1996: 26–7). Reader-response theory will be considered in Chapter 6, 'The rich landscape of children's literature'. On reflecting on his earlier views, Dixon himself considered that participant kinds of language, language to do with operating in the real world rather than the world of the imagination, in English lessons were at risk of being neglected if the 'personal growth' model was followed to the letter.

Questions to discuss with colleagues

1.   What do you think was valuable in the 'skills' and 'cultural heritage' models? How might they be adapted to deserve a place as part of the English curriculum today?
2.   How broadly would you define the 'skills' element in English in the light of new technology?
3.   What do you think are the strengths and limitations of the 'personal growth' model as described by John Dixon?
4.   Dixon felt later on that he had neglected 'participant' activities in the English lesson. With reference to your age phase suggest how you might introduce and develop a topic

   a.   involving children in research and debate;
   b.   writing factual accounts for the class or school magazine.

(See Section 3 for more about 'participant role' and 'spectator role' activities and language.)

Section 2: Play as the forerunner of cultural activity and the enjoyment of stories, drama and art

Extract 2

Source

Britton, J.N. (1971) The role of fantasy. *English in Education*, 5 (3), 42–3, 44.

Much has been written about the role of play in the learning of young children. In his article 'The role of fantasy' James Britton makes the link between early play and cultural activities of all kinds which come later on. He reminds us that play is essentially a voluntary activity and that although there may be images of the real world in children's play, the credibility of what they pretend is not a main concern. Britton sees the arts, including literature, as highly organised forms of play.

   I want to see play, then, as an area of free activity lying between the world of shared and verifiable experience and the world of inner necessity – a 'third area', as Donald Winnicott has called it (1971: 102–3). The essential purpose of activity in this area for the individual will be to relate for himself inner necessity with the demands of the external world. The more the images that clothe inner instinctual needs enter into the play activity, directly or indirectly, and the more they engage and relate to images from the world of shared experience, the more effectively, it seems to me, is the activity achieving its assimilative function. In the range of activities that come into the category of play as we have defined it, some will take up more of the demands of the inner world and are likely for that reason to include features that are inconsistent with our everyday notions of reality. It is activities towards that end of the scale that we shall most readily, and rightly, call 'fantasy', whether they are children's own creations or the stories they read ...

Culture, the common pool of humanity, offers the young child witches and fairy godmothers, symbols which may embody and work upon the hate and love that are part of a close, dependent relationship: he will read of witches and tell stories of his own that arise directly from his needs. In doing so, he performs an assimilative task, working towards a more harmonious relationship between inner needs and external demands. Culture offers him, at a later stage perhaps, *Alice in Wonderland*, which among other matters must certainly be concerned, if covertly, with *scale* – with bigness and littleness – and so with the difficulties a small comparatively powerless creature may feel in facing the demands of a world of full-grown, powerful adults.

If the Freudian view is right, there will be children whose ability to operate in the 'third area' has been so severely restricted in infancy that we as teachers can do little to help them. For the rest, it is important that we should recognise their need to 'play', understand as fully as we can the nature and value of such activity, and provide the cultural material on which it may flourish.

Extract reference

Winnicott, D.W. (1971) *Playing and Reality*. London: Tavistock Publications.

Comment

Britton argues that as well as being satisfying and worthwhile for its own sake, early play helps create a 'space' where the growing child can harmonise their inner needs with the demands of the external world. He builds on the work of Donald Winnicott, who first identified this intermediate area lying between internal and external reality. Winnicott, a paediatrician and child psychiatrist, places the emphasis on the therapeutic aspects: the successful use of this 'space' makes it possible for an individual to live creatively and to find life worth living. Britton, a teacher and scholar, is most interested in the huge implications for classroom practice: here play is enriched by what the teacher offers – for example the stories and poems valued by the culture. Much has been written about the value of play. Britton's analysis remains important because of the link he identifies between play and the later enjoyment of all things cultural. He hints at the impoverishment that might result where opportunities to play are not provided. There are, of course, different kinds of play but here the focus is on the free, imaginative play the special value of which Britton explores in the extract.

Questions to discuss with colleagues

1. What do you think Britton would wish us to include in our collection of 'cultural material' on which imaginative play flourishes? How has this range of material expanded in our age of new media and technology?

2. Do you still play? Are there games or play activities that you enjoy and which contribute to your sense of well being? Would any of these games be suitable for adaptation in the Early Years or primary classroom?
3. Identify some play and role play activities or themes that under-fives would enjoy and explain how you might bring them into daily practice in the Nursery Years to help learning and imagining.
4. How would you introduce children to the notion of play if it has not been part of their lives before they came to school?
5. How might play of the fantasy kind Britton concentrates on in the extract come into the school day of older primary school children?

Section 3: 'Spectator role' language at the heart of the English lesson

The extract in Section 2 linked early imaginative play to a child's capacity for later 'cultural learning' and enjoyment. This 'cultural learning' includes, of course, the activities that happen in English lessons: talking about experiences, whether one's own or those of characters in stories; the children's own personal and imaginative writing; role play and improvised drama. The next two extracts, the first from James Britton and Bernard Newsome and the second from Marian Whitehead, explore this 'cultural learning' in English lessons. In the analysis that follows, Britton and Newsome aim to give a theoretical explanation to illuminate these activities. The starting point is their observation that from early childhood every human being constructs an inner representation of the world. Included in this representation are the things we have gleaned from all we have experienced so far. This 'world picture' or inner representation is dynamic and changes in the light of further experiences causing us to modify our perceptions of the world.

There are two ways, these authors suggest, in which we can use our inner 'world picture'. One is to help us participate in the everyday world – finding our way round towns, doing household repairs or making a meal. Language associated with this way of looking at things is termed 'participant role'. The other use of the 'world picture' is to reflect on experience, to improvise, to ruminate and to share these reflections with others either in talk or perhaps in a story or poem. This way of using our 'world picture' and the kinds of language associated with it Britton and Newsome term 'spectator role'. You may not often come across the terms 'participant' and 'spectator'. The important thing is to know what is distinctive about the ways in which thinking, feeling and language are used in English lessons because this understanding is a helpful underpinning when planning the English curriculum.

In the following extract the authors suggest that language in the English classroom for learners of any age has a special job to do. It helps to home in on what is 'unique and personal' and is therefore to do with an individual's response to experiences, stories, poems, plays and ideas. The extract from Marian Whitehead's book brings us into the Nursery Years and explores the interesting connections that young children make between their own lives and the characters and events they encounter as they explore and share picturebooks and stories. There are some powerful examples of these 'spectator role' encounters.

Extract 3

Source

Britton, J.N. and Newsome, B. (1968) What is learnt in English lessons? *Journal of Curriculum Studies*, 1 (1), 71–3.

These authors argue that it is in English lessons that a child's individual response to experiences, ideas and literature is valued and developed.

> If we accept that man operates in the actual world by means of his representation of the world, it will follow that two courses are open to him. He may do just that – operate in the actual world *via* his representation, or he may operate *directly upon the representation itself*. This is a non-participant activity: let the world's affairs look after themselves while I contemplate my own past experiences, imaginary experiences – probable, possible or merely conceivable – and in doing so *improvise upon* my representation of the world. In daydreams I improvise situations that flatter my vanity; in gossip I may improvise upon the lives of my neighbours to satisfy my spite. In reading a novel I am also improvising, drawing upon the raw material of the past to give it a new shape in relation to the events of the story. I do so, normally, because I am not satisfied with the one humdrum life I have to lead.
>
> All these are uses of language in the spectator: a spectator may be deeply involved, deeply participating in the illusion, but to be in the role of participant in the way we are using the term he must participate in the affairs of the actual world. I may, to take a simple example, engage you in a discussion of my plans for the future: if I seek your help, your permission, or merely your good opinion of me, I am in the role of participant and am involving you as participant. If, on the other hand, I invite you merely to *enjoy* with me the prospect of my future – then we are both in the role of the spectator.
>
> We take up the role of spectator of other people's lives – whether chatting about last summer's holidays or in reading a novel – mainly for the reason already suggested: we enjoy tasting experiences at second hand that we have never had at first. We are, moreover, interested in the *possibilities of experience*, the unfamiliar and unlikely patterns that events may assume.
>
> We take up the role of spectator of our own experiences sometimes for similar reasons – to enjoy them, to savour them perhaps in a way that we could not while we were caught up in their happening: talking round the fire in the evening we enjoy the ardours and excitements of the day's walk, for example. But at other times we go back over experiences as spectators for other reasons – from need rather than for fun. If an experience proves too unlike our anticipation for us to adjust to it

while it is happening, we may need to go back to it in order to come to terms with it. We do this ordinarily in talk, but of course many stories and many poems are evidence that their writers have turned to writing in order to deal with recalcitrant experiences ...

When a child responds to a poem, this is a crucial process, for he is likely to be making his adjustments in accordance with our pattern of culture – values which we have derived by giving currency to the most mature and sensitive adjustments our society produces, those in fact of the poets and other artists.

As participants, we use language to get things done: to explain or persuade, to buy and sell, to acquire or pass on useful information, to pass examinations, to co-ordinate joint activity – and a thousand other ways of interacting with the environment. The point about language in the role of spectator is that it is disengaged from practical activity. When we take up this role, then, we are freed from certain responsibilities, and we use this freedom to do other things: in particular, we attend to the utterance itself, *as a form* or as a set of forms. We attend to the forms of language, its sounds and rhythms, to the pattern of events in a story, and to the pattern of feelings embodied – the changing kaleidoscope of tension and relief, fear and hope and love and hate ...

We use our freedom for another purpose also. As participants we evaluate situations in order to regulate our own behaviour in them: often enough we are aware of the need to go back over these events and re-evaluate against a broader frame of reference than we were able to use at the time. As spectators, we typically re-evaluate our own experiences and evaluate other people's in the full light of the attitudes, beliefs, values we have derived from living ...

We believe that language has a particular job to do (also) in English lessons, that English teachers have their own area of operating for language, and that what it is may be inferred from observing the best practice, past and present, in English teaching.

To select this area from the total learning function, we shall apply a different principle of selection from that we have referred to in talking of history, science, geography. In such subjects it is the areas of *common* concern and *common* curiosity that are selected. The experiences which are selected in English are those in which individuals *differ*: relations between the individual and other people: and relations – in so far that they are unique and personal – between the individual and his environment as a whole. By saying 'unique and personal' we put a stress, clearly, upon relations of feeling. It must be added that it is at the point of personal response that all experiences, all learning, must be integrated.

Extract 4

Source

Whitehead, M.R. (2004, 3rd edn) Playful encounters. In *Language and Literacy in the Early Years*. London: Sage Publications, 133–4.

The classroom experience of both Britton and Newsome was mainly in secondary schools. However, the 'spectator role 'activities and language examined above are important for English lessons for any age group. In this extract Marian Whitehead, an Early Years specialist, considers the responses of very young children to stories and rhymes. Referring to some well-established favourites, she notes that 'being an onlooker or spectator of literary events' frees young learners from having to respond in what she terms 'practical ways'. They question, savour and reflect on the characters and events in the stories and sometimes relate bits of them to their experience of events in the real world. The cumulative effect of being 'spectators of fiction events' is likely to enlarge the capacity for imagining and understanding.

The playful exploration of pictures and written narratives in books appears to be a major preoccupation with young children who enjoy literary encounters. Pictures and texts are often subjected to rigorous questioning and tentative reorganisation. Characters which appear lost or alone prompt such questions as, 'Where's her mummy (or daddy or granny)?' …

Such questioning is challenging and literally eye-opening for the adult reading partner, but for the young child it also marks the beginnings of encounters with totally new and surprising sets of possibilities. Suppose a tiger came to tea (Kerr, 1968)? Suppose you were always given hot water bottles for presents (Furchgott and Dawson, 1977)? Experiences found in literature begin to combine with bits of the child's daily life in rich and liberating ways. A small child can be comforted by a story or a book when away from home and familiar adults, or a threatening situation can be eased by the reassurance that a book or story character coped with this or similar difficulties. Success, joy and humour also migrate from the world of books into the every day world of the young child who is indulging in a little domestic mayhem like 'Noisy Norah' (Wells, 1978) …

One reason that young children (and older ones too) thrive on terrible tales is usually expressed as the reader or listener being an onlooker or spectator of literary events. In the case of fiction, we are reading or listening to an account or representation of imagined events in which we are obviously not participants. This non-participation gives us the time and the freedom to evaluate more sharply our feelings and attitudes about the events and characters represented – even very small children pick out the kind and the naughty, the dishonest and the brave in stories, but our ambiguous real-life motives and complex reactions involve heart-searchings, self delusions and frequent misunderstandings. Because literature and play free us from demands to respond in practical ways they allow distanced but very full evaluations, unblurred by personal confusions and involvement …

The cumulative effect of our many experiences as spectators of fictive events, feelings and personalities is an enlargement of our imaginative sensibilities and understandings. It is as if the fictional lives, events and emotions we encounter extend the range of our own responses and increase the resources we have for making sense of our own lives.

Extract references

Furchgott, T. and Dawson, L. (1977) *Phoebe and the Hot Water Bottle*. London: Deutsch.

Kerr, J. (1968) *The Tiger That Came to Tea*. Glasgow: Collins.

Wells, R. (1978) *Noisy Norah*. Glasgow: Collins.

Comment

Britton and Newsome, in Extract 3, argue that language in the 'spectator role' is evident in our day-to-day lives because we use it to explore our own experiences and in reacting to the experiences of others. We also use it when we talk about the experiences of characters in the books we read or in the films we watch. 'Spectator role' language is the language we use in English lessons. Our responses are 'unique and personal' and so feelings are more important than in most other curriculum subjects. This emphasis is characteristic of English activities – discussion about stories, dramatic improvisation and talking over personal experiences – with every age group from tiny babies playing peekaboo right through to the secondary school and university stages. In Extract 4, Marian Whitehead has shown how very young children are freed from other demands when listening to stories and can indulge in playful exploration of a range of things, not least the adventurous and even the dangerous.

Questions to discuss with colleagues

1. Britton and Newsome argue in Extract 3 that when we use language in the 'spectator role' we are able to 'attend to the utterance itself … to the forms of language, its sounds or rhythms, to the pattern of events in a story, and the pattern of feelings embodied …'. With reference to the age phase you teach, share with others your experience of children discussing the forms of language in a particular story or poem and suggest what you think (a) they learnt, (b) what you learnt. (You may find the paragraph in Extract 8 in Chapter 2 'Sharing connections' from Aidan Chamber's book *Tell Me* helpful in thinking further about this.)

2. Later in the book from which Extract 4 is taken, Whitehead explains that poetry and story introduce young children to the literary device of metaphor. Children sometimes puzzle over the meaning and use of metaphors like the 'diamond in the sky' of the nursery rhyme. How would you introduce either the Early Years or primary age group to the idea of imagery in fiction?

3. Do you agree with Marian Whitehead that the frightening aspects of stories can be helpful to young children? Are there some stories you would avoid introducing to your age group?

Section 4: A creative approach to English – towards a synthesising model

Issues around the competing philosophies underpinning English teaching and the models that follow from them are and will be endlessly debated. There will continue to be arguments that are far from good natured! At one end of the spectrum we have those who favour an exercise-based programme with traditional approaches to the teaching of grammar and spelling, a privileging of the phonic cue system in the initial teaching of reading and regular testing of children's progress. Those placing themselves at the other end of the spectrum are concerned with opportunities for children to be thinking, imagining and feeling beings, able to learn from risk taking in creative tasks, see more than one cue-system as contributing to the initial teaching or reading and tend to view assessment, formative as well as summative, as essentially part of the cycle of learning. Those writers, thinkers and teachers in the second camp often refer to a 'creative' approach to the curriculum subjects, not least English. These writers include, for example, contributors to Fisher and Williams' book *Unlocking Creativity: Teaching Across the Curriculum* (2004), Wyse and Jones' *Creativity in the Primary Curriculum* (2013), Clipson-Boyles *Teaching Primary English Through Drama: A Practical and Creative Approach* (2012). But I have chosen for this last extract in the chapter Teresa Cremin's visionary picture of what primary English teaching and learning could be like.

Extract 5

Source

Cremin, T., Reedy, D., Bearne, E. and Dombey, H. (2015, 2nd edn) *Teaching English Creatively*. Abingdon: Routledge, 1–4.

While recognising the importance of routines in English lessons and the need for direct teaching of reading, writing and language skills and abilities, Cremin argues that contexts that allow creative teaching and learning are those most likely to bring about children's active engagement in the full range of activities in the English lesson.

> Teaching and learning English is, at its richest, an energising, purposeful and imaginatively vital experience for all involved, developing youngsters' competence, confidence and creativity as well as building positive attitudes to learning. At its poorest, English teaching and learning can be a dry didactic experience, focused on the instruction of assessable skills, and paying little attention to children's affective or creative development as language learners and language users. Following apparently safe routes to raise literacy standards, interspersed with occasional more creatively oriented activities, does not represent balanced literary instruction. Such practice plays lip service to creative approaches and fails to acknowledge the potential of building on young children's curiosity, desire for agency and capacity to generate and innovate ...
>
> Teaching literacy creatively does not mean short-changing the essential knowledge, skills and understanding of the subject; rather it involves teaching literacy skills

and developing knowledge about language in creative contexts that explicitly invite learners to engage imaginatively and which stretches their generative and imaginative capacities. Creative teachers work to extend children's abilities as readers, writers, speakers and listeners and help them to express themselves effectively, to create as well as to critically evaluate their own work ...

Creativity emerges as children become absorbed in actively exploring ideas, initiating their own learning and making choices and decisions about how to express themselves using different media and language modes. In responding to what they read, view, hear and experience, children make use of their literacy skills and transfer this knowledge and understanding in the process ...

Creativity, in essence the generation of novel ideas, is possible to exercise in all aspects of life. In problem solving contexts of a mundane as well as unusual nature, humans can choose to adopt a creative mindset or attitude and trial possible options and ideas. It is useful to distinguish between high creativity and everyday creativity, between 'big creativity' (seen in some of Gardner's 1993 studies of highly creative individuals, for example Einstein and Freud) and 'little creativity' that Craft (2000, 2005) suggests focuses on agency and resourcefulness of ordinary people to innovate and take action ...

Creativity involves the capacity to generate, reason with and critically evaluate novel suppositions or imaginary scenarios. It is about thinking, problem solving, inventing and reinventing, and flexing one's imaginative muscles. As such the creative process involves risk, uncertainty, change, challenge and criticality ...

Finding a creative way forward

If teachers are to adopt innovative ways forward in their English teaching, they need to reconcile the tension between drive for measurable standards on the one hand and the development of creativity on the other. As children move though school they quickly learn how the system works and suppress their spontaneous creativity (Sternberg, 1997). Some teachers, too, in seeking to achieve prescribed literacy targets, curb their own creativity and avoid taking risks and leading exploration. More creative professionals, in combining subject and pedagogical knowledge, consciously leave real space for uncertainty and to teach for creativity. Teaching creatively involves teachers in making learning more interesting and effective, and using some imaginative approaches in the classroom (NACCCE, 1999). Teaching for creativity, by contrast, focuses on developing children's creativity, their capacity to experiment with ideas and information, alone and with others. The two processes are very closely related.

In examining the nature of creative teaching in a number of primary curriculum contexts, Jeffrey and Woods (2003, 2009) suggest that innovation, originality, ownership and control are all associated with creative practice. More recent research affirmed and developed this, showing that creative teachers in both planning and teaching, and in the ethos they create in the classroom, attribute high value to curiosity, risk taking, to ownership, autonomy and making connections (Grainger et al., 2006).

They also afford significance to the development of imaginative and unusual ideas in both themselves and their students. This work suggests that while all good teachers reward creativity and originality, creative ones depend on it to enhance their own well being and that of the children. They see development of creativity and originality as a distinguishing mark of their teaching. Perhaps, therefore, the difference between being a good teacher and being a creative teacher is one of emphasis and intention. The creative teacher is one who values the human attribute of creativity in themselves and seeks to promote this in others (ibid; Cremin, 2009). In the process, such teachers encourage children to believe in their creative potential and give them the confidence to try. Furthermore, they seek to foster other creative attributes in the young, such as risk taking, commitment, resilience, independent judgement, intrinsic motivation and curiosity.

Creative literacy teaching is a collaborative enterprise; one which capitalises on the unexpected and enables children to develop their language and literacy in purposeful, relevant and creative contexts that variously involve engagement, instruction, reflection and transformation. Such an approach requires that 'learning to read and write is an artistic event' (Freire, 1985) and one that connects to children's out-of-school literacy practices. Creative English teaching and teaching for creativity in English aims to enable young people to develop a questioning and critically reflective stance towards texts, to express themselves with voice and verve multimodally and in multiple media, and to generate what is new and original.

Core features of a creative approach

An environment of possibility, in which individual agency and self-determination are fostered and children's ideas and interests are valued, discussed and celebrated, depends upon a climate of trust, respect and support in the classroom. Creativity can be developed when teachers are confident and secure in both their subject knowledge and their knowledge of creative pedagogical practice; they model the features of creativity *and* develop a culture of creative opportunities.

A creative approach to teaching English encompasses several core features that enable teachers to make informed decisions, both at the level of planning and in the moment-to-moment interactions in the classroom:

1. profiling meaning and purpose;
2. foregrounding potent, affectively engaging texts;
3. fostering play and engagement;
4. harnessing profiling and agency;
5. encouraging collaboration and making connections;
6. integrating reflection, review, feedback and celebration;
7. taking time to travel and explore;
8. ensuring the creative involvement of the teacher.

Extract references

Craft, A. (2000) *Creativity Across the Primary Curriculum: Framing and Developing Practice*. London: Routledge Falmer.

Craft, A. (2005) *Creativity in Schools: Tensions and Dilemmas*. Oxford: Routledge Falmer.

Cremin, T. (2009) Creative teachers and creative teaching. In A. Wilson (ed.) *Creativity in Primary Education*. Exeter: Learning Matters.

Freire, P. (1985) *The Politics of Education: Culture, Power and Liberation*. USA: Bergin & Garvey Publishers inc.

Gardner, H. (1993) *Creating Minds: An Anatomy of Creativity Seen Through the Lives of Freud, Einstein, Picasso, Stravinsky, Eliot and Ghandi*. New York: Basic Books.

Grainger, T. and Barnes, J. (2006) In J. Arthur, T. Grainger and D. Wray. *Creativity in the Primary Curriculum: Research Report for Creative Partnerships*.

Jeffrey, B. and Woods, P. (2003) *The Creative School: A framework for Success, Quality and Effectiveness*. London: Routledge.

Jeffrey, B. and Woods, P. (2009) *Creative Learning in the Primary School*. Oxford: Routledge.

National Advisory Committee on Creative and Cultural Education (NACCCE) (1999) *All Our Futures: Creativity, Culture and Education*. London: Department for Education and Employment (DfEE).

Sternberg, R.J. (1997/9) *Handbook of Creativity*. Cambridge: Cambridge University Press.

Comment

Cremin adopts what might be termed a 'democratic' view of creativity. According to this view there can be creativity in everyday activities as well as in the 'big creativity' of famous artists, scientists and writers. Making connections in thought, movement and language needs to be recognised as creative acts, just as much as the production of a finished piece of writing or a poetry performance. By taking on this perspective Cremin opens the way to achieving creativity in everyday classroom activities. Skills and knowledge are not sidelined, as it is argued that a creative approach gives full weight to the importance of developing children's knowledge about language and acquisition of the skill aspects of literacy. Indeed, they are motivated to build this knowledge so that their creative efforts can get full and proper voice. These elements in the English programme, argues Cremin, can be situated in creative contexts. Another insight which emerges from this extract is that teachers as well as children need to be allowed to be creative – in their planning as well as their teaching – there's nothing drearier, for teacher or class, than following someone else's lesson plan. Cremin's classroom research pinpoints some core features of creativity and these are helpfully summarised at the end of the extract.

Questions to discuss with colleagues

1. Cremin sees possible tension between 'subject knowledge' and 'pedagogical knowledge' – that is knowledge about how children learn. Do you agree with this part of her analysis? If so, share with others your own experience of this tension.

2. Explore some ways in which Cremin's approach has some of the features of Dixon's 'personal growth' model and pinpoint some possible important differences.
3. Can you think of some interesting ways to connect creative work in school with out-of-school literacy activities?
4. It is suggested in the extract that 'multimodality' – to do with combining design, artwork and writing to make and communicate meaning – has potential for children's creativity as readers and writers. Children's picturebooks for the under-elevens often provide experience of multimodality. Choose two books and suggest how the different modes work together in each picturebook to entertain and communicate.
5. New media are emerging constantly and have an important place in the English classroom. Explain how you have used, or encouraged children to use, a non-print medium to encourage innovative work.
6. If, as Cremin and others have suggested, 'risk taking' is one of the features of 'creativity', how might teachers promote this in a climate favouring the achievement of measurable standards?

Further reading

Clipson-Boyce, S. (2012) *Teaching Primary English Through Drama: A Practical and Creative Approach*. London: David Fulton. Drama can be a flexible tool in supporting English. This author shows how drama and role play can create powerful and helpful context for different kinds of talk, reading and writing, including script writing.

Johnson, C. (2004) Creative drama: Thinking from within. In R. Fisher and M. Williams (eds) *Unlocking Creativity: Teaching Across the Curriculum*. London: David Fulton. In the spirit of the fine work of Dorothy Heathcote, Johnson shows how children can be helped to understand and use their creative understandings. I find inspiring her case study of a teacher and her Year 2 class exploring through improvisation Sendak's *Where the Wild Things Are*.

Kress, G. and van Leeuwen, T. (1996) *Reading Images: The Grammar of Visual Design*. London: Routledge. How do images communicate meaning? These authors explore visual literacy by drawing on examples of children's drawing, on textbook illustrations and on photographs as well as three-dimensional forms like sculptures.

Plowden, B. (ed.) (1967) *Children and their Primary Schools: Plowden Report*, vol. 1: The Report. London: HMSO. This seminal report favoured child-centred approaches and emphasised the central role of language – talk, story-telling, drama and writing – in education.

Wyse, D. and Jones, R. (2013, 2nd edn) *Creativity in the Primary Curriculum*. London: Routledge. Chapter 2 'English' explores how children's creativity in writing, drama and response to literature can be enhanced by their teachers' encouragement of curiosity and exploration. Case studies, interviews with teachers and children, and suggestions for using film and role play make this analysis interesting and useful.

Speaking and listening in English lessons

Story-telling, drama, booktalk and debate

Introduction

When children start to talk they acquire a powerful means of organising their thinking and of communicating with others. Thereafter, language shapes and refines all their activities, and is a major tool for learning in every lesson. Across the curriculum, talk between teacher and child accompanying learning to read and learning to write is a powerful facilitator of progress. In English lessons children have the opportunity to integrate ideas and knowledge about the things that matter to them and to express their feelings about all of this. So there is a well-deserved place for discussion about issues in the news, about school events, about personal relationships and about social and ethical issues – for example about the environment and critical questions round advertising.

But if asked to say what are the kinds of speaking and listening at the very heart of the English lesson teachers would, I think, respond with the following: oral story-telling (including anecdotes told by teachers and children); improvised drama; talk about fiction. So the extracts in the first three sections of this chapter are concerned with these. However, the kind of talk that helps planning, debate and assessment is another important part of the English curriculum and it is this kind of talk that is taken up in the later part of the chapter.

The first Extract, Section 1, is about story-telling: Mary Medlicott argues that good story-telling is an art and one that can be learnt. Teachers of children in the Early Years and Primary Years will find her suggestions for 'preparing to tell' of great practical help. Hearing someone tell a story with animation, gesture, facial expression and perhaps some props is not just deeply involving and enjoyable for its own sake, but it also refines a child's developing sense of narrative.

Role play and improvised drama also contribute to developing sense of narrative, as Lesley Clark shows in Section 2, Extract 7. She argues, too, that such activities give young children the space to explore social roles and assimilate everyday experiences. Furthermore, 'play language' is a bridge to the patterned language of rhymes and stories.

'Booktalk', talk about books and poems of all kinds and in all media, is a hugely important part of the English curriculum at every age. In Section 3, Extract 8, Aidan Chambers explains how 'three sharings' – of enthusiasms, of puzzles and of patterns – can help shape and enliven children's talk about fiction. Many teachers have found Chambers' approach both stimulating and of genuine practical help and, in Extract 9, we join a class of older primary school children as they respond intensely to a short story by Philippa Pearce with some help from the teacher, help that is informed by Chambers' three 'sharings'.

Extract 10 also takes us directly into the classroom. Learning to 'read' visual images, in print or on screen, and to understand how they relate to written text is an important part of work in English lessons. The children in this extract are deeply engaged in talking about the illustrations at least as much as about the written text in *Rose Blanche*, a picturebook that tells the story of a young girl's terrible experience in war time. Catriona Nicholson argues passionately for the power of 'book-share' in creating sensitive readers – for collaborative talk about texts between members of small groups. There is more about the qualities of picturebooks and their contribution to children's reading development in Chapter 6, Extract 46.

Then, turning to the extracts in Section 4, 'Talk to plan, assess and debate', these are about children using language to reflect and to get things done. In the first of two short extracts from Mallett and Newsome's research report, *Talking, Writing and Learning, 8–13*, older primary children plan a presentation on the life of St Patrick for the younger children in the school. This was a genuine task and the nine-year-olds show considerable understanding of the needs of their young audience. The second extract lets us listen in on children discussing their recent improvisation about the journey of the Three Wise Men. How far was this successful and how might they improve it?

Another satisfying kind of collaborate talk occurs when children are encouraged to assess their own and their peers' writing, with the possibility of this leading to changes and refinements. In Extract 13, Jonathan Rooke reports on research published by the National Literacy Trust, which shows how teachers may create a 'dialogic space' and use a visualiser to facilitate whole-class discussion of children's writing. The teachers involved in this research remarked that constructive and collaborate discussion seemed to encourage children's interest in writing and to move them forward in understanding how to recognise and even improve successful writing. (There is another extract from this research project in Chapter 8 'Planning, assessing and recording progress in English: the learning cycle' which focuses on approaches to marking and peer talk about teachers' written comments on children's writing.)

Section 1: Story-telling

Extract 6

Source

Medlicott, M. (2004, 2nd edn) Story-telling. In P. Hunt (ed.) *International Companion Encyclopedia of Children's Literature*, vol. 1. Abingdon and New York: Routledge, 619–21.

The chapter from which this extract is taken begins with the author's observation that story-telling combines the art of the tale, which is 'worth more than all the wealth in the world', with the human propensity for 'seeing life in the form of stories'. A sense of narrative structure begins early: even the very youngest children are able to talk about things that happen in their daily lives and retell stories that have been told to or read to them. In this extract Mary Medlicott, a well-known story-teller who has written widely on story-telling and made presentations in many hundreds of Nursery and primary schools, offers advice about how to make story-telling involving and dramatic. Although this advice is helpful for anyone telling a story to any audience, I think it will be particularly useful for the classroom teacher.

The art of story-telling

Story-telling is a live, expressive form in which story-tellers have a number of instruments: voice, facial expression, body movement, eye contact and, when they are used, musical instruments and props. Setting, too, is important and, as in the theatre, arrangements of the venue can also be part of the art.

Voice is the major instrument. Use of it varies enormously between tellers and cultures. Sometimes the emphasis is on an evenly paced narrative style, sometimes more on dialogue and mimicry, for example of animal noises and birdsong. Some tellers use the actor's ability to put on different voices; others rely on change of tone and pitch rather more than accent. Ability to draw on dialects is almost always admired. As well as pace, rhythm and dynamics of speech, the story-teller draws on the value of silence. Pausing is essential to give the audience time to move through the mental images summoned by the tale. The length and weight of a pause is as vital as in music.

Use of facial expression and body movement also varies greatly. Some tellers enact; others recount. Much also depends on venue. On the glow of a fireside telling, voice assumes unique importance; large gestures will seem out of place. In other settings, hand gestures, for example, may play as expressive a part as in the associated art of shadow-play.

With children eye contact is the aspect which most strongly differentiates story-telling from story-reading. It gives a host of advantages, ranging from the freedom to observe which children are restless to being better able to establish rapport and communicate emotions. Some story-tellers use cloths or interesting objects to focus interest or enhance the story. Sound-making instruments may also be used, either for effects within a story or to punctuate the telling. Where props are used, it is vital to consider the size and arrangement of the audience. Whether people are able to see is greatly affected by whether the teller sits, stands or moves about. With children, it is important not to adopt a position which might feel intimidating. For seated tellers, a low seat is often ideal and, considering the arm movements that may be used, a stool is often preferable to an armchair.

Preparing to tell

Preparation involves attending to the story as well as the circumstances in which it may be told, the nature of the event and the kind of audience. Getting to know the story is the greatest challenge and is easiest when the story has been heard and not read. Being able to remember a story that has been heard probably means that the previous story-teller has told it in a memorable way, the words, sounds and meaning already shaped and patterned for telling. With a story found in a book, the work of bringing it to life has to be done from scratch. In either case, preparation involves making the story your own.

Imagination is crucial and strongly linked with memory. Remembering a story requires making a relationship with it and visualisation, essentially the act of making pictures in the mind, is an important technique. (Significantly, story-tellers in several traditions have often been blind.) The mental pictures on which the story-teller subsequently draws during the telling may be formed from all kinds of information, visual, aural, olfactory and textural. They may also be fed by research. Another primary technique involves getting to know the story's underlying shape and structure, a task which is also helpful in identifying different types of stories and their inter-relationships ... Words are also important. In traditional story-telling, freshness and beauty are important requirements but so is the reassurance of phrasings that sound well settled, honed by time and repeated use. According to Alan Garner, the writer and collector of folk tales, 'folktale is no dull matter that anyone may touch, but more a collection of patterns to be translated with the skill, bias and authority of the craftsman, who, in serving his craft, allows that craft to serve the people' (Garner, 1980: 10).

The word stock of oral tradition consists of a wealth of phrases, refrains, formulaic runs, dialect words and proverbs and riddles. Alliteration is a frequent feature: 'There wasn't a stone but for his stumbling, not a branch but to beat his face, not a bramble but tore his skin.' Metaphor, too, is common. A person may disappear 'into the night of the wood' or run 'as swift as the thoughts of a woman caught between two lovers'. Also available are patterned beginnings and endings. 'Crick!' says the West Indian story-teller. 'Crack!' the audience replies. 'There was, there was not ...' might be a starter in Ireland. Other starters summon another kind of time: 'When birds made their nests in old men's beards ...'

Endings soften the return to reality: 'They lived happily, so may we. Put on the kettle, we'll have a cup of tea'. One common Armenian ending reminds the audience of the oral tradition. 'Three apples fell from heaven: one for the story, one for those who listened and one for those who first told the story long, long ago.'

Particularly important with children are refrains and chants encouraging participation. 'Run, run, as fast as you can. You can't catch me, I'm the gingerbread man': chanted or sung, such choral forms are also a peg for memory. Where they have not been handed on, it is worth making new ones. Where research can dig them out, it is good to bring them back into currency, adapted or in their original form. Bringing stories to life in these ways is something which children can enjoy practising as much as adults.

Extract reference

Garner, A. (1980) *The Lad of the Gad*. London: Collins.

Comment

Being told a story is a different experience to having one read from a book. Mary Medlicott believes that for children the important difference is the greater opportunity for the teller to make eye contact with the listeners. This connects teller and told very directly. She remarks that the way the voice is used varies between different cultures. However, all tellers vary in such things as how far they use dialogue and the way in which they use facial expressions and gesture to reveal character. It is encouraging that Mary Medlicott believes that the craft of story-telling can be learnt. But adults telling stories to children need to do some preparation, including giving some thought to such practical things as an appropriate venue or setting for the particular story and the need, perhaps, for simple props. She writes interestingly about the role of the imagination in a successful telling and about how visualisation – making pictures in the mind – aids memory. One thing that Mary points out rings true to me: children like to hear stories with refrains and when they tell stories themselves these are an aid to memory.

Questions to discuss with colleagues

1. In the extract, it is noted that the venue or setting in which a story is told can inspire. Have you used a setting which proved to be an exciting or atmospheric backdrop to a particular story told to your age group?
2. Stories incorporating rhymes can provide 'pegs' for memory. Can you think of examples of stories with chants or rhymes which might help children to begin to tell stories?
3. What do you think Mary Medlicott means by 'softening endings' and how would you do this in particular tellings?

Research inquiry

Choose a story to tell to a group or whole class of children.

Decide on a suitable venue, taking account, of course, of the age of the children and the nature of the story. Teachers of very young children sometimes go outside to the park or the school garden to tell a story about the creatures that live there. For older children, something as simple as pulling the classroom blinds down and telling the story in torchlight can add atmosphere.

Ask the children, after the telling, what they thought of the story, and if the venue (and perhaps any props used) added to their enjoyment.

Write a short account of your findings, if possible including direct quotations from what the children said.

Further reading

Daniel, A.K. (2011) *Storytelling Across the Primary Curriculum*. Abingdon: Routledge. Chapter 1 explores the social nature of story-telling and suggests how teachers and children can tell a tale together. See also chapter 6, 'Words, words, words: storytelling, language and literacy'.

Drever, C. (2015) Words on the wind – storytelling in the woods. *English 4–11* (autumn 2015). In this lyrical account, eleven-year-olds tell stories in a woodland setting and listen to their teacher telling an ancient fairy tale.

Graham, J. (2011, 3rd edn) The magic must not vanish: Traditional tales in the classroom. In P. Goodwin (ed.) *The Literate Classroom*. Abingdon and New York: Routledge. See chapter 15. Judith Graham reflects on her own practice and concludes that children benefit greatly from hearing the creative use of language in story-telling.

Harrett, J. (2009, 2nd edn) *Tell Me Another … Speaking, Listening and Learning Through Storytelling*. Leicester: United Kingdom Literacy Association (UKLA). This booklet offers help with choosing stories, including traditional stories, to tell to different age groups. Advice is also given about encouraging children's story-telling.

Kucirkova, N. (2014) *iPads and Tablets in the Classroom: Personalising Children's Stories*. Leicester: UKLA Minibook 41. Since the 2000s technology has changed how we think about children's spoken and written story-telling. This author shows how 'personalised stories' can be 'socially relevant and culturally sensitive'.

Smith, C. (2014) *147 Traditional Stories for Primary Children to Re-tell*. London: Hawthorn Press. This book from the founder of 'Storytelling Schools' has an index linking stories to topics, plot and lands of origin.

Section 2: Role play and improvised drama

Extract 7

Source

Clark, L. (2001) Foundations for talk – speaking and listening in the early years classroom. In P. Goodwin (ed.) *The Articulate Classroom: Talking and Learning in the Primary School*. London: David Fulton, 87–8.

After considering how the teacher can make story-telling come alive, attention turns in the next extract to children's story-telling through role play. Role play allows children space in which to explore different roles and social situations; this helps them to understand their world and to make sense of their own experience of that world. During the Early Years children enjoy creating satisfying narratives. Sometimes these are retellings of stories they have read or had read to them. Lesley Clark suggests that play narratives are a bridge from spoken language to the patterned language of nursery rhymes and stories for the very young.

The language of play and role play

Research into children's play repeatedly demonstrates the richness and range of language employed: 'by engaging in children's story making in an active and participatory manner I have uncovered depths of understanding and complexity of ideas that are difficult to tap in the ordinary everyday activities of the best classroom' (Hendy 1995). Young children may use a stylised running commentary to sustain their individual play. This includes, singing, rhyming and gesture together with descriptive detail of what and how they are directing the action in their storying. Thus, a child playing with 'Brio-Mec' hums and sings the journey his train takes, using repetition and noises to punctuate the script. Collaborative play and role play offers authentic purposes for exploring different types of talk. Negotiating and confirming roles and responsibilities, sharing resources and deciding how they are going to be played with, are very demanding. Such play is often fluid and requires frequent re-directing, so arguing and persuading, reaffirming and explaining are required to sustain it. Negotiating and sustaining storylines allows children to direct their play. By sharing in and celebrating these play narratives, teachers can make links with the patterned language and structures of shared readings and story-tellings. Observing retellings, often supported by puppets or props, provides teachers with insights into children's understanding and enjoyment of story. Take, for example, this extract from a video *The Foundations of Learning* (Barrs *et al.*, 1999), which shows a group of nursery children collaboratively reconstructing the story of Three Billy Goats Gruff using a wooden brick bridge and a mask for the Troll:

Child A: Who's that tripping-trap over my bridge?

Child B: It's only me – little one.

Child C: AAAAHHH! Leave my little brother alone!

(The voice of Little Billy Goat Gruff surprises all! The troll prompts goat on bridge.)

Child A: You've got to say 'Wait for that one.' Go on …

Child B: No you …

Child C: LEAVE MY BROTHER ALONE!

(This impassioned plea leads a passing boy to intervene.)

Child D: I'm gonna see what's going on … (He kicks wooden block bridge that is supporting troll.) I knocked your house down.

Acting out stories provides safe ways to explore strong emotions, supported by an attentive adult whose empathy (and sense of humour) allows him or her to maximise experiences for the children. Role play provides children with opportunities to demonstrate their understanding by tapping into experiences, voices and contexts beyond the classroom. Messages, lists, receipts, cards, invitations, official forms, environmental print or finding out what's on television invite the explorations of 'everyday' literacy. This realism energises role play with a range of purposes and audiences. By involving children in initiating and resourcing role play areas, teachers can rehearse scenarios and highlight and model literary acts. Repetition and patterning of play facilitate teacher intervention, often in role, to extend the learning, while ensuring control remains with the children. These factors combine to motivate children towards taking risks and exploring literacy in ways they may find more problematic in more structured work. Hall and Robinson (1995) provide examples of the skilled use of role play to support writing, such as the teacher writing in role. Whole-class talk can then be used to validate and extend their play.

Extract references

Barrs, M. *et al.* (1999) *The Foundations of Learning.* London: Centre for Language in Education (CLPE). (Now Centre for Literacy in Education.)

Hall, N. and Robinson, A. (1995) *Exploring Writing and Play in the Early Years.* London: David Fulton.

Hendry, L. (1995) *Playing, Role Play and Dramatic Activity in the Early Years,* vol. 15, No. 2. Stoke-on-Trent: Trentham Books.

Comment

Lesley Clark first notes that young children's spontaneous role play often centres on everyday events. In my experience, the sort of themes that might inspire engaged role play include going shopping, searching for a lost toy or picnicking in the park. Young children find this kind of play deeply satisfying and it helps them understand about social roles, to have feelings about others and to develop their language. Clark then looks at story as a starting point for improvisation with attention to a particular example – the acting out of 'The Three Billy Goats Gruff'. Here, the story provides a structure for role play and the opportunity to collaborate. There is evidence that the children are taking over some of the language and patterning in the story – 'Who's that tripping-trap over my bridge?' Clark's analysis supports the belief that role play, whether around everyday events or inspired and structured by a story, expands and enriches spoken language. She claims that the best role play and early attempts at improvised drama, carefully monitored by the teacher, introduce and nurture some kinds and uses of language difficult to encounter in any other context.

Questions to discuss with colleagues

1. In the extract from Lesley Clark very young children act out a story they have been read. The teacher is present but does not intervene. How might you lead discussion about the characters and the plot with the children when the improvisation has ended?
2. What do you think the teacher might learn from the 'Troll' improvisation about the children's understanding of both the development of plot and the patterns of language typical of stories?
3. Suggest some other stories you might read to this age group which could lead to improvisation. Some of the themes which seem to appeal include: need for adventure versus need for security; making friends; losing and then finding precious things; overcoming fears and worries.
4. If your chosen age group is the middle or later Primary Years, how would you develop improvisation either round social and environmental issues – for example people objecting to building projects – or by using a story as a starting point? (I have found that Anthony Browne's picturebook *The Tunnel* has often led to imaginative improvisation on the theme of sibling rivalry.)

Research inquiry

Choose a children's story or picturebook for your specialist age group which throws up an involving theme. Working with the whole class or a small group, help the children improvise the story or part of the story.

If possible, record or film the drama and after studying it make some notes on the children's understanding of:

- the development of the plot;
- the feelings of the characters;
- social issues inherent in the story.

Further reading

Clipson-Boyes, S. (2011, 3rd edn) The role of drama in the literate classroom. In P. Goodwin (ed.) *The Literate Classroom*. Abingdon and New York: Routledge. Provides an overview of drama in the primary curriculum and shows how in drama contexts speaking, listening, reading and writing 'are interlinked in useful and meaningful ways'. There are suggestions for drama and talk round literature: 'Goldilocks and the Three Bears' (Early Years Foundation Stage), the early chapters of Jan Mark's *The Snow Maze* (Key Stage 1) and chapters 1 and 2 of Ted Hughes' *The Iron Man* (Key Stage 2).

Cremin, T. and McDonald, R. (2014, 2nd edn) Developing creativity through drama. In R. Jones and D. Wyse (eds) *Creativity in the Primary Curriculum*. London: David Fulton. Shows how drama can draw out children's ability to be creative in exploring social roles and situations.

O'Neill, C. (ed.) (2015) *Dorothy Heathcote on Education and Drama: Essential Writings*. Abingdon: Routledge. Dorothy Heathcote is known for her drama work with all age groups and in many countries. Her 'teacher in role' and 'mantle of the expert' strategies have been used across the curriculum to promote children's learning. For the use of stories as a framework for drama, see the chapter entitled 'Stories as context in Mantle of the Expert'.

Wyse, D. and Jones, R. (2013, 3rd edn) Drama and texts. In *Teaching English, Language and Literacy*. London: Routledge, 106–8. Describes two examples of drama, one using the story of 'Little Red Riding Hood', the other using the first chapter of *Goodnight Mister Tom* by Michelle Magorian. Here, drama techniques like questioning characters in role, picturing scenes as they might appear in film, mime, hot seating, taking on the mantle of the expert and freeze framing are explained.

Section 3: Booktalk – talk round stories, poems and novels

Extract 8

Source

Chambers, A. (2011 edn) The three sharings. In *Tell Me: Children, Reading and Talk* (published in this edition with the companion book *The Reading Environment: How Adults Help Children Enjoy Books*). Stroud: Thimble Press, 103–7.

Who was it who remarked that talking about books in school should, as much as possible, be like a conversation between friends? I seem to remember it was a secondary school teacher called John Walsh who also wrote poems for younger children, including *The Bully Asleep* (the bully asleep, available at http://technology.tki.org.nz, accessed 17 November 2014). Aidan Chambers, an author of children's books and of novels, plays and books of literary criticism, identifies the important elements in such conversations in this extract from *Tell Me*. The fact that this book has been published in North American and Australian editions and in nine foreign language editions shows how wide has been its influence on all those who care about involving children with books. Whatever new media and technological discoveries bring, I believe that this framework and these insights will be of continuing value, a lasting guide to how adults can help children understand and enjoy texts.

Sharing enthusiasms

When friends start talking about a book it's usually because one of them wants to share her enthusiasm. 'I've just read this amazing book,' she says. 'Have you read it?'

We all know the variations on that opening ploy, and how the conversation then continues. If others in the group haven't read the book, they want to know what it is about. But what does 'about' mean? Most people simply reply by giving the plot and the characters or the story's setting. What they don't talk about is significance. They tend to say something like: 'oh it is about these three older men who go off on a sailing trip leaving their families behind and then ...' Much less often they say: It's a novel about family politics and the strains on family life in a post-feminist society.' That is, they do not summarize meaning as an academic critic would. Rather, they tend to retell the story and talk about what they liked and didn't like – which might be anything from the nature of the story and characters and setting to the form, the way it is told.

If the others have read the book, the talk tends to slip at once into the kind of sharing that begins with such ploys as: 'Did you like the part where ...' or 'Didn't you think it was funny when ...'

In everyday gossip, people seem to delay discussion of meaning (interpretation and significance) till they have heard what their friends have to say. In other words, the meaning of a story *for that group of readers* emerges from the conversation; it isn't set up at the start and then discussed, which is what happens in formal academic 'booktalk'. These book-reading friends are sharing two kinds of enthusiasm:

- ■ *likes:* enthusiasms about elements in the story that have pleased and attracted, surprised and impressed them and made them want to go on reading;
- ■ *dislikes:* aversions to elements in the story that displeased them, or put them off reading for one reason or another.

It is important to understand that readers are often as vehement about what they have disliked as about what they've liked. You see the effect of this in gossip. If friends like the same things and find themselves in complete agreement, the gossip is less interesting and ends sooner than if there are elements that inspire opposing responses.

Sharing puzzles (i.e. difficulties)

A reader will often express dislike for elements of the story that have puzzled him – things he found difficult to understand. 'What did it mean when …' he'll say, or: 'Did you understand the bit where …' Sometimes we hide our puzzlement in such comments as, 'I didn't like the way the story ended, did you?' or 'I wasn't convinced by the teacher as a character, were you?' Or 'What was it you liked so much about the scene where … ?'

One of the friends will try to provide an answer. (How this is done is considered below in 'Sharing connections'.) It is in this part of the talk that meaning – an interpretation of the story – is most obviously being negotiated. The friends discuss the puzzle and the suggested explanation, and out of this comes an understanding of (or an agreement to disagree on) what the text is 'about' – what it 'means' – to that group of readers at that time.

I say 'that group of readers at that time' because a different group of readers might well discover a different emphasis of meaning. As indeed might the same group of readers at a later date. The meanings of any text shift according to the context of the readers' own lives and their needs at a particular time …

Which is why we now accept that, as Frank Kermode wrote, 'the illusion of the single right reading is possible no longer'. In any text, no matter how simple, there is always the possibility of multiple meanings.

In sharing and solving difficulties over the puzzling elements of a story we may discover what that piece of writing means for each of us now.

Sharing connections (i.e. discovering patterns)

We solve puzzles, we resolve difficulty, by finding significant connections between one element in a text and another: elements, for example, of language, motifs, events, characters, symbols and so on. Human beings cannot bear chaos, meaninglessness, confusion. We constantly look for connectedness, for patterns of relationship between one thing and another that make meaning we can understand. And if we can't find a pattern, we tend to construct one out of the disparate odds and ends of raw material in front of us. We do this with everything in our lives, and we do it as we read.

We can only 'read' when we can recognise in the marks on the page the patterns called words and sentences. But learning to read stories isn't only a matter of learning to recognise these verbal patterns. It is also a matter of learning to use the formal narrative patterns of the story itself.

Think of it like this: a building is made of bricks and stone and wood and steel, which we identify when we see them. But these materials are used to create a pattern of shapes that make rooms of different kinds, and stairs and roofs and windows and doors, which in turn create different kinds of building – in a house, an office

block, a factory, a school – which we also learn to identify from our experience of knowing how each is used. Texts are the same. They are built of different elements of language used in various ways to create different kinds of texts. We learn to look for details of design, constructed in patterns that tell us what kind of building, what kind of story we have in front of us.

When the 'Tell Me' approach is being used, children sometimes have trouble understanding what we mean by 'patterns'. Try drawing their attention to the story patterns in familiar folk tales (the three sons, the third one of which performs three tests in order to win the prize, for example; the repeated 'I'll huff and I'll puff and I'll blow your house down' in 'The Three Little Pigs'); the pattern of rhythm and rhyme in a limerick; and the visual patterns in illustrations and decoration that help us 'make sense' of a picture. They'll soon catch on and extend the range of their pattern-finding. Not that all the patterns come from the text itself. There are extra-textual patterns that can be brought to the reader's aid. Two of these and another, third, are important in booktalk and the making of meaning.

- Critics call the first one *world-to-text*. This means comparing the events or characters or language of a story with events or people or language known personally to the reader. We bring our own world to the world of the text and by comparing them discover meanings in one or other or in both.
- In the same way readers sometimes *compare one text with another*. They describe how one book is like another or how it differs. Or they compare a character in one story with a character in another, understanding both a little better by thinking about their similarities and differences.
- Both of these comparisons rely on *memory*: memory of our own lives, memory of other texts we've read. The play of memory provoked by a text is an integral part of the experience of reading and a source of its pleasure. Very often in ordinary book gossip all the talk will be concentrated on the memories the book has brought to mind.

These features in book gossip do not occur in any formal order. They are mixed up as the talk meanders about, apparently without conscious arrangement. In fact, the talk is guided by immediate need: the need to express satisfactions, the need to articulate new thoughts in order to hear what they sound like, the need to 'bring out' disturbing elements provoked by the story so that we can contextualise them – hold them up – so to speak, look at them, and thus gain some control over them. Like ordinary gossip, 'Tell Me' booktalk is not orderly and linear, not what some experts call 'totalizing discourse'. It is not the sort of discussion that looks for specific answers to questions asked in a prescribable order, one question 'logically' following another.

In essence, talking about literature is a form of shared contemplation. Booktalk is a way of giving form to the thoughts and emotions stimulated by the book and by the meaning(s) we make together out of its text – the imaginatively controlled messages sent from the author that we interpret in whatever way we find useful or delightful.

Comment

The 'repertoire of questions' which Aidan Chambers offers here helps teachers and children to talk about books and the feelings they awaken. It has been used successfully with children of different ages and has informed the approach to talking about literature in many classrooms. Now that reading visual texts has become important, many are finding that the Chambers' framework of questions about enthusiasms, puzzles and patterns works well.

Questions to discuss with colleagues

1. This question requires a member of the discussion group to bring a story to the session. (It may be a work of fiction for either adults or for children.) After the first few pages have been read out loud, ask the reader to begin a group discussion about 'enthusiasms and puzzles' that arise from the text. Next, evaluate this way of approaching an appraisal of a work of fiction.
2. Following on from the question above, do you agree with Chambers that 'readers are often as vehement about what they have disliked as what they liked?' Do you find this is the case with children? If so, which books, characters or incidents in books have you found children in your specialist age group dislike? (I am reminded of the time I saw a child throw a nursery rhyme book out of a window as she found the 'Wee Willie Winkie' rhyme and illustration made her feel uneasy.)
3. Aidan Chambers argues that in successful booktalk there arises a 'shared contemplation'. How would you help children who are making a rather tentative start begin to share the feelings and memories awakened by the story or poem under discussion?

Research inquiry

Following Chambers' advice about helping children to recognise patterns in literature, choose a story, picturebook or poem and help a small group of children in your specialist age phase to recognise some of these patterns. For example:

■ patterns in numbers – common in fairy tales which may be about three sons, three wishes or twelve princesses;
■ patterns in language – repetition is common in poetry and in folk tales; language to do with a theme or setting – for example words to do with water, heat or fear;
■ if the chosen text is a picturebook discuss patterns in the illustrations of perhaps colour, form or iconography and how these connect with the written text.

Make a series of notes and either present your findings in a talk to colleagues or write them up as a short paper or article.

Extract 9

Source

Mallett, M. (1997) 'Can you say a little more about that?' Helping children make their response to fiction explicit. *Education 3–13*, 25 (1), 11–17.

In the following extract, taken from a longer transcript, a group of six children in their last term in primary school are helped to make their understandings about the underlying meanings in a short story explicit. The story, *What the Neighbours Did* by Philippa Pearce, was read aloud and discussed over the course of an afternoon. In the previous extract, Aidan Chambers identified some of the important elements in 'booktalk'. He explained that the 'enthusiasms', 'puzzles' and 'patterns' which are important elements in such conversations do not occur in any particular order but 'meander about' and so it is in this case.

> *What the Neighbours Did* is a first-person narrative revealing events through the eyes of a child who becomes unwittingly involved in one neighbour's theft from another. At particular moments there are revelations or 'epiphanies' where the child becomes aware of the different values and attitudes human beings have. Moments of revelation occur in all fiction, but in short stories these illuminating moments have to be particularly sharply focussed. I wanted to tune them in to the type of fiction we were about to read.
>
> *Adam*: (leafing through the story) This seems quite long for a short story!
>
> *Teacher*: Well it's shorter than the stories Mrs Mac reads to you a chapter at a time.
>
> *Christine*: Yes ... shorter than *Stig of the Dump* or *Carrie's War*.
>
> *Teacher*: You can usually read a short story through at one time ... what do you think a writer of a short story has to bear in mind?
>
> *Scott*: I think you haven't so many words and you need a short sharp start and probably a short ending but with a longer middle.
>
> *Christine*: Yes but it has to be a good ending.
>
> *Scott*: And have a main character.

I wanted the children to recognise that an author's choices are partly shaped by the conventions of the genre or kind of writing. Scott and Christine are beginning to appreciate that many of the features of the short story are to do with its length. The main characters have to be introduced early and the setting swiftly established. Endings cannot be lingering, but they need to be satisfying and may have an intriguing twist. Building on the children's points, I suggested to them that every word, phrase and sentence in a short story is important and included for a reason. There is careful, economical language as there is in poetry.

Responding to character, plot and ideas

There were two interventions to share responses to the author's creation of character. First Scott asked us to pause to discuss the part of the story where one neighbour's secret – a dog hidden in the garden shed – is discovered by his wife.

Scott: Shall I read it? 'Mr Macy came out first, with his head down and his arms sort of curved above it: and Mrs Macy came out close behind him, aiming at his head with a light broom – but aiming quite hard.'

Teacher: Can you say why you wanted to draw attention to this bit?

Scott: Well it describes it well – how he came out.

Teacher: Yes it does. Can you say a little more about that?

Scott: Well he's holding his hands above his head to protect it from the broom. His arms are 'curved' to protect it.

Teacher: Yes. We get a strong picture of how he was running along, curving his arm to cushion his head against any blow from the broom. This tells us something about both the Macys.

Adam: He's frightened of her.

Joanna: She's not a nice person.

Teacher: Is there any other detail which tells us more about the Macys? (Pause while children scan the text so far.)

Adam: I can't find the bit – but somewhere it says she put his food out of the kitchen window while he's doing jobs in the garden. I think that's cruel. He has to eat alone.

Teacher: Could Mr Macy be partly responsible for his wife's attitude and behaviour?

Scott: Yes because he's weak. Can't stand up for himself and he can't help the dog that he likes.

Adam: I've found that bit … page 118. 'He was retired and every morning in all weathers Mrs Macy'd turn him out into the garden and make him stay there until he had done as much work as she thought right. She would put his dinner out to him through the scullery window.' That bit shows how unkind she is.

Teacher: And perhaps also how weak Mr Macy is to put up with it.

Here, with some support, the children have been able to see how an author reveals a person's nature by relating particularly telling incidents. By inviting further scrutiny of the text we can show there is often a cumulative effect of such revelations. The scullery example is of a piece with the broom-chasing episode. The children needed encouragement to go beyond Mrs Macy's behaviour to examine the flaws in her husband's character that may have contributed to the kind of relationship it seems to be.

The second passage chosen spontaneously, this time by Joanna, shows that children are often moved on in their thinking not by the bland and 'cosy' view of life but by things that are troubling or even unpleasant ...

Joanna: I've got a bit that isn't very nice ... about Mr Macy when he wants the boy to take the money back to Dick. (To the others.) It's on page 126 near the top. 'There was a tiny bit of froth at one corner of his mouth, as though he had been chewing his words in advance. The sight of his mouth made me not want to stay; but then the way he looked at me made me feel that I had to.' It's horrible when people have bits of food that you can see ...

Teacher: Why do you think that the author included that detail?

Joanna: ... the boy had to go on looking at it because he wants to hear what Mr Macy is going to say.

Teacher: Yes and just as the things Mr Macy is going to own up to are unpleasant so is the appearance of his mouth. Do you think the author uses something repulsive like frothing food as a sort of symbol of the unsavoury things the character is going to say? A symbol is something that represents something else isn't it?

Joanna: Yes because it says it was as if he had been chewing his words. He wants the boy to put the money back. That's cowardly because he stole the money and now he regrets it.

Christine: Sometimes bad people in films look horrible as well as doing horrible things ...

We take up the transcript again at a point when Scott, invited to read out loud part of the story, chooses the part where the young narrator tells his family that their neighbour, Mr Macy, has been forced by his wife to abandon the old blind dog he has been protecting.

Inference and deduction

Scott (reads) 'There was a pause, when even Nora seemed to be thinking.'

Teacher: Pause there, Scott.

Scott: I think the boy is hoping he can be allowed to keep the dog and the others are thinking they don't want it. Because the next bit tells you – 'Dad said at last: that's bad. But we've got four people in this little house and a dog already, and a cat and two birds. There's no room for anything else.'

Joanna: Mrs M, a lot of people think pets are a lot of trouble and especially if it is an old creature and blind as well. Do you watch Animal Hospital? A man threw a dog out of the window.

Adam: Somebody left two dogs without food in a house and one dog ate the others.

Scott: Can I read the next bit?

Teacher: Yes — top of page 121 — the father suggests the boy take the dog to the police station and explain it is a stray.

Scott (reads) ' "But what will they do with it?" Dad looked as though he wished I hadn't asked that, but he said: "Nothing, I expect. Well they might hand it over to the Cruelty to Animals people." "And what will they do with it?" Dad was rattled. "They do what they think is best for animals …" '

> *Scott:* The boy keeps on asking the question but the Dad doesn't want to answer because he doesn't want to tell him that an old blind dog might be put down by the RSPCA.
>
> *Michael:* Sometimes they let people that want a pet choose them.
>
> *Adam:* Not much chance of that sort of one being chosen.
>
> *Terry:* Yes because blind dogs can cause accidents if they try to cross the road and they can't see a car.
>
> *Scott:* Mrs M, can I ask everyone something? Do you think a dog can be blind and still happy?
>
> *Christine:* If it has a kind owner.
>
> *Adam:* If a dog or a person loses their sight sometimes they can hear and smell better.
>
> *Teacher:* So, Scott, perhaps having smell, touch and hearing make it possible for a creature to still get some pleasure from life. But, as Christine says, you need a kind owner.

I think the small group context and close attention to the text make it possible for the children to reflect and go deeper into the issues that the story raises. Scott, in particular, has been able to think about characters' motivations. Because he has lived a bit longer than his son the father can see that, while they all feel sorry for the dog, their own quality of life might be under threat if they took it on. Scott has noted the tension between the boy's relentless questioning about the dog's likely fate and the father's reluctance actually to put in words the probable outcome. The other children have been put in a context where they have had to consider and reflect on a small piece of text more deeply than they might otherwise have done. Their ability to read between the lines, to infer more than the text actually makes explicit, has been sharpened …

When it came to choice of vocabulary the children tended to break in during the reading of the story. On one occasion Michael broke in to ask what 'contradict' meant. The text tells us that the theft was confirmed not by Dick volunteering the information, but by his 'not contradicting' those who suggested this was the case. Asked to help, Christine gave an example: 'If your Mum said – your hands are dirty and you said no they are not, your Mum might say – don't contradict me.' Scott admired the word 'lumbered' to describe the movement of the old dog when the shed door was opened.

> *Scott:* It means very slow movement.
>
> *Terry:* 'Slowly' would be more boring.

Joanna: Also 'lumbered' makes it sound as though it could almost be tripping over itself.

Teacher: Yes it sounds like a clumsy movement, the movement of an old blind creature.

Adam: It is one of those words where the sound is like the movement – lum-bered.

Christine: Lumbered sounds more interesting. I know a dog that lumbers along.

Extract reference

Pearce, P. (1994) *What the Neighbours Did.* In J. Mark (ed.) *The Oxford Book of Children's Stories.* Oxford and New York: Oxford University Press, 117–31.

Comment

Some of the elements in Aidan Chambers' analysis of booktalk in Extract 8 are recognisable in this conversation. The talk flows from discussing 'patterns' in the behaviour of one of the characters, Mrs Macy – she is consistently unkind to her husband with small acts of meanness. Then Joanna's thoughtful observations about Mr Macy's frothing mouth when talking to the boy who narrates the story can be conceived of as a 'puzzle'. Talking with her peers about what she says is 'not very nice' helps her see the author's intentions in including something that reveals character. But, above all, this conversation between a teacher and a group of children shows what Chambers points out – the importance of the memories and feelings a work of fiction awakens. His 'world-to-text' principle is at work when Joanna comments that people think a dog can be a lot of trouble 'especially if it is an old creature and blind as well'. Reading the story about the dog's plight brings back memories of a television programme some of the children have viewed at home called *Animal Hospital*.

Questions to discuss with colleagues

1. Why do you consider the teacher nudges the children back to the text at points in the discussion?
2. What are the signs that some of the children are making progress in inferring meaning not made explicit in the text?
3. In Extract 8 from Aidan Chambers' *Tell Me*, he mentions the value of 'shared contemplation'. At which points in the transcript do you feel that the children and teacher are achieving this?
4. At which points in the transcript do you think the children's comments suggest they are becoming more aware of the writer's craft, for example in making linguistic choices?

Further reading

King, C. and Briggs, J. (2011) *Literature Circles: Better Talking, More Ideas.* Leicester: UKLA Minibook 36. These authors argue that the kind of talk encouraged in 'literature circles' promotes adventurous and critical reading.

Reedy, D. (2011, 3rd edn) Talk in guided reading sessions. In P. Goodwin, P. (ed.) *The Literate Classroom*. Abingdon and New York: Routledge. A scholarly account based both on transcripts of children talking about books, including Jan Mark's short story *Nothing To Be Afraid Of* and Anthony Browne's picturebook *Gorilla*, and informed by research into the power of dialogue as a way of learning and understanding.

Extract 10

Source

Nicholson, C. (2011, 3rd edn) Reading the pictures: Children's responses to *Rose Blanche*. In P. Goodwin (ed.) *The Literate Classroom*. London and New York: Routledge, 108–10.

The children whose conversation about a short story is set out in Extract 10 concentrate hard to read and make sense of a written text. But becoming literate today is not just a matter of learning to read and write print texts, it is also to do with interpreting and evaluating both static and moving images. A very real opportunity to develop visual literacy in English lessons occurs when teacher and children read and talk about picturebooks together. In the following extract Catriona Nicholson, for many years a primary school teacher and tutor on advanced courses on children's literature, observes children reflecting deeply on the visual images in *Rose Blanche* and make connections between the pictures and the spare written text. Full-page illustrations seem to convey what would be difficult to explain in words. This engrossing, haunting and much praised picturebook tells a moving story about the sad realities of war and particularly those of the Second World War. Everything that happens is seen through the eyes of Rose, a young German girl, who discovers starving children held behind a concentration camp fence near her village. I chose this extract because it is an example of creative and successful classroom practice informed by careful scholarship and set within a theoretical framework.

From theory to practice

As with all good classroom practice, the concept of book sharing is underpinned by theoretical principles. Iser's (1974) study of the phenomenology of reading and the subsequent work of Aidan Chambers (1985/2012) establish frameworks of reference for examining the responses of the children who shared *Rose Blanche*.

I have selected, from several hours of taped book-share conversations, extracts from the opening and closing discussions as they exemplify Iser's assertion that the act of reading is a 'sense-making activity' (Iser, 1978). The group of four Year 5 children was unfamiliar with the book but the two Year 6 boys had briefly examined it in the previous year. The responses of the two boys support Iser's view that a second reading of a text elicits 'a kind of advance retrospection'. The responses of all six readers show how 'impressions that arise will vary from individual to individual' (Iser, 1974). By way of introduction to the book, both groups concentrated on 'reading' the jacket illustration and, as they began to interpret the puzzle of its

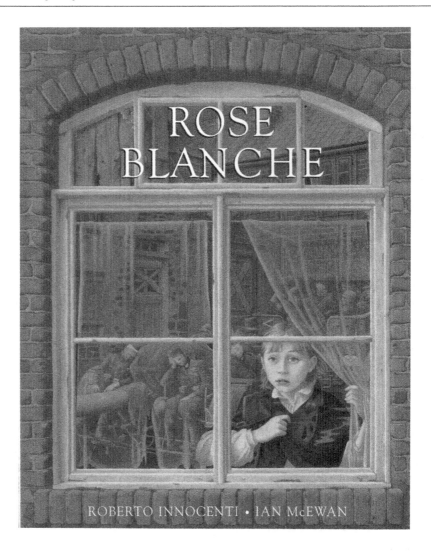

Figure 2.1 Front cover of *Rose Blanche* by Ian McEwan and Roberto Innocenti (illustrator). Artwork reproduced with the permission of The Random House Group Ltd.

reflected war images, they began the process of 'establishing connections – filling in the gaps left by the text'. Rose Blanche stares from behind a curtained window on to an unseen outside. Behind, but apparently within, her inside world are reflections of injured soldiers. There is compelling engagement between her disquieting gaze and the eye of the reader. Chambers (1985/2012) reminds us that, 'In books where the implied reader is a child, authors … put at the centre of a story a child through whose being everything is felt … the child is thus wooed into the book … and led through whatever experience is offered.'

Articulating responses

Ian and David, encountering the book for the second time, having offered me remembrances of their initial reading, were clearly 'wooed' into the book:

David: She seems like she's an angel with the innocent blue eyes and yellow hair ... she just needs curled hair and a fancy dress and she could live literally in a forest and be another Snow White.

CN: Can you describe her gaze?

David: Her eyes are just innocent.

Ian: She's someone who doesn't seem to belong to anything because of the war ... her eyes have no depth ... it's as if she is trying to get out the feelings of all the killing and hatred. The illustration does not give her eyes any depth ... she is trying to repel something, she's just horrified. This reflection is the other side of war.

CN: Does what you see on this front cover encourage you to open the book?

Ian: It does me. If I was seeing it for the first time I'd think, 'well, what's inside?'

Discussing the impact of Rose Blanche's face on the cover, both boys confirmed once again Chambers' proposal that the child reader is led through the book. Ian said:

'I can see the war through Rose Blanche's eyes because that's how the words have been written but with the pictures you kind of feel an onlooker at times because all through the book I remember you can see her and you can always see something in there which tells you that's where she was or that's where she is now.'

David similarly demonstrates how 'advance retrospection' directs his thoughts as, with the benefit of a previous reading, he recalls the impact of the book:

'With the killing and the cruelty to come, if you try to shut it out you can't because of Rose Blanche. If she wasn't there you would shut it out.'

The responses of the younger group bore out Iser's theory that a literary text (illustration) is 'something of an arena in which the reader and the author engage in a game of the imagination'. He refers to reading as a 'dynamic act of recreation' and proposes that the process is neither smooth nor continuous but one which:

'In its essence relies on interruptions of the flow ... we look forward, we look back, we decide, we change our decisions, we form expectations, we are shocked by their non-fulfilment, we question, we muse, and accept, we reject ... we oscillate between the building and the breaking of illusions.' (Iser, 1974: 288)

The unwritten narrative of the cover promoted animated discussion as the four readers made predictions, modified them and oscillated between the 'building and breaking of illusions'. They began to make sense of the cover illustration by constructing scenarios for the forthcoming narrative:

Sophie: Who is the girl?

James: She is looking out of a window but the men went off to the war but ... um ... didn't come back and she is seeing their ghosts ... meeting their ghosts.

Rachel: 'Cos if you look at the window you sort of see cobwebby things hanging … Maybe it's after the war.

Anthony: I think it is the middle of the war.

Rachel: Maybe she's like a Florence Nightingale. She's been helping these people who are ill and … she's been helping those people put bandages round their heads.

James: I think it is a reflection in a mirror …

Anthony: Maybe she's imagining it all. It's a reflection.

James: Yes, it's a reflection.

Rachel: Normally. If there's a reflection it would be a different way round. I reckon she may be looking out of it.

Anthony: She looks as if she has been evacuated.

Rachel: Maybe her father has been killed … or her mother.

Sophie: Is she the reflection?

As this group searched for narrative information, located pictorial clues, discarded ideas, hypothesized, hovered between sudden revelation and the conflict of uncertainties, they demonstrated how their expressive and varied conjectures verified Iser's (1974: 280) view that in reading, 'the opportunity is given … to bring into play our own faculty for establishing connections – for filling in "gaps" which are often so fragmentary that one's attention … is occupied with the search for connections between the fragments.'

Extract references

Chambers, A. (1985) *Booktalk*. London: The Bodley Head.
Chambers, A. (1993/2012) *Tell Me: Children, Reading and Talk*. Stroud: Thimble Press.
Iser, W. (1974) *The Implied Reader*. Boston, MA: Johns Hopkins University Press.
Iser, W. (1978) *The Act of Reading: A Theory of Aesthetic Response*. Baltimore, MD and London: Johns Hopkins University Press.
McEwan, I. and Innocenti, R. (1985) *Rose Blanche*. London: Jonathan Cape.

Comment

Following the writing of such educationists as Wolfgang Iser and Aidan Chambers, Catriona Nicholson argues that a good telling of a story, in this case through pictures as well as through words, enables readers to create for themselves the meanings in the text. Roberto Innocenti's evocative illustrations, with their atmospheric settings full of detail, engage the children's attention and inform their speculations about the unfolding story and its meaning.

Although readers, whatever their age, make an individual response to a work of literature, sharing those responses and listening to what others think contributes to what Nicholson terms 'communal understanding of a text'. So a member of the conversing group might express an opinion on the motives of a character, but if someone points to another way of construing things, first thoughts and opinions might be modified.

The transcripts of the four younger children's intense conversations about the meaning of the cover shows them responding to each other's theories as they 'read' the visual messages. They note the young girl's empty stare and wonder if the soldiers behind her are really there or are ghostly images. Later, they turn their minds to the meaning of the illustrations inside the book; the transcripts show their efforts to 'read', speculate about and reach some understandings of the messages in a visual text. Nicholson pinpoints quality talking and active listening in small group contexts as crucial in helping children become sensitive and critical readers.

Questions to discuss with colleagues

In preparation for discussion, at least one copy of *Rose Blanche* needs to be available as well as copies of other picturebooks members of the group consider have something to teach us about visual literacy.

1. How far do you agree with Nicholson that *Rose Blanche* is a creative work which 'compels children to respond'? Can you think of other children's picturebooks which have this effect? Do you think that such compelling books usually show events, in words and particularly in their illustrations, through a child's eyes?
2. With reference to the illustrations by Roberto Innocenti in *Rose Blanche*, what do you consider can be communicated better visually than verbally?
3. 'I believe that children at the right stage of development can, through engagement with stories that offer what Nina Bawden (1980: 17) refers to as "emotional realism", receive a faithful account of the human condition by glimpsing, from the safe distance of a book, a darker side of life.' Do you agree? And, if so, what do you think pictures can convey more successfully than words?
4. If you agree with Nicholson that book-share sessions in small groups are a potent way of helping children become critical readers of fiction, how would you overcome potential management problems in building such sessions into English lessons?

Research inquiry

Choose a picturebook for your specialist age group in which the illustrations carry much of the narration. Read and talk about the book with a small group of children over two sessions.

Talk in the first session about:

- their first response to the story and characters – sharing enthusiasms and puzzles, and the feelings the picturebook awakens (along the lines of Aidan Chambers' framework, see Extract 8);
- the details in the pictures that enrich understanding of particular characters and/or events;
- how the illustrator creates a particular mood, whether happy, sad or puzzling, by for example, varying the palette or showing telling facial expressions and gesture;
- the interplay between words and pictures.

In the second session, share another reading of the book and ask the children:

- if they notice certain patterns or connections, again along the lines of Chambers' framework;
- if they think returning to the story helped them refine their understanding and particularly to notice new things in the pictures.

Either present your findings in a short talk to colleagues from notes you have made and/or write up a paper on (a) what the children learnt, and (b) what you learnt from the children's conversation during the two sessions.

Further reading

Arizpe, E. and Styles, M. (2015, 2nd edn) *Children Reading Pictures: Interpreting Visual Texts.* Abingdon: Routledge. Reports on research showing that children, including those from diverse backgrounds, can talk with insight about subtle messages, emotions and moods when perusing pictures.

Bawden, N. (1980) Emotional realism in books for young people. *The Horn Book Magazine,* LV1 (1), 17–33.

Dean, G. (2010) Rethinking literacy: Points for practice – every picture tells a story. In C. Bazalgette (ed.) *Teaching Media in Primary Schools.* London: Sage. Extract 10 homes in on children talking about picturebooks; this book has a wider remit, looking at the development of children's visual literacy through discussing media texts like film, photographs as well as interpreting print images.

Stafford, T. (2010) *Teaching Visual Literacy in the Primary Classroom: Comic Books, Film, Television and Picture Narration.* Abingdon: Routledge. There are suggestions for activities for children across the Primary Years to help expand the concept of what it means to be literate in the digital age.

Section 4: Talk to plan, assess and debate

Extract 11

Source

Mallett, M. and Newsome, B. (1977a) The life of St. Patrick. In *Talking, Writing and Learning, 8–13.* London: Evans/Methuen for the Schools Council, 153–4.

Talk is a powerful tool to plan, direct and assess activities in and out of school, and in English and in other lessons. The first two extracts in this section come from a Schools Council Report and show two episodes of work from the same primary school in Northern Ireland. In the first example, nine-year-olds plan an assembly presentation for younger children with their teacher. The conversation is particularly rich and fruitful because the teacher welcomes a speculative approach and the story-telling approach unites English and history and the possibility of bringing in drama. There has been some talk about dates on which events occurred and we break in at the point at which a pupil protests about this preoccupation.

PUPIL 1 What I mean is we've got to get the people in the hall interested and I don't think history is interesting if it's all dates ... I mean if you just say how old he was, that'll be enough, you don't really need to know when and where he went.

PUPIL 2 He stayed in Ireland for six years and then he left when he was twenty-six years old.

TEACHER To let them know the framework of the stories we have to have a general outline.

PUPIL 1 I'm sure the little ones, say in P3, wouldn't know what AD means ... or BC or any of those things.

PUPIL 3 ... And they would be shuffling around ...

PUPIL 4 You could say, um, a few hundred years after Christ's birth Patrick was born.

PUPIL 5 Do we have to do it all reading – couldn't we do a bit of drama as well? I was watching a drama programme the other day and I think we can put a bit of drama in or something like that.

PUPIL 4 This is beside the point, but do we know his second name?

TEACHER Does anybody know? Did people have second names in those days?

PUPIL 6 Shouldn't think so.

PUPIL 7 Must have because when Jesus was born there was Judas Iscariot, and that was his surname.

PUPIL 1 Some people did then. People like blacksmiths would be called just Smithy.

PUPIL 8 There was Ben Hur too.

TEACHER I think people tended to be known by the name of their occupation. You would be known – as someone suggested – Smith – so Patrick the Smith.

Comment

The teachers' contributions are interesting in this conversation – for a 'real' conversation it certainly is. Taking her cue from the pupils, she often invites a member of the group to take up and expand another pupil's point. Even contributions which some would consider off the point are not ignored. The teacher takes up interesting speculations and ensures they are not overlooked by others – 'Does anybody know? Did people have second names in those days?' The researchers go on to note that because she is able to see relevance in the pupils' terms, the teacher helps them to make progress. Nevertheless, she tells the children that they do need to provide a general framework of St Patrick's life story to help the young audience.

This conversation gets its energy from being directed towards a genuine task and one the children both understand and find interesting. They show knowledge of their intended audience – the younger children in the school – and awareness of what might bore them and what might enthuse them, for example they think that integrating some drama into the programmes would help. The signs are that the children are developing imaginative insight into the needs of others. One pupil comments 'I am sure the little ones, say in P3, wouldn't know what AD means'. It is a sign of a genuine conversation when everyone, teacher and children, is comfortable asking and answering questions.

Questions to discuss with colleagues

1. What other kinds of context might there be for this kind of planning talk where it is informed by a sense of purpose and audience?
2. How do you think this teacher sees her role in promoting children's confidence and their learning?
3. Should we try to make time, sometimes, to follow up children's spontaneous expression of interest? How might a teacher develop the children's interest, expressed in the transcript, in second names?

Further reading

Alexander, R. (2004) *Towards Dialogic Teaching*. York: Dialogos. The author explores different kinds of talk and the impact of each kind on children's learning. He explains the importance of 'dialogue' in achieving understanding through questioning and discussion.

Goodwin, P. (ed.) (2011, 3rd edition) *The Literate Classroom*. Abingdon and New York: Routledge. See introduction, pages 1–12, for an analysis of the role of talk in thinking, reading and writing.

Myhill, D., Hopper, R. and Jones, S. (2005) *Talking, Listening and Learning*. Milton Keynes: Open University Press. These researchers found evidence that teachers tend to dominate classroom conversation and suggest how contexts can be created to encourage learner participation.

Reedy, D. (2011, 3rd edn) Talk in guided reading sessions. In P. Goodwin (ed.) *The Literate Classroom*. Abingdon and New York: Routledge. Enriched with transcripts of children's talk, this analysis concludes that children's talk is most likely to be successful if a teacher has a clear intention in mind, while being flexible enough to respond to children's responses.

Extract 12

Source

Mallett, M. and Newsome, B. (1977b) Evaluating drama: The Three Wise Men. In *Talking, Writing and Learning, 8–13*. London: Evans/Methuen for the Schools Council, 157–8.

From the same research project as Extract 11, this one homes in on the sort of talk children use to reflect on their improvised drama with a view to improving it next time. The researchers believe that improvisation, and the talk that assesses it afterwards, generates a particularly rich and varied use of language. Here, a group of ten-year-olds assess their first attempt at improvising the story of 'The Three Wise Men'.

> WISE MAN 1 The king, Herod, would ask them to speak when he wanted them to, not by themselves really. But you asked us what business we had and we told you. But you wouldn't be saying it in an angry voice, because you only just knew about it.
>
> WISE MAN 2 But there were three things that we forgot. One of them was a merchant ...
>
> WISE MAN 1 They weren't all actually kings – they were just rich travellers ... trying to find the place ... saying the star told us ... the angel told us ... they were Melchior ... and Balthazar ... And Caspar.
>
> WISE MAN 3 We'll have to think about our places, and how we should come in, and all that ... and what mood Herod would be in. The three travellers would be tired, worn out with the journey ...
>
> HEROD Then I come in, and all my high priests and my chancellors discuss it – they haven't heard about it – and then we ask certain people to keep an eye on them.
>
> WISE MAN 1 Yes, there might be some people in the village who are on their side but you – Herod – don't really like this king who might take over the place.
>
> WISE MAN 2 We have to make up our minds if Herod would believe them or not believe them ...
>
> WISE MAN 1 ... And then the king has a dream.
>
> WISE MAN 2 Does he have a dream?
>
> WISE MAN 1 Yes ... they made connections with the stars. In that film we saw, they'd gone to visit Mary, Joseph and the baby, and they were sleeping somewhere, weren't they? ...
>
> GUARD Of course we don't know whether they would talk slang or posh do we? The Romans I mean.
>
> WISE MAN Well Herod would be quite ruthless, but a king couldn't be all that rough and ready.
>
> WISE MAN 1 But they would be tired, and they would not bring forth answers straight away – they would be hoping you would give them a rest.

Comment

Unlike the St Patrick conversation in the previous extract, the talking group in Extract 12 does not include the teacher. Later in the book, the researchers pinpoint two challenges for the group discussing their first attempt at improvising the story of 'The Three Wise Men'. First, they need to understand the story themselves. What was it like to live in this far-off time and what predicaments did the different people in this story face? Of course, life was experienced differently by people in different social groups and the children recognise that these different groups might use spoken language differently – 'we don't know whether they would talk slang or posh do we?' Second, the children want to use these insights and understandings to make their improvisation convincing. This involves, they think, showing that the Wise Men are almost incoherent with weariness and that Herod was concealing raging fury under a pretence of calm. Their conversation shows that they have confidence in their ability to work out theories, drawing on impressions they have built up over time and integrating these with fresher insights and ideas, some resulting from viewing filmstrips and reading books about the period of the Roman occupation.

The confidence these children show in expressing their opinions on their first attempt at improvising the visit of the three kings to Herod suggests they have had opportunities for this kind of monitoring talk for some time. The transcript offers an example of mature collaborative talk in which the children listen and respond to each other's observations and comments.

Questions to discuss with colleagues

1. There are many demands on the time of teacher and children during the school week. How would you defend making time for children to talk in groups to assess their own progress on tasks in English lessons?
2. If you believe, as many teachers and researchers do, that spoken language is central in children's thinking and learning, what do you consider the children talking about their improvisation learnt?
3. What are the advantages and possible limitations of children's collaborative talk without a teacher's participation?

Research inquires (Extracts 11 and 12)

Either:

■ Record for about 20 minutes the talk of a group of children in your class age range planning a presentation – of a story reading or some improvised drama – for their class (or another class).

Or:

- Record, again for about 20 minutes, the evaluative talk of a group who have just improvised a story or part of a story.

In either case, depending on the age and maturity of the children making up the group, decide whether to be a participant in or an observer of the conversation. Write up a short paper to share with colleagues and include an evaluation of:

- the children's understanding of their task;
- the responsiveness of individuals to the comments and questions of others;
- how far the conversation moved on the children's thinking;
- what you have learnt from your analysis and how this might affect your future practice.

Further reading

Alexander, R. (2010) *Children, Their World, Their Education.* Abingdon: Routledge. He reports that classroom research suggests that talk between teacher and learners and talk between learners that goes beyond mere transmission of information is underestimated. There are suggestions for promoting the kind of talk, including 'dialogic' talk, that enables leaps in thinking, insight and understanding.

Johnson, C. (2012) Dynamic talk: Speaking, listening and learning through drama. In D. Jones and P. Hodson (eds) *Unlocking Speaking and Listening.* Abingdon: Routledge. Colleen Johnson explains the value of discussion both in and out of role.

Extract 13

Source

Rooke, J. (2013) Teachers created dialogic spaces for children to collaboratively talk about and assess their writing. In *Transforming Writing – Final Evaluation.* London: National Literacy Trust, 50–1.

The four language processes – talking and listening, reading and writing – are mutually enriching and this key perception is recognised in every chapter in this *Guided Reader.* For example, in Extract 9 earlier in this chapter, children talk about a short story they have read to reflect on the themes and characters; the importance of children talking about their reading and writing is also recognised in Chapter 4 'Writing in English lessons'.

Jonathan Rooke, author of the report from which the extract that follows is taken, has been a primary school teacher and is now a college lecturer working with student teachers, and a researcher and writer. That talk can be a way of helping plan and assess writing was one of the findings of the National Literacy Trust research on writing. We take up the report at the point at which teachers and researchers reach some conclusions about the best ways in which to involve children in their writing progress.

The comments and questions that precede and follow the extract are those of the author and not necessarily those of the writers of the report or the National Literacy Trust.

Teachers frequently required the children to display their writing to the whole class, and then developed a whole class discussion that collectively assessed its quality. Teachers believed this to be a powerful way of teaching children both how to assess writing and how to talk about writing with a focus on assessment.

It was motivating. Children were curious to know what other children had written and were mostly keen to have their own writing evaluated and assessed by their peers. They wanted to engage with their peers in a dialogue about the quality of their writing and teachers believed it motivated them to think about how they were using the writing goals (toolkit) and the effect their composition choices would have on their audience.

To facilitate this whole class dialogue, a visualiser was used. These devices are ubiquitous in primary schools, and enable a teacher to place a child's writing beneath the lens and throw an enlarged image of it on the whiteboard to provide a focal point for class analysis and assessment. Teachers have the flexibility to create this whole class dialogic space for assessment talk at any point in the sequence of lessons, e.g. planning, first draft, final presentation. Using a visualiser means assessment can be done at the point of writing, i.e. during writing as well as immediately after writing, while the words are 'still warm' and closely connected to the writing and thinking processes that formed them in the young writer's head. Crucially, teachers could responsively integrate whole class collaborative formative assessment of writing at a point in the lesson when children were immersed in the composition task and engaged in the creative and focused writing 'atmosphere'.

This focused atmosphere takes time for a teacher to build. Teachers felt that if they could assess writing at that time and 'that place' as one teacher described it, it was particularly powerful and made a significant difference to the children's learning about how to assess writing. It also sent out a powerful message that revision is not something to do at the end of a linear unidirectional writing process – it is a reciprocal process and writers are constantly looping back on what they have just written to assess its likely impact and quality and how far the writing is meeting the intended writing goals. Such immediate and collaborative assessment is likely to support the development of children's metacognition about their own writing – their understanding of the processes they are using to achieve writing.

Comment

This research supports the argument that talking about writing helps children revise and improve earlier drafts. The visualiser used by the teacher researchers made it much easier for children to revise their work while writing was in process, rather than waiting until the task was completed. Of course, when something new is tried enthusiasm is generated, but it does seem that these researchers were convinced that involving children in the assessment of their own and of their peers' writing was motivating.

Questions to discuss with colleagues

1. If you are convinced by this research team about the benefits of children's involvement in assessment, how would you make sure that children learn to comment constructively on their peers' writing?
2. How far do you consider that the collaborative approach favoured in this study is likely to encourage children's awareness of 'audience' when they write?
3. Do you agree with the research team's argument that assessing and revising a piece of writing should take place as it proceeds as well as at the end? What do you consider are the advantages and possible disadvantages of this approach?
4. The research was to do with writing across the whole curriculum. Intervention when children are immersed in non-fiction kinds of writing seems unproblematic. Do you see any potential problems in intervening when children are 'immersed in the composition task' of a story or poem?
5. From what age would you consider children would benefit from being involved in the assessment of their writing?

Research inquiries

Either:

■ Ask two or three under-eights to write a story on a topic of their choice. Read the stories out when they are finished and invite the children to say what they liked about each other's work. Write what the discussion revealed about the children's developing knowledge about story writing and their ability to comment constructively and critically.

Or:

■ Ask a group of at least three children aged eight or older to write a story on a theme of their own choice. Pause the writing after each has written their first sentence and ask them to read it out loud. Invite discussion and comment with a view to them making changes – only, of course, if they agree that these changes improve their work. Pause for discussion of progress at intervals during the writing task. Read the stories out at the end of the session. Ask the children whether or not they found the interventions and discussion helpful and, if so, why.

Write a short analysis of your observations making it clear how far you agree with interventions while the words are 'still warm'.

Further reading

Bearne, E. (1998) *Making Progress in English*. London: Routledge. See page 173, 'Making progress in speaking and listening', and page 186, 'Evaluating talk and using talk for evaluating'.

Dimitriadi, Y., Hodson, P. and Ludhra, G. (2012) Emphasizing the 'C' in ICT: Speaking, listening and communication. In D. Jones and P. Hodson (eds) *Unlocking Speaking and Listening*. Abingdon: Routledge. With reference to case studies of children using digital video, voice-activated software and programmable toys, these writers share their thoughts on the new technologies and how they can provide future contexts for oracy. Such innovations also have implications for assessing talking and writing.

Reading and responding to texts in English lessons

Introduction

The four language processes, speaking and listening, reading and writing work together as children think and learn in every part of the primary school curriculum. And so there are strong links between this chapter and Chapters 2 and 4. Chapter 2, on speaking and listening, has already shown that much talk goes on between teacher and learners in English lessons, about issues to do with all the thoughts, experiences and feelings important to human beings. Also explored here is the value of a special kind of conversation, known as 'booktalk' – so important to children's journey towards critical and sensitive reading of fiction. Chapter 4 explores children's development as writers and we know that the processes of reading and writing are very much intertwined in children's learning about different texts. There are also significant links between this chapter and Chapters 6 and 7, 'The rich landscape of children's literature' and 'Non-fiction literature in English lessons', which explore the genres included in the Early Years and Primary Years school book collections.

This chapter, however, is concerned with how we can best support children on the path to becoming increasingly confident and critical readers of fiction and those kinds of non-fiction that find their way into English lessons.

This journey starts when children first begin to learn to read because it is at this early stage that attitudes and, most importantly, enthusiasms are formed. There are different viewpoints, often passionately held, about how the initial teaching of reading can best help children on their way to success and independence. Margaret Perkins, in Extract 14 of Section 1 'The initial teaching of reading', explains that beginner readers need to be helped to make sense of written language as a symbol system. However, before formal teaching begins on sound symbol relationship, Early Years teachers employ playful games and activities to build phonological awareness. They also ensure that the reading environment is rich with books and resources, supported by much talk.

Children build their reading abilities in every lesson, but traditionally English lessons have been thought to have a leading role in their becoming literate. It is also true, in the United Kingdom at least, that the teacher co-ordinating or managing English, language and literacy leads and inspires colleagues as they create a reading programme and select the best books and resources for each age group.

How do children learn to become sensitive and critical readers of fiction, of the 'spectator role' texts described by James Britton and discussed in Chapter 1? The extracts in Section 2 are concerned with reading fiction, the reading material at the heart of the English lesson. Margaret Meek, in Extract 15, asks how children from about age eight can be helped to acquire reading stamina when reading narrative fiction: an important part of becoming a sensitive and critical reader of these texts, she argues, involves becoming able to 'get into the story' and to tolerate uncertainty. Then in Extract 16, Nikki Gamble sets out the key principles of reader-response theory and explores the ideas of reader-response advocates like Rosenblatt who believe meaning does not reside in the text alone. Children, like adult readers of fiction, respond both cognitively and affectively. What, asks Gamble, is the point of children being able to talk about such things as narrative structure and cohesion 'if they are not moved, excited, delighted, challenged or changed by what they read?' This has implications for teachers' choice of books and poems for their age group and so Section 3 explores some principles for choosing texts for children in the Early Years and for those in the later primary school years.

Extract 18 in Section 4 presents Tim Stafford's analysis of some aspects of what is involved in helping children to become visually literate. He argues that in the English lesson visual literacy is often developed through narrative and story-telling and suggests some terminology for children's critical comment on visual texts, including comics.

What contribution do non-fiction texts, in different formats and media, make to children's developing literacy in English lessons? This is considered in Section 5, and there are links with other chapters, especially Chapter 4 'Writing in English lessons: finding a voice' and Chapter 7 'Non-fiction literature in English lessons'. Becoming able to recognise bias and distortion in non-fiction texts is a very important part of becoming a critical reader. English teachers have long included a study of advertisements, news reports and other persuasive texts in the reading programme. Autobiography and biography also need a critical eye because writers wanting to present a certain perspective or interpretation may be selective in what they offer the reader. Sometimes inspiration for debate round texts arises from issues that have come up in lessons in other parts of the curriculum – about for example environmental concerns arising in science or geography or contemporary news reports in history. The issues arising from these can be powerful and affecting and worth debating in English lessons. In Extract 19, Horner and Ryf address the kinds of non-fiction texts, on-screen and in print, used in English lessons to develop critical literacy.

Reading and writing on screen is well integrated into good practice in school and in the culture in general. Extract 20 considers some important differences between reading print books and reading on screen.

Section 1: The initial teaching of reading

Extract 14

Source

Perkins, M. (2011, 3d edn) Making space for reading: Teaching reading in the early years. in P. Goodwin (ed.) *The Literate Classroom*. London and New York: Routledge, 21–3.

Margaret Perkins is an experienced teacher across the whole primary age range and she has a particular research and practical interest in the teaching of reading. The early part of the chapter from which the extract is taken is a thorough consideration of how Early Years teachers prepare to teach reading. She covers how they recognise and build on the language knowledge children bring to school and they make space in the classroom for all kinds of texts that children will enjoy and learn from. In the extract she recognises the need for children learning to read to understand how the symbolic system works, but believes that phonological awareness needs to be nurtured by enjoyable activities like drama, clapping and music before explicit teaching about how sounds are represented in print begins. Attitudes to reading are formed early on, so it is most important that children's reading environment is rich and encouraging.

There are times when the phonic strategy is not the most useful one, and then I will encourage the children to choose another strategy. They might:

- leave the word out and read on;
- go back to the beginning of the sentence and re-run;
- look at the picture;
- think about what they know about the story;
- look for words they do know inside the new one, e.g. 'sun' inside 'sunshine'.

In guided reading I will focus the children's attention on one particular strategy, choosing carefully the text they are reading to ensure that it is appropriate. I can then remind the children of what to do when they come to an unknown word, demonstrating the strategy with other words so that when they read independently they will have that strategy in the forefront of their minds.

There is no doubt that for beginning readers the main element of learning to read is the process of making sense of written language as a symbol. If children are to become independent readers they need to know how that symbolic system works and they need to be able to use and manipulate the 'code'.

Essentially, written language is a relationship between sound and symbol but, unfortunately, it is not a simple relationship. We have about 44 phonemes (or sounds) in the English language, which are represented in print. Our starting point, therefore, is work on 'phonological awareness'. Classroom experiences related to phonological awareness will involve a lot of drama, movement, singing, clapping, listening and music. All these activities become reading lessons as the children learn to hear, identify and discriminate between different sounds ...

Space needs to be given for this phonological awareness to be firmly established before explicit teaching about how sounds are represented in print is given. An independent effective reader is in control of written language and that is the purpose of our teaching. There are many resources available that give ideas for classroom activities ... but I do not want to list them here. Rather I want to recall some key principles of phonic teaching:

- The purpose of phonic teaching is to enable independent access to the meaning of the text and that must remain at the forefront of our thinking and planning. Phonics can be fun when we play with language and use texts like the Dr Seuss books, nursery rhymes, or the brilliant *Tanka Tanka Skunk* by Steve Webb (2003).
- Sounds are represented by the symbols; the letters do not 'say' anything themselves. Children can become confused by our careless use of language and we must be careful that we do not over-simplify and so be less accurate.
- There are no rules in phonics. There are more common ways of representing sounds, but often well-known words do not conform to usual patterns. Think of the phoneme /ie/. It can be represented in many different ways: light, tie, eye, kite, I, climb, height, fly. Which is the most common? Which is the most unusual? Collecting words and sorting them is a powerful way of helping children to understand how the English language uses symbols to represent sounds.
- Children need to understand that there are some differences that matter and some that don't. In their previous experience, a chair has always been a chair whichever way it is facing and whichever way up it is. Letters do not work like that. Playing with letters becomes a way of becoming familiar with their forms – magnetic letters, letters made from sandpaper, fur fabric, satin, wood, written on a partner's back, letter shapes I can make with my body, letters drawn in wet sand, in rice, in sawdust, letters painted in water on the playground, grown in cress on blotting paper, made out of Play-Doh. It is important to give children every possible opportunity of becoming familiar with the shapes of letters.
- Listening to sounds and playing with them does not stop when we move to more focused phonic teaching. This can still be text-based. There are many wonderful texts that play with language; jokes and poetry are a useful way of accessing this.

... children's enjoyment of texts and experiences of reading for pleasure are the key to successful reading and so it follows that effective teaching of reading focuses on the texts that children can and want to engage. Our teaching needs to give children the strategies to enable them to access the texts independently, and that is what teaching at sentence and word level does ...

However all this must be done in a context in which children experience the purposes and functions of reading and the pleasure reading can offer.

Reading is an extremely complex and diverse process and yet one that is rewarding and exciting. In my classroom I want the teaching of reading programmes to reflect that complexity, diversity and excitement. To do that I need to make space: physical space for the wide variety of different types of texts, temporal space for reading and talking about reading; cultural space to recognise and exploit the different interpretations of reading and text that children hold; social space to allow interaction and talk between adults and children, and children and children; conceptual space to recognise and accept uncertainties and questions and to use them as starting points for exploring texts. Above all, I need to allow children the space to enjoy reading and to share their personal response to the variety of texts they encounter both in and out of the classroom, for therein lies the magic that is reading.

Extract reference

Webb, S. (2003) *Tanka Tanka Skunk*. London: Random House.

Comment

This scholarly, yet very passionate and very practical analysis of some issues in the teaching of reading explains that phonological awareness, gained through playful activities and language experiences, is the best forerunner to learning about the matching of sound to written symbols. The advice given emphasises the importance of making the whole reading environment exciting and encouraging so that children find learning to read enjoyable. This includes providing a rich selection of all kinds of texts with appeal for the very young.

Questions to discuss with colleagues

1. How would you explain to parents the need to develop children's phonological awareness through language activities like saying rhymes and enjoying drama and music before and alongside more systematic teaching of reading?
2. Should teachers of older children be informed about the early stages of learning to read? If so, discuss for what reasons, and suggest how a school might encourage collaboration between teachers of different age groups.
3. Many early books to support learning to read are fictional narratives. Why do you think teachers regard these as important in shaping children's attitudes to reading? What qualities would you look for in selecting these?
4. How would you bring in the other cue systems than the phonological one to help beginning readers?
5. Discuss the factors that Margaret Perkins considers help children to find learning to read a pleasurable experience.

Research inquiries

Either:

- Look in libraries and bookshops for picturebooks, nursery rhyme collections and poems which you consider deserve a place in the Early Years classroom. Write up an annotated list organised in sections to share and discuss with colleagues. This would be a useful enquiry for teachers of older age groups as well as for those preparing to teach beginning readers.

Or:

- Research electronic resources to support early reading and make a list and write a short analysis about why these should be included in classroom resources.

Further reading

Cremin, T. and Arthur, J. (eds) (2014, 3rd edn) The phonics debate. In *Learning to Teach in the Primary School*. London and New York, 531–4. Provides a careful explanation of the differences between synthetic and analytic phonics.

Dombey, H. (2010) *Teaching Reading: What the Evidence Says*. Leicester: United Kingdom Literacy Association (UKLA). Recommended here is a 'comprehensive, integrated and flexible approach' to the initial teaching of reading.

Goswami, U. and Bryant, P. (1990) *Phonological Skills and Learning to Read*. London: Psychology Press. In this influential book the importance of developing children's phonological awareness before and alongside learning to read is explained. The authors stress the relationship between spoken language and literacy and the role of rhyme in reading acquisition.

Graham, J. and Kelly, A. (2007, 3rd edn) *Reading Under Control*. London and New York: Routledge. You will find this book, which has become something of a classic, on many education book lists. It sets out research results, discusses issues about the teaching of reading and applies all this to classroom practice.

Johnston, R. and Watson, J. (2014, 2nd edn) *Teaching Synthetic Phonics*. London: Learning Matters. These authors took part in the Clackmannanshire research, which they consider pointed to synthetic phonics as being the most effective kind of phonics teaching for aiding reading. The interpretation of the research results has been questioned by other researchers and reading specialists. Do we want to direct all English schools up the Clackmannanshire cul-de-sac? This is what Henrietta Dombey asks in *Teaching Reading: What the Evidence Says* (2010: 4).

Lewis, M. and Ellis, S. (eds) (2006) *Reading Phonics: Practice, Research and Policy*. London: Sage, with UKLA. Here we have a balanced debate about how children learn to read and how early phonics helps.

Lockwood, M. (2008) *Reading for Pleasure in the Primary School*. London: Sage. How do teachers promote reading for pleasure from the earliest stages? Michael Lockwood sets out his arguments and supports it with classroom case studies.

Section 2: Learning to read fiction

Extract 15

Source

Meek, M. (1988) *How Texts Teach What Readers Learn*. Stroud: Thimble Press, 30–1.

Margaret Meek, Emeritus Reader at the Institute of Education, has long been concerned with the connection between literacy and literature. In her classic text *How Texts Teach What Readers Learn*, a book she refers to as 'a workshop rather than an essay or lecture', she identifies her main point – the proposition that we learn to read by becoming truly involved in what we read. So it follows that the quality of the texts we offer children matters. She demonstrates how the picturebooks and stories of writers of literary power and merit, for example John Burningham, Pat Hutchins, Shirley Hughes and Janet and Allan Ahlberg, give important reading lessons. We join the analysis when Meek turns her attention to how readers of about age eight or above can be helped by books of subtlety and wisdom to tolerate uncertainty and ambiguity.

> The signs of genuine reading development are hard to detect as they appear, and bear little relation to what is measured in reading tests. For me, the move from 'more of the same' to 'I might try something different' is a clear step. So a growing tolerance of ambiguity, the notion that things are not quite what they seem, even in a fairly straightforward tale about, say, a family seaside holiday or the unexpected behaviour of parents …
>
> The crossing point from reading and understanding 'what happens' to the Iron Man to interpreting the mythic implications comes for most children when, in answer to the question 'if we had Mr Hughes here, what would you like to ask him about his book?' the child says, 'Where did he get the idea from?' The idea is the meeting place of reader and writer, the intersection of culture and cognition; the readers are now writing as they read.
>
> By the time they are eight, or a little later, children are generally expected to choose books for themselves. Those who know that authors help them make sense of the story are more patient with the beginnings of books than those who expect to recognize straight away what they have to understand. The common phrase for this process is 'getting into the story'. Practised readers tolerate uncertainty; they know that sometimes the author is building up suspense and that puzzles will be resolved if they just keep reading. I wish I knew more about how we learn to tolerate uncertainty in our reading and what we are really doing. The poet W.H. Auden says we go on reading books we only partly understand if they have been

given to us by someone we like and we want to be thought well of by him or her. Many a good tutor has let fall the title of a book, implying that of course the student will want to read it. Remember the early untaught lessons of approval and virtue? I doubt if this kind of suasion is very prevalent nowadays but surely, surely we should continue to help young readers to 'get into books' until they are confident that they need not be daunted. We needn't do more than reduce some of the uncertainty; the author will take over where we leave off.

Extract references

Hughes, T. (1968) *The Iron Man*. London: Faber & Faber.
Mark, J. (1980) *Nothing to Be Afraid Of*. London: Viking Kestrel.

Comment

It occurred to me as I re-read this that it has many implications for teachers' knowledge about books. In the school context at any rate, they are the ones who select texts for the school collection and for particular lessons and they are the ones who talk about them and all the issues they raise with the young readers. Margaret Meek expresses her belief that teachers through discussion can help children to feel more confident – in her words 'less daunted' – as they approach more challenging books, for example Ted Hughes' *The Iron Man* (1968) and Jan Mark's *Nothing to Be Afraid Of* (1980). It would follow from her argument that teachers need to select some books which take readers on to the next stage, and in the case of children of eight years and older this may well be a stage where they move from safe and predictable books with familiar themes towards some that, as she says, require readers to 'tolerate uncertainty'. This might be rewarding but also unsettling, but such reading material is likely to help children become more experienced and more skilful readers. It is also true that the uncertainties found in fiction are also experienced in our lives. This gives us the possibility of doing what reading scholars suggest, to connect life to books and books to life.

Extract 16

Source

Gamble, N. (2004, 2nd edn) Teaching fiction. In P. Hunt (ed.) *International Companion Encyclopedia of Children's Literature*, vol. 2. Abingdon and New York: Routledge, 755–9.

For many years Nikki Gamble has both taught and researched about the importance of children achieving literacy and children's literature. Well known in schools and colleges, she founded and directed 'Write Away', an internet site giving news and advice about children's books and information about conferences. Later she opened

'Just Imagine', a story centre and specialist book shop which offers events for children, teachers, writers and families. The article from which the extract has been taken begins with a discussion of some issues about selecting texts for children. But the extract homes in on that part of the article where reader-response theory and a number of ways of encouraging children's involvement with and enjoyment of fiction are considered.

Developing response to fiction

In the 1960s and 1970s a paradigm shift in the teaching of literature occurred. Researchers became increasingly interested in children's responses to the books they read. Typically, this interest has been characterised by asking questions about what happens in the minds of young readers: how do young readers respond to fiction? Response is a general term that is used to describe a range of processes including personal responses – the pleasures and new understandings derived from the experience – and literary responses – responses to literary qualities and critical appreciation. Responding to literature is more than the sum of the parts. While students might talk confidently about point of view, narrative structure or cohesion, this is to no purpose if they are not moved, excited, delighted, challenged or changed by what they read.

Reading fiction is a cognitive and affective activity and educators are concerned to develop both emotional and intellectual responses. The importance of generating pleasure in reading is a recurring theme in discussions about literature teaching. Nodelman's list of the pleasures of children's literature is extensive and includes items such as 'the pleasure of gaining insight into history and culture', 'the pleasure of experiencing something new' or the pleasure of repeating a comfortable experience' (Nodelman, 1992: 20–1).

The recognition of children's abilities to respond personally and imaginatively to fiction has been informed by Reader-Response Theory, which challenges New Criticism's belief in the authority of the text. In education, Rosenblatt's work has been particularly influential, though not always acknowledged. First published in 1938, *Literature as Exploration* proposes that meaning does not lie exclusively within the text but is created in the interaction between author, text and reader.

'The special meaning, and more importantly, the submerged associations that these words will have for the individual reader will largely determine what the work communicates to him. The reader brings to the work personality traits, memories of past events, present needs and preoccupations, a particular mood of the moment, and a particular physical condition. These and many other elements in a never-to-be-duplicated combination determine his response to the peculiar contribution of the text.' (Rosenblatt, 1938/1970: 30–1)

Rosenblatt was involved in teacher training, and her second major work, *The Reader, the Text, the Poem* (1978) specifically considered the application of transactional theories to the classroom, challenging teaching approaches that focused too narrowly on literature instruction. It is now widely expected in education that when a reader encounters a text, the new meanings that are generated are greater than those intrinsic to the text or indeed the reader's previous understandings. Although the author may have an 'implied reader' in mind (Iser, 1979), the 'real reader' brings to the text a set of cultural and social expectations and previous knowledge and experience which is highly individual and which may lead to different interpretations of the text. Vygotsky argues that in engaging with higher psychological processes, as we are when reading, we draw on our 'socio-cultural origins' (Vygotsky, 1978: 46). The greater the differential in reader's and author's experience and culture, the greater the potential for divergence in the sense made of the text.

Rosenblatt argued that there can be a number of readings and interpretations of a text but that some readings can be considered superior to others according to particular criteria: 'Always therefore, a full understanding of literature requires both a consciousness of the reader's own angle of refraction and any information that can illuminate the assumptions implicit in the text' (Rosenblatt, 1938/1970: 115) …

While a text has unlimited personal significance, interpretation is constrained by features within the text. Culler proposes the term 'making sense' rather than 'meaning', as meaning suggests 'a property of text', whereas 'making sense' implies the reader's active engagement with the text, and 'links the qualities of a text to the operations one performs on it' (Culler, 1981: 50).

Eliciting and analysing children's response to text is not as straightforward as it may appear. Crago states that we cannot know what actually happens when a child reads – we can only study what children choose to show us of their response, and that 'the act of articulating one's inner responses changes that experience' (Crago, 1991: 121). He illustrates this with an account of his own reading log, written in response to Jill Paton Walsh's *A Chance Child*. This detailed commentary demonstrates his engagement, his unease at some of the content, and both his appreciation and criticism of the author's style. He makes hypotheses based on his experience of reading related texts, including Hans Andersen's *The Little Mermaid*, Nesbit, Tolkien, Browning, T.S. Eliot and *Dr Who* demonstrating a range of cultural referents.

Benton and Fox suggest that in reading we enter a 'secondary world', which 'lies in an area of play activity between the reader's inner reality and the outer reality of words on the page'. Like Crago, they advocate encouraging written response to attempt to explore how readers move on a 'journey' through a text, often changing their perceptions as they gather more information. Asking students: 'What pictures do you have in your mind's eye?' facilitates this reflection. They also, like Crago, attach importance to the first page of the book and suggest pausing for recording individually, then sharing initial responses in groups (Benton and Fox, 1985: 7) … Keeping journals, making notes and visualising are part of a process for developing critical readers, which can be combined with other teaching strategies to encourage reflection … Chambers (1985) categorises different levels of response to text in defence of children as critics. He proposes three levels of sharing that take place when talking about books: sharing enthusiasm, sharing puzzles and connections, and discovering patterns ...

Vygotskian theory illuminates the teacher's role as a model for developing readers. Modelling takes place through a range of classroom activities. For example, expressive reading aloud attunes students to the language and rhythms of fiction as well as enabling them to sample the excitement and pleasure of reading ... Campbell (1989) has shown that teacher modelling is also vital in the effective implementation of Sustained Silent Reading (SSR), which research has shown to have a positive effect on students' recreational reading. Incorporating sharing sessions into the SSR routine provides opportunities for teachers to talk about books they are reading. By sharing their thoughts about how, for example, the main character develops through the course of the book, or the surprises and disappointments they encounter as they read, teachers extend students' thinking about the process of reading and develop their knowledge and awareness of cultural experience ... In recent years, teachers have been encouraged to scrutinise the quality of booktalk and consider what constitutes good questioning ... Statements and prompts such as: 'I wonder why the author chose to narrate this story with an alternating first- and third-person narrator'; 'I'm not sure what I think about Mrs Coulter's feelings for Lyra'; 'I've changed my mind about what this writer is saying about friendship' provide children with a model for tentative thinking about literature. The aim is to get children to internalise the process of asking questions and to generate their own questions (Hobsbaum *et al.*, 2002) ...

Analytical activities such as story transformation, where, for example, students rewrite or perform a traditional story as a soap opera or thriller, facilitate reflection on what they know, understand and have learnt about the genre. Storyboarding a film trailer for a book can stimulate response to mood, language and narrative structure, and the creation of sociograms can be used to promote analysis of character relationships (Johnson and Louis, 1985).

Drama is frequently used as a means of exploring fiction, bringing together learning in the cognitive and affective domains. Drama strategies are used to explore aspects of fiction such as conflict, character motivation, narrative structure ...

Author study, particularly popular in the USA, is another approach to studying fiction (Jenkins, 1999). Students might study the body of an author's work alongside autobiographical and biographical material to stimulate interest and develop contextual understanding. Author study is also used as a means of developing student awareness of authorship. Looking at writers' drafts and redrafts to illuminate the writing process might also be undertaken ...

Looking ahead: new technologies are likely to have further impact on the way fiction is taught in schools. It is already common practice for students to look at the diversity of fictional narratives especially film, picturebooks and, to a lesser extent, video games. Interactive gaming, role-playing and storymaking are certainly likely to have a significant place in the classroom of the future.

Extract references

Benton, M. and Fox, G. (1985) *Teaching Literature – Nine to Fourteen*. Oxford: Oxford University Press.

Campbell, R. (1989) The teacher as role model in silent reading. *Reading*, 23 (3), 179–83.

Chambers, A. (1985) *Booktalk, Occasional Writing on Literature and Children*. London: The Bodley Head.

Crago, H. (1991) Roots of response. In P. Hunt (ed.) *Children's Literature: The Development of Criticism*. London: Routledge.

Culler, J. (1981) *The Pursuit of Signs: Semiotics, Literature, Deconstruction*. London: Routledge & Kegan Paul.

Hobsbaum, A., Gamble, N. and Reedy, D. (2002) *Guiding Reading*. London: University of London Institute of Education.

Iser, W. (1979) *The Act of Reading: A Theory of Aesthetic Response*. Baltimore, MD: Johns Hopkins University Press.

Jenkins, C.B. (1999) *The Allure of Authors: Author Studies in the Elementary Classroom*. Westport, CT: Greenwood Press.

Johnson, T. and Louis, D. (1985) *Literacy Through Literature*. Sydney: Methuen.

Nodelman, P. (1992) *The Pleasures of Children's Literature*. New York: Longman.

Rosenblatt, L. (1938/1970) *Literacy as Exploration*. London: Heinemann.

Rosenblatt, L. (1978) *The Reader, the Text, the Poem: The Transactional Theory of Literacy Work*. Carbondale: Southern Illinois University Press.

Vygotsky, L. (1978) *Mind in Society*. Cambridge, MA: Harvard University Press.

Comment

What strikes me about this analysis is that Gamble moves seamlessly from literary theory, particularly reader-response perspectives, to suggestions for interesting and effective classroom practice. She also draws from a rich landscape of cognitive theory, demonstrating how Vygotsky's work on how the young reader brings a set of cultural and social expectations to reading texts can inform the teacher's role in making children enthusiastic readers of fiction. As she points out – reading fiction is both a cognitive and affective activity and so the kind of teaching and learning which encourages children's personal and imaginative response to texts is what we are after.

Questions to discuss with colleagues (Extracts 15 and 16)

1. Margaret Meek believes it is at around age eight that children are ready to move to more adventurous reading, in the sense that they are ready to cope with uncertainty. Share with colleagues your ideas for books you feel would suit children at this stage in their reading development.

2. If you agree with Nikki Gamble about the merits of 'reader-response theory', how would you explain the principles that underpin it, and how would you put these into practice in your approach to teaching literature, at a curriculum evening for parents?

3. Is it important to read aloud from books, even to older primary children who are competent and independent readers?

4. What are some of the best ways to help structure children's talk about fiction?

5. How would you use writing to help children on their journey through a book shared by the whole class?

6. Do you agree that as children move through the Primary Years they can be helped by acquiring a metalanguage, a language to talk about narrative structure? How can we teach about such things as narrative structure and cohesion while making our priority, in Gamble's words, that children are 'moved, excited, delighted, challenged or changed by what they read'?

7. At the end of Extract 16, it is recognised that the advance of new technology is likely to continue to change and widen how learning fiction is taught. How do you see the diversity of fictional narratives developing in the classroom?

Research inquiries

Either:

■ With a group of Early Years children, read out loud from a picturebook and then read it again more slowly, giving more attention to the pictures and text and providing space for the children to respond. Ask the children what they think the characters are feeling and if they have a favourite part of the story or a favourite character and why. Give the children the opportunity to act out the story. Write some notes on how you invited children to make their thoughts about the story explicit and about the nature of the children's responses.

Or:

■ Following from the first question for discussion, with a small group of eight to nine-year-olds read aloud from a book that you consider helps them to 'tolerate uncertainty' as they read. (The writers Philippa Pearce, Anthony Browne and David Almond spring to mind here.) After reading the early part of the book to them, pause and give the children space to gather their thoughts and share their impressions. Try some other strategies to help them 'get into the story'. For example, you could take up Benton and Fox's suggestion, in the extract from Nikki Gamble's account, by encouraging the sharing of initial responses in some written notes to read out to the group. You could suggest some questions to address in the writing: what is your impression of the main character so far? Why do you think the author decided to write the account in the first/third person?

You could either continue to read the story together over some more sessions, perhaps continuing the journey through the book with the help of writing as well as talking, or offer the children the choice of taking turns at borrowing the book and reading the rest of it on their own. When everyone in the group has read the story, it would be satisfying to share a final discussion. You could structure this by addressing Aidan Chambers' three sharings: enthusiasms, puzzles and patterns/connections. (Extract 8 from *Tell Me* in Chapter 2 would help here.)

Further reading

Bearne, E. (2009) And what do you think happened next? In M. Styles and E. Arizpe (eds) *Acts of Reading: Teachers, Text and Childhood*. Stoke-on-Trent: Trentham books. If we want children to become *committed* and lifelong readers, it is a matter of 'engaging hearts and minds'. This author draws attention to the importance of making bridges between the kinds of reading children do at home and their reading in school. While continuing to value print texts, children and teachers benefit from being informed about and open to the ever-changing and developing array of new texts – multimodal and multimedia – that are part of our modern world.

Martin, T. (2011, 3rd edn) Readers making meaning. In P. Goodwin (ed.) *The Literate Classroom*. London and New York: Routledge. Martin explores the ways in which readers and texts interact. He suggests how a teacher can approach class discussion of a story or novel using *Who's Afraid?* by Philippa Pearce as an example.

Section 3: Choosing fiction for Early Years and primary school children

Extract 17

Source

Mills, C. and Webb, J. (2004, 2nd edn) Selecting books for younger readers. In P. Hunt (ed.) *International Companion Encyclopedia of Children's Literature*, vol. 1. London and New York: Routledge. (a) 771–2, (b) 774, (c) 775–7.

All young readers have preferences when choosing books to read or have read to them. However, when teachers choose texts for the class and school library they are guided by some general understandings about what will appeal at particular ages and stages and which will support reading development. Here, in Extract 17, Colin Mills and Jean Webb, who both have long-standing teaching and research interest in children's literature of all kinds, share their insights. The extract is divided into three parts: Part a – 'Three questions', Part b – 'Five to seven' and Part c – 'Seven to ten'.

Part a: Three questions

… we have proposed three general questions that may be of interest and assistance. In work with adults over many years, we have found these questions (beginning 'Does this book … ?') practical and helpful.

Does this book give the young reader access to ideas, themes and possibilities, while keeping the 'surface' accessible?

The task for any writer (or artist) working for the young is to keep the 'surface' of the text accessible, in terms of readability, text format and content. The 'look' of the page, and the interplay between text and pictures, has to be appropriate. Yet, within this frame of accessibility, there has to be challenge in terms of ideas and themes. What can, or could, this story tell the young about the business of being a child, of growing up, of dealing with the themes of change, with feelings, or of coping with adults? ...

Does the book give the young readers possibilities for growing as thinkers and imaginers, while keeping the pleasure of reading in the forefront?

As choosers of books for the young, we know that reading, with the possibilities of entering into other times, locations and value systems, gives us the possibility of growing and changing as thinkers. Yet the driving force in our reading is often our need to follow a narrative and to find out 'what happens next'. Books that we select for the under tens need to combine these two features. Is there scope within this book for extending children's power to think, empathise, imagine and create new ideas and patterns of thought? Is there enough in the story to take readers in and along through the patterning of language, pictures (often), character and action? Now, writers and artists for the young borrow and use the forms of TV, cartoons, computer games and adult genres to tell their tales. Stories such as Jon Scieszka's and Lane Smith's *The Stinky Cheese Man*, a postmodern collection of fairy tales (see Thacker and Webb, 2002: 163) show how big and challenging ideas can be enjoyed by the young through a combination of the playfulness, parody and subversion that has always been lurking beneath the surface in books for the young.

Does the book help children in their growth as readers?

Good books for the young give valuable lessons in reading and literacy; teachers, librarians, parents and others involved should take notes of the ways in which texts 'work' for children. Being aware of some of these ideas, and looking and listening to what young readers make of the books we give them, help us to be more attuned to the powerful reading lessons that good books give the young. In books such as Eric Hill's *Where's Spot?* and Pat Hutchins' *Rosie's Walk*, the very young are encouraged to read to anticipate, predict, make sense of what is implicit and have their 'guesses' confirmed or changed during the course of their reading. Stories with clear 'patterns' such as John Burningham's *Mr Gumpy's Outing*, teach young readers the value of repetition, the role of dialogue in moving action on, the strong sense of anticipation that will be crucial when they come to read longer texts. Those who select books for the young should be aware of the possibilities and need to be able to track the developments in children's literary competences. We have some good models. Smith's work (2001) has been significant in demonstrating the ways in which sophisticated texts develop children's understanding of narrative patterns. Sensitive and guided selection of books can help children in their writing (Barrs and Cork, 2001).

Part b: Five to seven

Children's developing awareness of the structure of stories, and the importance of them hearing stories read, is obviously crucial to their growth as readers as they get older. Stories that are memorable are often ones that come out of an oral tradition. Of particular value and enjoyment at this stage of childhood are collections of folk and fairy stories that have been shaped by centuries of re-telling. These stories are powerful in their content, too, dealing as they do with themes of archetypal significance, feelings and fantasies that are part of the inner experience of childhood. When reading is new to children, stories are inextricably linked with their play. The fantastic has its roots in the workaday and the domestic playthings, toys, animals are anthropomorphised as friends. Novice readers have to understand stories as a particular kind of imaginative activity. An important category of books is made up of those which seem particularly good at teaching the game of reading. Books such as *Where's Spot?* (1980) by the British artist Eric Hill, or *Beware of the Storybook Wolves* (2000), an award-winning book by Lauren Child, invite children to join in, predict, set up expectations about what happens next …

Five- to seven-year-olds have a taste for realism, an insatiable curiosity about how things are, and what people do. It is, however, simplistic to label stories which deal with the homely as 'realism'. The best stories for five- to seven-year-olds slow down, and turn into art, the action, sounds, sights, feelings of childhood. The universal experiences – birthdays, starting school, having a baby brother or sister, losing a tooth, being left awake at night, fussy eating – are shown to be the same for everyone. Form is important. When one reads stories by the best writers in the genre – Jacqueline Wilson's *Lizzie Zipmouth* (2000), Dorothy Edwards *My Naughty Little Sister* (1969 and sequels) (one of the very few nameless characters in all fiction), Lauren Child's *I Will Not Ever Never Eat a Tomato* (2000) one sees how deceptively simple techniques can work. The length of chapters and the interplay of episodes help story-tellers to catch the slowness of childhood. Events often happen all in a day and can be held in the head. Crude divisions into 'realism' and 'fantasy' ignore the fact that for children at this age, the line between the two is not a clear one.

Part c: Seven to ten

The most potent change that comes about between these ages in Western society is that children have a more extended and more diverse relationship with the social world. Friends, teachers, groups or gangs, clubs or societies have an increased importance to them. They develop more sophisticated modes of thinking, experience a wide range of emotions. Their stamina in terms of literacy and literary competence increases. Children's own social groups become more important to them … Many significant writers have skilfully integrated the jokes and superstitions within children's games and culture into stories and poems. The work of British poets Michael Rosen and Allan Ahlberg, especially the latter's *Friendly*

Matches (2001), provides good examples of demotic language meeting mainstream literature.

From the 1970s onwards, writers for children have explored sometimes complex aspects of children's lives ... The domestic can still be an appropriate setting for children's stories, but such settings can lead out to fantastic explorations in classics such as E. Nesbit's stories and C.S. Lewis's Narnia tales. Domestic settings can also lead inwards to explorations of relationships, to the interplay between children, their siblings and their parents. Of particular note here is the work of the British writer Philippa Pearce. *A Dog So Small* (1962) deals with a solitary child's longing for a fantasy companion. *The Battle of Bubble and Squeak* (1978) deals with sibling rivalry and relationships between step-parents and children. Pearce's work shows how books for this age range can become more complex and sophisticated in their moral viewpoint and in the range of themes that can be addressed. *Tom's Midnight Garden* (1958) and *The Way to the Satin Shore* (1983) are subtle but very readable explorations of time, of past secrets and of the relationship between the young and the old.

Two other writers deserve mention here to show how simple seeming stories can give developing readers the challenges that they need. One, Margaret Mahy, is a New Zealander who has produced an impressive body of work since 1969, from picturebooks to novels. Her collection of short stories, *The Great Chewing Gum Rescue* (1982), for example shows a writer at the peak of her power. In Britain, Philip Pullman's work for older readers has been much celebrated, but two of his novels, *Clockwork* (1996) and *The Firework-Maker's Daughter* (1996), have become favourites for nine- to eleven-year-olds beginning to enjoy a challenge in their reading. Pullman's preface to *Clockwork* guides the young reader in the mode of reading needed to deal with a challenging metaphorical text.

One of the fascinating features of children's reading in this age group is that it shows greater understanding of the ways in which literature works for them (Meek, 1988). It is also possible to probe the development of children's grasp of the sort of textual devices that writers use. Comprehension of conventions within stories builds upon their prior reading, and can lead to more sophisticated texts ...

Children's sense of humour becomes more sophisticated. They enjoy the possibilities of logic and common sense being turned on their heads. Like Carroll's Alice, children at this stage have to battle their way, without a map, through an adult world which often appears ridiculous.

Extract references

Barrs, M. and Cork, V. (2001) *The Reader in the Writer.* London: Centre for Literacy in Primary Education.

Meek, M. (1988) *How Texts Teach What Readers Learn.* Stroud: Thimble Press.

Smith, V. (2001) All in a flap about reading: Catherine Morland, Spot and Mister Wolf. *Children's Literature in Education*, 32 (3), 225–36.

Thacker, D. and Webb, J. (2002) *Introducing Children's Literature: From Romanticism to Postmodernism.* London: Routledge.

Comment

Mills and Webb's three questions (see Part a of Extract 17) to ask of the texts we choose for children are useful and would inform discussions at meetings of teachers making purchasing decisions. However, no one book is likely to have all the qualities suggested. Rather, we would seek to secure these qualities within the classroom and school library collections as a whole. The first question 'Does this book give the young reader access to ideas, themes and possibilities, while keeping the "surface" accessible?' has strong implications for choosing books for the younger end of the age range. The best picturebooks will do this well.

The second question homes in on the need to choose books that give young readers 'the possibilities for growing as thinkers and readers and imaginers while keeping the pleasure of reading in the forefront'. The authors mention postmodern picturebooks as having the potential to combine these qualities. For older children, I would also include short stories by such writers of imaginative power as Michael Morpurgo and Joan Aiken, and the novels of David Almond, Anne Fine and Jacqueline Wilson.

The third question 'Does the book help children in their growth as readers?' relates strongly to the previous two questions. If the answers, applied to a particular book, to each of the first two questions is a positive one, we might expect it to follow that the book in question would contribute to a young learner's growth as a reader. While agreeing with all that these authors suggest, I do think that children, like adults, sometimes want to read for sheer fun and pleasure or to seek out the comfort of a familiar and well-loved book. I remember a nine-year-old saying to me she liked the novels and short stories the teacher shared with the class, but added 'I love reading my comic when I get home from school'.

Part b of Extract 17 reminds us that some of the best books for five- to seven-year-olds, including picturebooks for example, are good at teaching the game of reading: they help young readers 'predict, set up expectations about what will happen next'. Stories for children in this age range often reflect the slow pace of a young child's life, so some tell of events taking place within one day. Mills and Webb advise against a simple division of stories under 'realism' and 'fantasy' as these often intertwine.

They continue their developmental approach to choosing texts for children in Part c of Extract 17. Favourite texts for older primary children include those which tap into their life experiences, preoccupations and other insights into more mature thinking and feeling. But these authors, following Meek (1988), also point out that children who love reading also become aware of the conventions writers use and this leads to their being able to enjoy more and more sophisticated texts. Beyond the chosen extract, Mills and Webb go on to say, importantly, that these are learned behaviours and that parents and teachers have an important role in developing them.

Questions to discuss with colleagues

It would be helpful to prepare for the discussion by remembering the books that meant most to you as a child and those you have found inspirational in the classroom with your specialist age range. There is much to be gained also from being well informed about texts for children both younger and older than your specialist age range. Chapter 6, 'The rich landscape of children's literature', gives examples of children's books in different genres.

1. How useful is it to think of ages and stages when selecting books and resources for the classroom?
2. Do you think we sometimes make too ready an assumption about what will appeal to boys and what will appeal to girls?
3. What do you consider Mills and Webb mean when they say (following Margaret Meek, 1988) that good books can provide for young readers and listeners 'powerful reading lessons'?
4. What is the contribution of children's books which have their settings in new places and cultures to children's growth as readers? Discuss with reference to particular books.
5. What do you consider is the appeal and value of traditional tales to children in the early and the primary school years?
6. Do you enjoy sometimes reading for sheer fun and enjoyment? How would you provide for children's love of humour and perhaps the ridiculous in the school collection?

Research inquiry

■ Choose two books for your specialist age range – picturebooks, short stories or novels – and write a short analysis explaining how the books do, or do not meet the qualities set out in Mills and Webb's three questions in Extract 17, Part a. Present your account to colleagues as a starting point for discussion.

And:

■ After considering some of the qualities we look for in children's texts at different ages and stages, select two or three texts for the age group either below or above your specialist age range and write a short account about what you have learnt.

And:

■ If you have not already done so, begin to make a resource by listing children's books under categories like picturebooks, traditional tales, short stories and novels. The lists will be particularly valuable if you annotate them. Collaborate with colleagues to share ideas.

Further reading

Arizpe, E., Farrell, M. and McAdam, J. (eds) (2014) *Picture Books: Beyond the Borders of Art, Narrative and Culture*. London and New York: Routledge. A multi-disciplinary approach.

Bunting, J., Nicholson, D., McGonigles, S. and Barrs, M. (2007) *BookPower: Literacy Through Literature*, Year 6, CD included. London: Centre for Literacy in Primary Education.

Suggestions for helping children respond to such books as David Almond's *Skellig* and Philip Pullman's *Northern Lights*. (There are other books in the BookPower series for Years 1–5.)

Centre for Literacy in Primary Education, *Core Booklist*. Free online resource available at: www.corebooks.org.uk.

Evans, J. (2014) Do you live a life of Riley? Thinking and talking about the purpose of life in picturebook response. In E. Arizpe, M. Farrell and J. McAdam (eds) *Picturebooks: Beyond the Borders of Art, Narrative and Culture*. London and New York: Routledge. Janet Evans suggests how teachers of older children can help children respond deeply to picturebooks that tap into philosophical debates.

Gamble, N. (2013, 3rd edn) *Exploring Children's Literature: Reading with Pleasure and Purpose*. London: Sage. This book has a helpful theoretical underpinning covering narrative and reader-response theory, but it also helps teachers nurture a love of reading in young learners with many suggestions for books and resources.

Lockwood, M. (2008) *Promoting Reading for Pleasure in the Primary School*. London: Sage. A life-enhancing book – see chapter 3 for ideas for inspiring Early Years readers and chapter 4 for inspiring readers in the later Primary Years.

Mallett, M. (2010) *Choosing and Using Fiction and Non-Fiction 3–11: A Comprehensive Guide for Teachers and Student Teachers*. London and New York: Routledge. This book covers the wealth of texts for the age range, with suggestions for classroom use together with critical commentary.

Safford, K., O'Sullivan, O. and Barrs, M. (2005) *Boys on the Margin: Promoting Boys' Literacy at Key Stage 2*. London: Centre for Literacy in Primary Education. An important book presenting a classroom research project in which teachers of older primary children try to enthuse 'children who are on the margins of literacy', and particularly underachieving boys. What did they find? Social interactive approaches seemed to work. Working with three quality texts led to a creative response. These were a poem ('What has happened to Lulu' by Charles Causley), a traditional tale (*The Seal Wife* retold by Kevin Crossley-Holland) and a contemporary novel (*There's a Boy in the Girls' Bathroom*).

Sainsbury, L. (2005) Chronotopes and heritage: Time and memory in contemporary children's literature. In K. Reynolds (ed.) *Modern Children's Literature: An Introduction*. London: Palgrave Macmillan. This is an interesting look at how time permeates children's literature, including picturebooks and novels.

Whitehead, M. (2010, 4th edn) *Language and Literacy in the Early Years 0–7*. London: Sage. Chapter 7, 'Books and the world of literature', provides principles together with helpful suggestions for choosing and using books.

Section 4: Visual literacy in English lessons

Extract 18

Source

Stafford, T. (2011, 2nd edn) Reading visuals. In *Teaching Visual Literacy in the Primary Classroom*. Abingdon and New York: Routledge, (a) 9–11, (b) 57–9.

The growing variety and sheer number of images in the different media that impinge on our everyday life make an ability to read and comprehend visual texts part of a current definition of literacy. Out of school, children are exposed to these images as they use tablets and the internet, watch films, television and DVDs, play computer games and read comics and graphic books. All these can be brought into the classroom if we want to make links between texts at home and texts at school. This can be the first step towards applying a critical approach to visual images. You will find visual literacy features in extracts in other parts of the book. There is a transcript of children reading pictures as well as the written text in the picturebook *Rose Blanche* in Chapter 2, and in Chapter 6 Eve Bearne suggests how teachers can introduce a range of media, including film, to help children understand and enjoy some of Charles Dickens' stories. In Chapter 6, Section 6, 'Multimodality and "popular culture" texts', there is more about graphics and comic strip.

Tim Stafford, who has taught in primary and secondary schools and now teaches English to undergraduates, has long had a keen interest in and wide ranging knowledge about contemporary approaches to teaching literacy and English. He believes that visual literacy in primary English lessons is particularly bound into narrative and story-telling. In the book, he sets out principles to do with teaching visual literacy and offers some ideas for the study and enjoyment of picturebooks, film, television and comic books. In the first of two extracts he suggests some basic vocabulary for teachers and children to use to talk about visual images. The second extract homes in on the vocabulary important in reading and talking about comics.

Part a: Reading visuals

As with any subject area, a definition of key terms and concepts is necessary to begin with. Admittedly, we are not working towards an unnecessarily complex or overly theoretical study of visual language with children here, but there is no reason not to introduce and clarify some of the more straightforward ideas. As with many of the terms encountered in academia, the more we search and the further we hunt for a definitive meaning, the faster we realise that singular definitions are almost impossible to locate. If we consider the term 'icon', for example, we are offered a plethora of subtly diverse meanings. A traditional definition of an icon is that it is 'an image or statue … a painting or mosaic of a sacred person' establishing the term firmly in a religious context (Oxford Reference Dictionary, 1986: 408). However, meaning has undoubtedly widened beyond these parameters over recent years, as acknowledged by a more recent definition of an icon as an 'abstract or pictorial representation of ideas, objects and actions' (Sassoon and Gaur, 1997: 12) …

I would offer a slightly different way in which to consider the concept of image, icon and symbol. It is easier to consider 'image' as an umbrella term, meaning 'the visual material which we are looking at'. In this sense the number of items depicted is irrelevant, for example we could be looking at a drawing of hundreds of people, yet we would still apply the singular term 'image' to it. The idea of a 'frame' helps here. Whether an image has a literal frame (such as a traditional painting in an art gallery) or a figurative one (such as a photograph, which has no physical frame to speak of but does have boundaries or edges which the image cannot cross), we can usually define an image or anything we see within a given frame. As these examples suggest, image is a cross-media term. Any two-dimensional photograph, painting, sketch or even mark on a page can be considered an image and in terms of film and television (commonly referred to as the moving image) an image would be what we would see when the film or television programme is paused. Therefore 'image' is used here as a general term but certain images (or elements within an image) can be described by the specific terms 'icon' and 'symbol'. An icon is a two-dimensional representation (drawn, painted or printed) of something tangible, such as a dog or a horse, or even something intangible such as fear or thoughts. An important point to make here is that icons are indeed *representations* of real life.

This is not simply a pedantic semantic point but rather a key idea we need to establish early on in our study of visual literacy: an icon is, by its very definition, a depiction of something and not the object itself. As McCloud asserts, a drawing of flowers is 'not flowers', just as a drawing of a face is, in actuality, 'not a face' (1994: 26). Of course the concept of icons can only be correctly used in terms of painted, printed, or drawn images – images which are interpretations of reality. You would not, for example, look at a photograph of your friends and say that the people in it were icons, because even though the picture is undoubtedly only a representation of reality, the camera has in fact simply exposed light and has not offered an artistic interpretation of the subjects.

The third term to define here is 'symbol'. A symbol is a specific kind of icon which represents more than just an object or idea. Here we can turn to literacy studies to aid our understanding …

The image-symbol-icon model is only a suggested approach, which will hopefully simplify any reading of images while at the same time showing that there is a specific and appropriate terminology that can be used. It is not completely without disadvantage however. It is perhaps a little too complex for younger children, for instance, and it is not always easy to classify something as a single image using the frame idea (if, for example, we were looking at several paintings on a cave wall, how would we tell if we were looking at one image or many?). Yet it does serve as an introduction to a vast and complex subject area and even if we do not introduce children to these terms immediately it will help clarify the approach before teaching it. In addition, viewing visual material as icons and symbols reinforces the basic tenets of visual literacy, reminding us that we are in fact looking at representations and interpretations of things, not the things themselves, and that these icons may often possess a deeper, less obvious meaning if we consider them carefully.

Part b: Comic books

Panels are to comics what prose is to novels. They are the fundamental building blocks of the text, the static images which tell the story through the sequencing. They usually take the form of vertical or horizontal rectangles but can also be square, circular or any shape imaginable and, in all but the most basic comic texts, are liable to change shape over the course of the comic or even over the course of a page. Each panel is read as a complete, self-contained image, usually forming part of a row which we read across the page from left to right, before moving down the row immediately underneath. The most exciting and liberating aspect of panels, however, is that writers and artists may choose to vary the traditional format and change layouts from page to page, so that even the most experienced readers have to pay careful attention in order to work out the correct sequence ...

The way in which they are ordered and structured is absolutely crucial to our understanding of the text as a whole and they are often inextricably linked with the tone and emotional effects of the story. For example if the pace of the story is frantic and exciting, the panels, like sentences in a book might be small and numerous, showing a number of images which the reader can scan quickly to create an impression of speed and action. Conversely, a scene which requires a more sombre tone might employ fewer panels but make each one larger, forcing the reader to spend longer looking at each and thereby slowing down the pace of the narrative. In addition, the shape of the panel can create its own feeling. A moment of particular violence or aggression may be depicted within a jagged frame evoking an explosion of broken glass, whereas a gentler image may be contained by a softer, curved and less rigid line. Similarly, the power and strength of characters such as superheroes can be reinforced when artists depict them transgressing the boundaries of the frame around them, as if the panel has failed to contain them. Comics expert Will Eisner terms these variations in framing 'the "language" of the panel border' (2001: 44).

Speech balloons, narrative boxes and sound effects

Comics show speech by depicting the words coming out of a character's mouth contained in what are known as speech balloons or speech bubbles. These are one of the fundamental elements of comics and one which the majority of readers understand from even an early age. The understanding that speech balloons represent spoken dialogue is not to be taken for granted, however. In a visual medium like a comic book, it shows quite a sophisticated level of understanding in children who can quickly ascertain that while the other icons in the picture are supposed to be actual 'real' visible elements within the world depicted (for example, a dog), the speech balloons and the words within them are not and are in fact merely representing what can be *heard* not *seen*. Like panels speech balloons can vary in appearance so that extra information can be provided for the reader. A jagged balloon outline could imply a loud noise or a jarring screech and a large or small font size within the balloon often tells us if the character is shouting or whispering ...

Another related feature of comics is the thought balloon. This is like the speech balloon but instead shows what a character is thinking – their inner monologue. Traditionally these are demarcated by a bumpy, cloud like shape to the balloon, as opposed to the usually smooth line of the speech balloon ...

Another way in which written text is used in comics is through what I term narrative boxes. These are small rectangular boxes which appear in the corners of panels to help provide extra information which the dialogue or thoughts of the characters cannot. They might be used to show where the scene is set (for example, London) or the time – especially if the story is telling a flashback to many years before …

A final, but important, combination of words and pictures in comic books is the sound effect. Again comic readers quickly learn that the large and colourful examples of onomatopoeia splashed across panels are not supposed to be objects which are visible to the characters in the story but are ways in which the writer and artist compensate for the fact that comics, unlike films, have no aural element. The most obvious example of this would be 'POW!' of a punch or the 'CRASH!' of glass breaking. However, far from being a humorous or stereotypical part of comic aesthetics, the sound words often constitute extremely creative and novel ways of representing specific noises.

Extract references

Eisner, W. (2001) *Comics and Sequential Art*. Tamarac: Poorhouse Press.
McCloud, S. (1994) *Understanding Comics*. New York: Kitchen Sink Press for Harper Perennial.
Sassoon, R. and Gaur, A. (1997) *Signs, Symbols and Icons*. Exeter: Intellect Books.

Comment

In Part a of the extract, Tim Stafford shares his thinking about visual literacy and how we might use terms to analyse and discuss the images in print books and electronic media that are part of our cultural world. Although he hopes that we can help children to become able to use terms like 'image', 'icon' and 'symbol' as they move through the Primary Years, he notes that teachers need themselves to become familiar with the vocabulary and the concepts the terms describe.

In Part b of the extract, Stafford continues his analysis of terms to discuss visual texts with special attention to comics. Comic books used to be unwelcome in the classroom and low down in the genre hierarchy. What Stafford refers to as 'the rise of the comic book' has led to comics being considered as worthy of critical attention and part of the literature collection in schools. Not only do children read comic books, they also find some of the features of comics in the picturebooks, magazines and newspapers they read. So Tim Stafford's examination of a vocabulary to describe these features so that children can learn to read and discuss the genre critically is helpful. Perhaps surprisingly, he does not use the term 'multimodal' in his comments on texts since this term is increasingly used to describe texts which combine design with words and pictures.

Questions to discuss with colleagues

It would be helpful to bring some comics and storybooks with comic and graphic book elements to the discussion.

1. How soon do you consider it is appropriate to bring in some of the vocabulary Tim Stafford suggests that is to do with visual texts when discussing them with children?
2. Being able to read symbols is important in developing visual literacy. How would you help children find deeper meanings in picturebooks by coming to recognise and understand the significance of symbols? (These occur in many picturebooks, for example *The Lion and the Unicorn* by Shirley Hughes and *The Tunnel* by Anthony Browne.)
3. What do you think the best comics might contribute to children's developing sense of narrative?
4. Many comics are about male superheroes and there is a tendency to think that this genre appeals more to boys than girls. How far do you agree with this assumption? How would you ensure that girls as well as boys have the chance to enjoy comics and storybooks with some comic style features?
5. What do you understand 'multimodality' to mean? Discuss picturebooks for different age groups that you would describe as 'multimodal'.

Research inquiries

Either:

■ Display some comics and books with comic features about superheroes (*Traction Man* by Mini Grey, for example) for a class or group of Early Years children. Children may like to bring their own comics to add to the display. Talk to the children about what they think a comic is and how it is different from an ordinary storybook. In pairs, ask the children to read a comic together that they have brought in or one you have provided. Ask the pairs to choose a page of their comic. Put the page up on the whiteboard or visualiser and ask the children what the story is about and what is happening on their chosen page.

Or:

■ With an older class or group, begin by showing on the whiteboard some scanned pages from a comic. Ask the children to help you make a list on the whiteboard of the features of the comic genre. How does it differ from other texts? Help them to use some of the terms mentioned by Tim Stafford in the extracts like 'panel', 'speech bubble' and 'narrative box'. Creators of comics write a storyline first and then do the illustrations. Ask the children to work in pairs to write a simple script for a comic-style version of 'The Three Little Pigs' or another well-known traditional tale for younger children. Having a sense of their audience will help them to write an appropriate script. It is probably best for everyone to work on the same traditional tale.

Ask some of the pairs to read their script aloud, perhaps putting their narratives on a visualiser or whiteboard. Then ask each pair to plan and sketch the first page of their comic story, deciding on panels and selecting from their script some text to go in the speech bubbles and text to go in a narrative box. Ask them to do rough sketches of the pictures which can be refined and worked on later. Show some of the pages on the visualiser and ask the pairs to explain their decisions – for example why some panels are larger than others.

The project could be extended into completing a whole comic narrative if time allows, and some of the pairs wish to do so. A splendid final stage of the project could be a showing on the visualiser or whiteboard of one or more of the comics to a younger class.

N.B. These suggestions for research are based on some of the ideas in the book from which the extract is taken, *Teaching Visual Literacy in the Primary Classroom*. Tim Stafford includes detailed sections giving teaching ideas for using picture-books, comic books and film. For my own suggestions for texts which incorporate comic strips and graphics for different age groups, see the annotated list in Chapter 6, Section 6.

Further reading

Arizpe, E. and Styles, M. (2003) *Children Reading Pictures: Interpreting Visual Texts*. London and New York: Routledge. A scholarly and enjoyable book with chapters on children interpreting ironic visual texts like Anthony Browne's picturebook *Zoo*, and on young bilingual learners responding to visual texts.

Maine, F. (2015) *Dialogic Readers: Children Talking and Thinking Together About Visual Texts*. London and New York: Routledge. When children are encouraged to use a special kind of talk round reading images, termed 'co-constructed talk', the author finds they bring a welcome energy and creativity to their learning. She suggests how teachers can nurture the 'social harmony' that is the foundation of successful collaborative learning.

Salisbury, M. and Styles, M. (2012) *Children's Picturebooks: The Art of Visual Storytelling*. London: Laurence King. This is a large, richly illustrated resource covering many aspects of visual literacy. There is a short history of the picturebook, and an explanation of how a visual language is created. It is a demanding read, but of great interest as it has a global reach and includes the perspectives of artists, illustrators, publishers and teachers. The authors illuminate the ways in which words and pictures interrelate and discuss children's responses to the picturebooks they read.

Wilson. A and Scanlon, J. (2011, 4th edn) *Language Knowledge for Primary Teachers*. Abingdon and New York: Routledge. See pages 151–4 for an analysis of a virtual world, 'Moshi Monsters'.

Section 5: Non-fiction reading in English – developing critical literacy through print and screen-based texts

Extract 19

Source

Horner, C. and Ryf, V. (2007) *Creative Teaching in English*. Abingdon and New York: Routledge, (a) 155–156, (b) 173–5.

Much of this chapter has concentrated on how teachers best support children's developing critical literacy when it comes to appraising as well as enjoying the fiction they read. This section turns to some of the non-fiction texts – both verbal and visual, in print and on-screen – that face children in their everyday lives and which aim to nudge them towards a particular viewpoint. Non-fiction texts in all media and formats are an important resource in lessons across the curriculum. Learning to read material on significant but less subject-specific topics, for example advertisements and news reports, is a well-established part of the English curriculum. It is of continuing importance since advertising material is more prolific than ever before and reaches into every format, context and medium. Access internet sites or use a mobile phone and advertisements constantly spring up. How do we help children to interrogate this kind of reading material and to question the motives of those who create it? In Part a of the extract Chris Horner and Vicki Ryf identify some of the issues and suggest some interesting activities to help put children in the driving seat as critical readers.

Part a: Critical literacy

Monitoring and questioning what we read or 'critical literacy' is a challenging but vital part of reading and writing information texts. As children are increasingly targeted as consumers and with the explosion and circulation of unsolicited information, understanding how and why texts are made is an essential part of learning how to read and write (Marsh and Millard, 2000). Critical literacy is essentially about comparing texts with our reality. This 'reality' will of course be different from reader to reader but of fundamental importance is the understanding that texts can tell us what the writer wants us to know. This can be very different from what we know to be so.

Non-fiction texts tend to have an authority quite different from fictional stories. They look serious and important and adults wrote them so they must be true. Challenging the accepted truth is an exciting and vital part of the creative classroom environment.

Barratt-Pugh and Rohl offer a useful framework of questions for reflection about texts that could be altered slightly to engage with any written or visual text.

What kind of text is this?
How can we describe it?
Where else have you seen texts like this?
What do these kinds of texts usually do?
Who would produce (write/draw) a text like this?
Who do they produce (write/draw) for it?
For what kind of readers (viewers/listeners) is this text intended?

(Barratt-Pugh and Rohl, 2000: 156)

Further activities to encourage questioning and critical readers and knowing writers could include:

Reading and writing catalogues. Collect images from catalogues and explore the differences between boys' and girls' toys – why do girls' toys always have to be pink? Who says so? Develop research into favourite toys and activities in the class. Any surprises? The children could develop class posters of Toys for All or Toys for Girls – the Truth!

Reading and developing greeting cards. Collect and collate images and words on greetings cards designated for particular people. Explore images of dads or grandparents, for example – my granny doesn't like roses and kittens, she likes motorbikes! Write alternative greeting and celebratory cards for use in the writing area.

Reading and filming TV adverts. How does the music make me feel? What is the filmmaker trying to sell me? How do I know? What do I need to tell the audience if I want to sell my bike?

Reading and making sweet wrappers. Look at a range of popular sweet wrappings and any related advertising. What do the pictures/words/fonts/colours tell me? Design and make and market a new sweet using the information gathered.

Extract references

Barratt-Pugh, C. and Rohl, M. (2000) *Literacy Learning in the Early Years.* Buckingham: Open University Press.

Marsh, J. and Millard, E. (2000) *Literacy and Popular Culture.* London: Paul Chapman.

Comment

Part a of the extract is from the chapter 'Teaching non-fiction at Key Stage 1' in the book by Chris Horner and Vicki Ryf, but some of the same issues also inform teaching and learning about persuasive kinds of text at Key Stage 2. Identifying the purpose and audience of advertising material and news reports is important at any age. The list of questions included to ask of a text can be adapted for any medium or format. The suggested activities are well matched to the children's age and likely experience, focusing as they do on toys, television adverts and catalogues. The next part of the extract, Part b, considers how older primary children can be helped further to develop their critical approach to reading texts.

Part b

Because many of the texts that we read are constructed to persuade rather than inform and, even if written to inform, are rarely neutral and context-free, it is important to provide children with strategies to help them distinguish fact from fiction. Sometimes the language provides an indication. Phrases like 'It would seem' or 'This suggests that' are not problematic, but whether we spot them depends on how they are slotted into the text. An opinion might be hidden, intentionally or unintentionally, amidst mainly factual writing and go unnoticed. Although we might teach critical literacy skills in English, it is essential that children have the opportunity to apply them in other curriculum areas. Omission of crucial pieces of information from non-fiction texts is common. For example a party political flyer for the local elections may list the positive initiatives they have carried out and leave out where they have failed. Historical accounts of a nation's achievements in war may omit the atrocities carried out. The creative teacher will not avoid such texts but remind the children to consider who the author is and their intention. Crucially the children should reflect on how the material might have been presented more fairly and accurately …

Different media

Television, radio, poster, magazine, newspaper and internet adverts can be examined in relation to the features of the different media and how they are received. The potential for exploration and critical reflection is enormous. Collect a selection of 'car' adverts saying where they come from, for example *The Observer, Capital Radio, ITV, AOL*. Give each group an example from two different media sources. What features do they notice about each advert? Use this information to formulate questions such as:

> How is a product shown on the radio as opposed to purely visual display?
> Why use jingles?
> What effect does music have?
> How are people portrayed in terms of age, gender, ethnicity, disability, class? …

As part of an extended project each group might focus on creating an advert for one of the media forms using the information that has been collected. The use of tapes, digital cameras and video camcorders, clip-art programs as well as typed text will enable the children to produce adverts in a range of forms.

As part of their own self-assessment and peer assessment children can devise an evaluation form to assess how effective the advert is and who they think the target audience is.

News reports

News coverage can also be explored in a similar way to advertising as the issues are similar. An important difference is that children might expect the reporting of news to be the reporting of facts and free of bias. By collecting evidence on what is presented and what is omitted, the more difficult questions of how and why can be broken down.

Give out photocopies of a news story taken from two different papers. Discuss as a class how a news story is presented in a newspaper, looking at headlines, sentence structure, vocabulary and photographs. How is the same story reported in another newspaper?

Comment

This analysis of how to help older primary children sharpen their critical thinking when reading persuasive texts like advertisements and news stories is full of ideas for activities to alert them to signs that a text is partial in the way it presents the information. Children also need to look out for texts that distort or omit part of the story. It is not a new idea to ask children to create their own advertisement. However, since advertisements now appear in so many formats and different media children are often invited to choose a media form and use such things as digital cameras, camcorder and clip-art programs in making their own advert. I particularly like the suggestion that children make their own list of criteria for a good advertisement in a chosen medium and use it to assess their own work and that of their peers.

Questions to discuss with colleagues

1. How would you support Early Years children in taking up a questioning approach to what they read and hear?
2. What do you understand by the term 'bias' in relation to reading material? How would you help children recognise different kinds?
3. How would you prepare children to take up a critical approach when carrying out book or internet research on such topics as those to do with environmental issues, the ethics of circuses and zoos, holiday destinations or research on a well-known sports person or performer?
4. Explain how you would go about creating opportunities for self and peer assessment of children's critical reading of an advertisement or news story.

Research inquiries

Either:

■ Ask a group or class of Early Years children what kinds of toys and games they like and list them on a flip chart or whiteboard. Then give out some catalogue pictures of toys and games. Discuss with the children if the catalogues are always right about what boys like and what girls like. You may prefer to carry out one of the suggestions in Horner and Ryf's list of activities in the first extract from their book.

Or:

■ Following Horner and Ryf's suggestion, give groups of middle or older primary school children photocopies of a news story from two different newspapers and ask them to compare them under headings like headlines, sentence length and structure, and illustrations.
■ This same approach would work with advertisements: give children photocopies of two or three advertisements for the same category of product, for example foodstuffs,

clothes or games. Compare them under categories like design, colour, language and depictions of people. Ask the children to amend any advertisement they consider biased, to create a more balanced version. Write a short analysis explaining what you consider the children learnt about detecting bias in advertisements.

Or:

■ Read to a group or class from biographies and autobiographies written for children. Discuss the issue of bias in this kind of material and make a list, with input from the children, on a flip chart or whiteboard of things to be aware of.

Further reading

Doyle, K. and Mallett, M. (1994) Were dinosaurs bigger than whales? Four year olds make sense of different kinds of text. *Early Years Journal of TACTYC*. Trentham. This case study suggests that even very young children can argue a case. Their teacher read to them about the blue whale and showed them photographs and explained that the creatures were endangered. The children said whales must be saved so that 'children like us in the future can see them'.

Lewis, M. and Wray, D (1997) *Extending Literacy*. Abingdon and New York: Routledge. This book shares the results of the EXEL project, which was a classroom-based investigation into practical ways to support children's non-fiction reading and writing. See chapter 9, 'A look at critical reading'.

Mallett, M. (2010) Argument. In *Choosing and Using Fiction and Non-Fiction 3–11*. Abingdon and New York: Routledge. See chapter 32, 'Argument'. Considers how children can be supported in gaining control over persuasive material through talk and then through reading and writing.

Riley, J. and Reedy, D. (2000) *Developing Writing for Different Purposes: Teaching About Genre in the Early Years*. London: Sage. See chapter 8, 'Developing control of argument/persuasive genre' for a very interesting and research-based analysis of how young children are not limited to narrative forms, important as these are, but can cope with persuasive texts with the help of skilled and sensitive teaching.

Extract 20

Source

Bearne, E., Clark, C., Johnson, A., Manford, P., Mottram, M. and Wolstencroft, H. with Anderson, R., Gamble, N. and Overall, K. (2007) *Reading on Screen*. Leicester: United Kingdom Literacy Association (UKLA), 24.

Children read screen-based texts at home and at school for entertainment and for information. These texts tend to have more visual information than paper ones and are more likely to be multimodal, combining design, illustration and written text. The multimedia nature of some on-screen texts makes possible the inclusion of sounds and moving images. So it follows that these texts are read differently to reading a printed page. They are for example, often more interactive as children can use hyperlinks to move between screens. *Reading on Screen* describes and evaluates a research project investigating the kinds of skills and abilities needed to be a successful reader of on-screen texts. The sources of data were extremely rich and varied and included evidence gained through surveys and questionnaires as well as videoed observations of children reading and interviews with children and teachers. On-screen reading for information, whether as a source of information for a debate in an English lesson or for a topic in another part of the curriculum, has become part of daily experience in primary schools.

One challenge for teachers is to ensure that children read texts from the internet as critically as they would print materials. In fact, critical reading is even more important on-screen: as Bearne and colleagues point out, screen-based texts are not edited in the way a print information book would be. The short extract from the research report draws on a case study with two Year 6 teachers and their classes showing how teachers can successfully create their own presentations for lessons, allowing them to maximise 'the use of multi-modal on-screen reading that they know the children appreciate'.

> ... the ability to design presentations for specific learning objectives is a great advantage. They (these teachers) also like the opportunities for tailoring the reading demands for their own classes using photographs, quotations and writing from different children to teach specific literary features. On the face of it this might not seem particularly different from using a chalkboard or whiteboard, but the flexibility of the software allows for focused attention on specific features. Colour, sound effects and animation add to the learning experience. Highlighter tools, particularly when used by the children themselves, can allow for direct teaching through annotation which can then be saved as examples, added to over an extended period of time and imported to computer screens for small group or individual work.
>
> As well as responding to the particular learning needs of the children in their classes the teachers also include their own writing in the presentations. Making writing public on the large screen is a powerful reading experience for the class. The children are particularly interested in how their teacher's style and choice of language appears when printed on-screen. For a cross-curricular PHSE and Literacy lesson about coping with change one teacher wrote about his feelings of apprehension when he left home to go to university.
>
> These teachers are developing the potential afforded by the large screen in their classrooms in a new and exciting way – they are actively demonstrating to the children how their own writing (both children's and teachers') can become a published text. Not only this, but the texts produced in the classroom look like the texts the children meet outside the classroom, bridging home and school text experience. The whole class experience of reading and commenting on everyone's writing means that reading contributes to the learning community in the classroom. In the hands of teachers who design their own texts as part of systematic planning for teaching reading, the big screen makes an important contribution.

Comment

I have chosen to share this vignette from a large research study as I find it an example of a truly creative use of the big screen, sharing as it does material carefully prepared and selected for a particular class and incorporating the children's and sometimes the teacher's writing. As Bearne and co-workers mention earlier in their research report, the large screen is not in itself 'a magic formula for transforming teaching' and needs to be incorporated in planning as part of a varied approach to teaching.

Questions to discuss with colleagues

1. How would you use a big screen to support children as they learn to read and use multimodal texts?
2. Websites may not be subject to the same level of editing as print texts. How would you help children keep their critical antennae alert?

Research inquiries

Either:

■ For a group or class of children in the Early Years, choose a television advert, perhaps for a toy or foodstuff, to show on a big screen. Discuss the purposes of the advert and who is the intended audience. Talk about the words used. Are there any jingles or little poems? Why do advertisers often use music and rhymes? What are the pictures, including any moving images, like? Do they use colour and humour to appeal to their target audience? If the children are enthusiastic about the work, it could lead to them creating their own advert and acting it out in costume, and perhaps to making a video to show another class. Write some notes on how far you think the children moved towards critical literacy during the project to present to colleagues for discussion.

Or:

■ Taking inspiration from the case study in the extract of the Year 6 work, choose a theme for a group or class of older primary children to research on the internet. Explain that you would like them to arrive at a viewpoint. You might choose a topic like an endangered species or a piece about an issue of local interest reported in a newspaper – say wind farms or fracking. Ask the children to hand in the fruits of their research – both writing and drawings – and make a page or pages for everyone to read and discuss on the big screen. If possible, include some writing of your own. Ask the children how your page design could be improved. The work could lead to a screen presentation to another class and to children's evaluation of the project.

Further reading

Bird, J. and Caldwell, H. (2014) *Lessons in Teaching Computing in Primary School.* London: Sage/ Learning Matters. Practical advice on helping children use technology as a tool to find and interrogate information.

Dooley, K. and Dezuanni, M. (2015) Literacy and digital culture in the Early Years. In M. Dezuanni and K. Dooley (eds) *i-Pads in the Early Years, Developing Literacy and Creativity.* Abingdon and New York: Routledge. Since smartphones and tablet computers have become part of children's daily experience at home, what might be their educational potential? This chapter, the first in a book based on research in Australia into digital literacies, looks at the contribution apps can make to teaching about phonics, shared reading and multimodal story-telling.

Kress, G. (2003) *Literacy in the New Media Age.* London and New York: Routledge. This influential book describes the move from page to screen and the increase in the importance of the visual and the multimodal as part of literacy in the twenty-first century.

Marsh, J. and Hallet, E. (eds) (2008) *Desirable Literacies: Approaches to Language and Literacy in the Early Years.* London: Sage, with UKLA. Chapter 7 is about multimodal literacies and chapter 11 considers media and literacy in the zero to eight years age range.

Vasquez, V. (2004) Creating opportunities for critical literacy with young children: Using everyday issues and everyday text. In J. Evans (ed.) *Literacy Moves On.* London: David Fulton. The everyday 'popular culture' texts used with four- to eleven-year-olds here include newspaper, magazine and television adverts, food wrappers and toy packaging. This author believes that teachers need to help children develop critical thinking as soon as possible. It should help them get an early grip on their social and cultural world.

Writing in English lessons
Finding a voice

Introduction

What kinds of writing are important in English lessons and how do teachers help and encourage children to find a 'voice'? 'Finding a voice', discovering your own distinctive way of using the written word to serve your purposes and to articulate your thoughts, ideas and feelings, is the key to fluency and control. A 'writing voice' develops and changes over time: writers go on shaping and refining theirs over their lifetime. The secretarial aspects of writing, which include learning to spell, to punctuate and to hand-write, are the meat of Chapter 5, freeing this chapter to concentrate on composition – how children learn to create and organise the content of what they write.

Section 1, 'What is involved in learning to write?', starts off on a broad canvass. In Extract 21 Dombey and a team of researchers deeply interested in children's writing identify all the different processes that a young writer has to bring together in 'almost any kind of writing'. They offer us a list headed 'What writing can do'. All the kinds of writing in that list have a place in English lessons, but I have chosen to focus on three which seem to me to be of special importance.

So first, in Section 2, 'Writing to share, clarify or reflect on experience', there is something about what James Britton termed 'expressive' writing – the kind of writing which is quite close to the talk that children (and sometimes adults) use when relating their own experiences, writing which often has a special spontaneity and vitality. This expressive kind of writing, together with early mark making, labelling and annotating drawings, is the earliest that young children achieve.

Then in Section 3, 'Writing stories and poems', five extracts explore how we can help children to write what Dombey and colleagues term 'aesthetically satisfying works' – the kind of writing we most associate with English lessons. The first extract, Extract 23, is taken from *An Experiment in Education,* Sybil Marshall's influential book in which she shares her experiences of her time teaching in a single classroom school in a Cambridgeshire village in the Fens. She sees the task of the educator as helping children to 'believe in their own potentiality for creativity' as a starting point for their journey towards being educated. Learning to write was, she believed, best done alongside the other arts, particularly painting and drawing. Teachers and children work in a different context and climate now, but this powerful 'voice' from the past can still inspire and remind us of some successful strategies we can use in order to make young writers.

Then, in the second extract, Extract 24, there is a glimpse into an inspiring and influential classroom research project, headed by Myra Barrs and Valerie Cork, which explores in some depth how children's reading can enrich their writing. Extract 25, from Horner and Ryf's book *Creative Teaching: English in the Early Years and Primary Classroom*, shares some ideas about how to encourage children's story writing through wide reading, inspiring starting points and carefully planned interventions. The two final extracts in this section turn to ways of helping children write poetry. In Extract 26, we find Ted Hughes' 'exercise' to promote that special, intense concentration necessary to create poetry. Finally, Wyse and co-workers in Extract 27 offer some guidance in providing frameworks for writing poems and on how to encourage experimentation.

While we tend to associate writing in English with personal and creative genres, some kinds of non-fiction writing can make a considerable contribution to the development of children's critical thinking and thus has a place in English lessons. So Section 4, 'Writing to plan and set out an argument' takes its theme from the list in Extract 21 from Dombey *et al.* (2013) 'Writing to order and extend thinking as in planning for action or developing an argument'. The two extracts in this section consider 'argument' – an important and challenging writing genre which takes in 'persuasion', which tends to present or at least privilege one viewpoint – and 'discussion', which presents more than one viewpoint, but ends up favouring one side.

Finally, Section 5 covers some other areas of continuing importance and interest to do with: 'young bilingual writers' (5.1), 'special writing needs' (5.2), ' gender and writing' (5.3) and 'writing multimodal, multimedia and "popular culture" texts' (5.4).

Section 1: What is involved in learning to write?

Extract 21

Source

Dombey, H. with Barrs, M., Bearne, E., Chamberlain, L., Cremin, T., Ellis, S., Goodwin, P., Lambirth, A., Mottram, M., Myhill, D. and Rosen, M. (2013) What writing is and how we go about it. In *Teaching Writing: What the Evidence Says.* Leicester: United Kingdom Literacy Association (UKLA), 2–3.

'Focus heavily on the basics, such as spelling and punctuation. Apply rigour, in the form of grammar teaching. Test frequently.' Is this a recipe for success in teaching children to write? Henrietta Dombey and her team challenge such assumptions held by many people not involved in primary school teaching. They do so by examining and sharing their thoughts on research evidence from English-speaking countries, research which points to some of the best ways in which to support young learners' journeys to becoming confident writers able to explore 'the rich possibilities that written text has to offer in enlarging their lives'. The extract starts where the authors set out what writing involves and go on to explain not only what writing can do now, but what it will do as the nature of text continues to change in an increasingly digital world.

What writing involves

If we are to teach children to write most effectively, we need to be fully aware of what writing is and what it can do. The act of writing is about constructing what the writer wants to say, in a visual form, using the communicative tools and practices available (Kress, 2013). So learning to write is more than the range of technical skills and transcriptional conventions that determine how words should be put down on the page or screen. Composition – the construction of meaning through words – is central. We should emphasise at this point that the evidence on the teaching that works best suggests that learning to write is most effectively achieved through approaches that balance communicative purpose and technical skills (Knapp *et al.*, 1995; Medwell *et al.*, 1998; Louden *et al.*, 2005).

In almost any piece of writing, from a substantial novel to a note on the kitchen table, a writer has to bring together:

- a sense of what has to be communicated – a purpose for writing;
- a knowledge of who might read the text and how to speak to them without the support of a shared context – a sense of audience;
- a familiarity with the explicit language of written text and its lexical, grammatical and presentational forms;
- an awareness of different types of writing, both paper-based and digital, and which might be best for the purpose and audience;
- a knowledge of punctuation and spelling;
- control of handwriting or digital technology;
- a readiness to review the writing after the first draft, checking for sense, for fitness of purpose and audience, and for technical accuracy.

Cremin and Myhill (2011) state that writing requires us to:

> Shape our thoughts into words, frame those words into sentences and texts which are appropriate for our intended audience and purpose, and pay attention to shaping letters, spelling words, punctuating sentences and organising the whole text.
>
> (Cremin and Myhill, 2011: 10)

What writing can do

However, writing is not just one, undifferentiated kind of activity: different purposes require different kinds of writing.

The writer can use writing to:

- record events, through log books, diaries etc.;
- work out ideas and shape emerging thoughts, through jottings, drawings and notes and wikis;

- order and extend thinking, as in planning for action or developing an argument;
- reflect on experiences, ideas or learning, through journals, logs and diaries;
- create aesthetically satisfying works, such as stories, poems and plays;
- communicate with others, both known and unknown, in a range of formal and informal ways, through texting, emails, letters, work reports, etc.

These purposes are not all mutually exclusive: some writing may be for the writer alone, but most writing has a communicative function, an audience in mind. In addition, engaging in the act of writing builds a cultural identity for the writer, an authorial persona. To write is to extend one's relationship with the world and one's role in it.

The changing nature of text

Writing these days is not just about words alone: in the world outside school the nature of texts has changed dramatically in the last few decades. Advances in digital technology have opened out possibilities, allowing texts to have a much stronger visual component with the added possibility of sound and video. Electronic texts of all sorts can be copied, modified and forwarded in ways that make them much less static than conventional texts and blur the boundaries between reading and writing. Today, text composition is as much about design as it is about verbal choice (Bearne, 2005; Kress, 2008).

Extract references

Bearne, E. (2005) *Making Progress in Writing*. London: Routledge.
Cremin, T. and Myhill, D. (2011) *Writing Voices: Creating a Community of Writers*. London: Routledge.
Knapp, M.S. and associates (1995) *Teaching for Meaning in High-Poverty Classrooms*. New York: Teachers' College Press.
Kress, G.R. (2008) *Reading Images: Multimodality, Representation and New Media*. Available at: www.knowledgepresentation.org/BuildingTheFuture/Kress2.
Kress, G.R. (2013) *Before Writing: Re-thinking the Paths to Literacy*. London: Routledge.
Louden, W., Rohl, M., Barrat-Pugh, C., Brown, C., Cairney, T., Elderfield, J., House, H., Meiers, M., Rivaland, J. and Rowe, K.J. (2005) In teachers' hands: Effective teaching practices in the early years of schooling. *Australian Journal of Language and Literacy*, 28 (3), 173–252 (whole issue).
Medwell, J., Wray, D., Poulson, L. and Fox, R. (1998) *Effective Teachers of Literacy*. Exeter: University of Exeter for the Teacher Training Agency.

Comment

Dombey and associates draw on a large number of studies when building a framework for thinking about writing and what it involves. They conclude that composition, 'the construction of meaning', is central to the task. However, many of the studies they assessed suggest that an approach that finds a balance between composition and the secretarial or transcriptional aspects is the most effective way to help young writers make progress. This seems in line with Wray and Medwell's research on handwriting, in which they suggest that achieving handwriting automaticity aids young writers in composing text (see Chapter 5). I have found the 'writer can use writing for' scheme helpful in identifying the kinds of writing most important and valuable in English lessons and therefore in structuring this chapter.

Questions to discuss with colleagues

1. Dombey and colleagues recommend that teachers seek a balance between teaching about composition and teaching about transcription. How would you set about achieving this balance when supporting children's writing development (a) with Early Years children, and (b) with older primary children?
2. In planning a writing programme for an Early Years class, how would you build in writing tasks and activities that encourage the development of a distinctive writing 'voice'? How would you support this development as children move through the primary school years?
3. What do you understand by (a) multimodal writing, and (b) multimedia writing? What is their potential value and how would you bring writing in these categories into the writing programme in English lessons?

Research inquiry

Either:

■ Work for several half-hour sessions with a young learner between age five and seven who has special writing needs, both in composing a story or account and with the transcriptional aspects of writing. Look together at a selection of their work, talk to them about it and plan together the sessions over a few weeks to help them make progress.

  Write a report giving your analysis of the difficulties they brought to the sessions, the strategies you put in place to help and your assessment of the progress made by the end of the project. What did the child learn and what did you learn about supporting writing development? Mention how you balanced support for composing with help over secretarial aspects. You may decide to present your report to colleagues.

Or:

■ Dombey and co-workers mention that children, like others taking on a writing task, need to have a sense of the audience for whom they are writing. Work with a pair or small group of children aged eight years or over to produce a story for an Early Years class. You might begin by asking the pair or group to visit the younger children to ask them what they would like their story to be about. Write an account of the work in a diary format and share what the children learnt and what you learnt with colleagues.

Section 2: Writing to share, clarify or reflect on experience

Extract 22

Source

Mallett, M. (2003) Ways of representing experience. In *Early Years Non-Fiction*. London and New York: Routledge Falmer, 6–7, 72–3.

Children's early mark making and writing includes labelling things they have included in their pictures as one way of ordering and clarifying the world around them. From this simple labelling, young writers move on to writing fuller annotations. Early Years teachers encourage this ability to comment on their experience by welcoming children's conversation about their 'news', often in a class group at 'circle time'. With some help, children soon become able to write their news in a book or jotter. Drawings are still important and the 'news' that children write is very often in the form of a picture with written annotation.

Early writing is about things that have meaning and importance in a young child's world. So we find them writing things like 'My friend would not play with me' or 'I had a Peppa Pig cake at my party'. More extended early writing, the 'expressive' kind close to speech, includes children's feelings about events and situations as well as thoughts and facts. Extract 22 revisits the work of James Britton explored in Chapter 1, Section 2 and looks at his model of how different kinds of writing develop from an 'expressive' core. He presents 'expressive' writing as a powerful tool for learning, enabling young children to share and reflect on all that happens to them.

Young human beings develop an inner representation of the world or 'world picture'. Before this happens babies know the world through action and perception, but once children can think symbolically – through images and through language – they can build a much more sophisticated inner representation. James Britton proposes that we can use our 'world picture' either as 'participants' to achieve something practical or as 'spectators' to reflect on and organise our experience. So I might use my 'world picture' of a recent train journey as a participant to remind myself or to explain to someone else how to get from Chislehurst to New Cross. Or I might, as a spectator, reflect on a conversation I had on the train and ruminate on its philosophical significance.

You might think that when we are in participant role the language that we use, whether spoken or written, is more likely to be informational in function than if we are in spectator role (which is to do with language to create stories, poems and anecdotes). You would be right – but when it comes to young children's use of language what we find is a quite flexible movement from one role to the other. A six-year-old, asked to tell the class about the elephant he had seen at the zoo, gave some information about size, colour and feeling and then said 'When it was time to go home I leapt on the elephant's back and rode all the way home.' This flexibility between fact and fiction is to be found in many texts for young children. Indeed many of the best texts are 'transitional' in that they have an informational function but also include some features associated with fairy tale and fantasy elements.

Britton brought his theory of participant and spectator roles to a more practical level with a model in the form of a continuum on which he placed three kinds of language. He placed 'transactional language' (all kinds of factual language) on the extreme left of the continuum and 'poetic' language (stories, poems, plays) on the extreme right. But what is particularly interesting is what Britton places at the mid-point of the continuum. Here he places what he calls 'expressive' language. This is talk or writing whose main function is to aid learning – rather like Halliday's heuristic function. Young children, as we would expect, see the world very much from their viewpoint. When they tell us about their visit to the park, their swim or when their pet went missing, their own interests and preoccupations are paramount. Children's early written 'recounts' are like this and Britton drew our attention to the fact that these early recounts are likely to serve an expressive function.

As children's control over language increases, their talk and writing develops, moving in two directions away from the 'expressive' heart. Early stories will still have an expressive flavour and their early attempts at factual writing will contain all those little 'expressive' touches that remind us that a young child is trying to organise their experience and response (Britton, 1970). Six-year-old Stephanie has word processed her recount of a class outing and includes 'expressive' touches like 'Getting messy was the best thing' and 'My mummy and daddy plus Darryl don't like gunge'.

A day out in Colchester

Yesterday we went on the train to Colchester group one went to the Minorities first. We did a picture of the seaside. I got very messy. Getting messy was the best thing. After lunch we went to the museum but they were closed. So we went to Castle Park which was fun, when we got an ice cream it was yummy. Then we went for a walk. We saw some ducks some of the children ran after a duck. I thought it was cruel so I told the teacher and she told them not to … we saw the lights were on so we could get a toy. In the end I got a pencil and some gunge. My mummy and daddy plus Darrell don't like gunge.

Britton's seminal book *Language and Learning* has remained in print since his death in 1994, but now other ways of categorising children's language hold sway … what now seems to be missing is official recognition that young children's language is grounded in the 'expressive' function. I believe we should welcome the 'expressive' touches children include in their early factual accounts because they signal that the child is actively 'making sense'.

Extract reference

Britton, J.N. (1970) *Language and Learning*. London: Allen Lane: Penguin Press.

Comment

It is in English lessons that a child has the opportunity to integrate thoughts, feelings and ideas in conversation, in drama and in writing. Of course we draw on our feelings when writing stories and poems but the argument, indeed the plea, in this extract is for making time and space for 'expressive' kinds of writing. This is because it provides an opportunity to order thinking, to express opinions and to explore feelings about things that are important to the writer. In James Britton's model of writing it is from 'expressive' writing that both informational kinds of writing and writing that has aesthetic merit – stories, poems and playscripts – develop.

Yet look in the content pages and indexes of official reports on writing and you may not find 'expressive' writing mentioned – not by name at least. In the extract we find a piece of writing by Stephanie at just age six showing she is able to give a very personal account of her experiences during a school outing. It reads very much as a conversation with the reader and she lets us know that she thinks some things are cruel, like chasing a duck, and that not everyone likes the same things – her family were not keen on her buying 'gunge' at the museum shop. So Stephanie is well on the way to finding her own 'voice' as she makes sense of her experiences.

Questions to discuss with colleagues

1. 'Expressive' kinds of talk and writing reflect young children's early thinking. In what ways and in what contexts might older children and adults find expressive language appropriate and useful?

2. How would you use published autobiographies to help children enrich their 'first-person' writing?

3. What do you think that children can learn about writing when they read and talk about books narrated by a fictional character, for example by Tracy Beaker or by Archie in *Archie's War*.

4. How far do you consider keeping a diary can help children 'explore what matters to them in their inner and outer worlds'? (Graham and Johnson, 2003)

5. I believe that just as it is important for children see their teachers as readers, it is a good thing for them to discover that their teachers can be writers too. Do you agree? If so, would you consider relating a personal anecdote as a starting point for the children's personal writing? (Let me give two examples. First, one of my students broke a foot during the half-term holiday. When he returned to his class he read them an account from his diary about the accident and, importantly, how he felt about it. Second, my children's guinea pigs were lost and I read out my account of how this caused distress to all the family and how we found them, many hours later, hiding under the garden shed. Both these anecdotes led to children's own written accounts of accidents and missing pets.)

Research inquiry

'Expressive' comments and asides often occur naturally in journal and diary writing. Stephanie's writing about the class outing with its 'expressive' touches shows that, from a young age, children are able to record events and how they feel about them. Making time for children to keep a diary in school reinforces the notion that some people write for themselves, to record and make sense of all the experiences they have. You may like to take up one of the following suggestions for helping children write diaries or journals and to share with colleagues what you think the children and you yourself learnt about the value of this kind of writing:

■ If there is a lunchtime or after-school writing club at your school, suggest keeping diaries or journals perhaps incorporating design features such as illustrations and memorabilia. Some members of a writing club run by one of my students wrote their autobiographies and read selected entries to the others. These children were eager to share their stories but the wishes of those who would rather not read out what might be quite personal observations must be respected. Some teachers write their own diary entries alongside the children and read some of these aloud. At the end of a writing session you might, as one teacher known to me did, lock the diaries away ready for the next time.

■ The diary format is sometimes used by writers as a literary device. Younger children would enjoy a class reading of one of the following books or a similar one before doing their own writing and drawing 'in role'.

> French, J. and Whatley, B. *Diary of a Wombat.* HarperCollins.
> James, S. *Dear Greenpeace.* Walker Books.
> Selway, M. *What Can I Write? Rosie Writes Again.* Red Fox.

■ Read one of the books listed below, or another book of this kind, with a class or group of older primary children and then suggest they take on a persona, perhaps of a person they are learning about in history, and write some diary entries in role. Young writers need to reflect on how this 'person' would cope with the challenges in their life and what they felt about them. This sort of writing task demands empathy and imaginative insight but, as it is more distanced from the writer than a personal account, children are usually happy to read out their efforts.

> Dahl, R. and Blake, Q. (illustrator) *Tales of Childhood.* Puffin.
> Williams, M. *Archie's War.* Walker Books.
> Williams, M. *My Secret War Diary by Flossie Albright.* Walker Books.
> Wilson, J. and Sharratt, N. *The Story of Tracy Beaker.* Yearling Books.

■ Children could be asked to write a holiday or weekend diary of all the things to do with language and culture they have enjoyed: watching television, films, DVDs, going to see a play, reading books or on screen, telling or reading stories to a younger brother or sister or engaging in computer activities. Some help from parents would be desirable, especially in the case of younger children. As Horner and Ryf point out, reading out parts of the diaries in school helps link home and school culture and activity (Horner and Ryf, 2007: 46).

Further reading

Clegg, A.B. (1964 edn) *The Excitement of Writing*. London: Chatto & Windus. In this anthology we find children's writing from what would now be called the Early and Primary Years, to the writing of older children in secondary school classrooms. Each piece of writing was annotated by the teacher and gave the date and context. Sir Alec Clegg, visionary Chief Education Officer of the West Riding of Yorkshire from 1945–1974, found the writing moving: it describes children's often harsh daily life in remote parts of the Yorkshire Dales in the 1950s and 1960s. One young writer wrote as follows: 'It's winter. At 5.00 a.m. I wake up and go down into the coldness. I make the tea. I shout up my Mum. I make porridge. I shout up my Dad.' Clegg, always interested in encouraging children's learning, concludes that decontextualised exercises are unlikely to result in such powerful and meaningful writing as exemplified in this brief piece.

Graham, L. and Johnson, A. (2003) *Children's Writing Journals*. Leicester: UKLA Minibook. These authors value children's journal writing as a way of exploring matters in their inner and outer worlds. Helpful case studies are set out and analysed.

Horner, C. and Ryf, V. (2007) Home language and literacy diary. In *Creative Teaching: English in the Early Years and Primary Classroom*. Abingdon and New York: Routledge, 45–6. A helpful account of the benefits of writing a diary to link home and school literacy.

Mallett, M. (1997) *First Person Reading and Writing in the Primary Years: Enjoying and Reflecting on Diaries, Letters, Autobiographies and First Person Fiction*. London: National Association for the Teaching of English (NATE). At the heart of this book is a classroom case study concentrating on the collaborative work of a group of older primary school children exploring first-person texts as readers and writers.

Mallett, M. (1999) Writing with expressive aims. In *Young Researchers: Informational Reading and Writing in the Early and Primary Years*. London and New York: Routledge, 129–30. This account suggests that older primary children continue to use expressive writing to learn and make sense of their experience in autobiographical and personal kinds of writing and in writing to get into new learning.

Plowden, B. (ed.) (1967) *Children and their Primary Schools: Plowden Report*, vol. 1: The Report. London: HMSO. Emphasises that children's writing is a creative activity.

Whitehead, M.R. (2010, 4th edn) *Language and Literacy in the Early Years*. London: Sage. Chapter 8 examines learning to write in the context of children's general language and literacy development. There are examples of early mark making and emergent writing and advice about creating an inspiring writing environment.

Williams, M. (2006, 2nd edn) Creative literacy: Learning in the early years. In R. Fisher and M. Williams (eds) *Unlocking Creativity: Teaching Across the Curriculum*. London: David Fulton. See chapter 3, pages 29–31 for ideas to encourage early mark making, drawing and writing through play and games skilfully mediated by adults.

Section 3: Writing stories and poems

The stories and poems children write take prime position among the 'aesthetically satisfying works' in the list 'What writing can do' (see Extract 21) and are what most people bring to mind when they think about the sort of writing that goes on in English lessons. Because these works draw on the inner world of the imagination as well as lived experience, writing them makes different demands on young learners to those arising from the personal and expressive kinds of writing explored in Section 2. In particular, when writing a story children have to create a structure, a setting, a plot and characters. The work and writing of the great educator, Sybil Marshall, can still inspire and guide good practice in meeting the challenge of creating a lively and supportive writing environment for children.

In Extract 23, she explains the importance of the 'writing books' she gave the children. When I re-read *An Experiment in Education*, published in 1963, I was reminded that she encouraged children to design the pages of their writing books so that they included all kinds of illustrations as well the writing itself. She would, I feel sure, be entirely at ease with the renewed value given to a multimodal approach in many classrooms today. One challenge in encouraging children as writers is how to provide help, even structure, while keeping children's own ideas and creativity central.

Teachers taking part in the project described in *The Reader in the Writer* by Barrs and Cork achieve this balance well. One of the findings in this classroom-based research was the importance of the teacher reading quality texts of all kinds aloud. From this book, Extract 24 shows how a teacher used a text as a model for writing 'the next chapter' in a story. The importance of children reading widely and hearing texts read aloud to nourish their writing is also made clear in Extract 25. Horner and Ryf share many useful practical ideas teachers and children can draw on to raise writing confidence. For example, visiting the websites of their favourite authors helps children discover where writers get ideas for their stories.

Extracts 26 and 27 turn to the ways in which young writers of poetry can be encouraged and inspired. First Ted Hughes, who wrote for adults and children, emphasises the sheer effort and concentration needed to catch the essence of a subject when making a poem. Then, in the final extract in this section, Wyse and co-authors offer their view about the place of poetry in the primary school literature programme, offering many useful starting points for children's writing. Readers may like to read this extract and Extract 26 in conjunction with Morag Styles' account in Chapter 6.

Extract 23

Source

Marshall, S. (1963) The writing books. In *An Experiment in Education*. Cambridge: Cambridge University Press, 110, 112.

Few have done more to discover what is involved in helping children find their writing 'voice' than Sybil Marshall. Born in 1914, she was the child of a smallholder in the Cambridgeshire Fens. After leaving secondary school she worked as an uncertified teacher. Following a long career in the classroom she went to university, taught at a college, contributed to the Granada schools television programme *Picturebox* and, in her old age, became a novelist. *An Experiment in Education* describes the years she spent in a one-room primary school in the village of Kingston from 1948 until the early 1960s teaching a class of twenty-six children ranging in age from four to eleven years. Written in the first person, it is one of the most powerful and inspirational accounts of the work of a teacher and her class ever written. I have chosen to draw attention to her work because she was a teacher especially able to help children achieve remarkable success in their writing, particularly with their poems and stories.

She found that what has often been called 'creative writing' could flourish when children were offered a rich artistic experience in which drawing and painting, but also model making, music and dance, all had a place. This fluidity, for at least some of the time, still informs the best Nursery school and Early Years practice and primary school project work. Regarded as a progressive educator, her ideas influenced those who participated in research for what became the *Plowden Report* (1967). But it is important to recognise that while her teaching was child-centred, it was not child-led: she considered the teacher had a crucial role in directing, supporting and resourcing children's work and activities.

When it came to children's writing, she believed that teachers need first to engage a child's imagination so that they can find that special quality of concentration needed for creative work. Each child in her class had a hand-sewn 'free writing' book made of sugar paper in which to gather their drawings, stories and poems. The selection of children's writing from the children's 'free writing' books in *An Experiment in Education* is well worth reading and the book can be accessed by typing the title into a search engine. In addition to 'free writing' books the children had a composition book in which they wrote a piece of English once or twice a week: this was carefully marked. Each child read out their writing and was offered critical comments from the rest of the class. The first of two short extracts explains the thinking behind the 'free writing' books, while the second shows us how one child created a series of illustrated books about the adventures of a cat. Part of Marshall's success as an inspirational teacher of writing was achieved by encouraging the children to share their work and by this sharing to create a community of young writers.

The writing books

These books are always profusely illustrated, the picture always being drawn before the appropriate text was written. Thought must precede written work, and the picture first seems to inspire and then order thought so that the words flow with confidence and clarity.

The second point is that once the children have acquired enough skill in writing English to write directly into the books with pencil, these books are not corrected in the ordinary sense of the word. Their authors know they can write what they please as long as it is legible and comprehensible. This does not mean that they are not read and appreciated. My usual practice is to take each child alone, with his book, reading it all, as it progresses, and 'correcting' a page here and there, by which I mean that I point out mistakes and allow them to be rubbed out and then corrections made by the owner …

As the children progress up the school, these books become more than a means of gaining confidence and skills and getting English to flow. They begin to serve a much deeper and more fundamental purpose, that of satisfying the need for ordering thought about life as they experience it, giving, as they do, a link between the tangible world and the intangibles of imagination, fantasy, desire and despair …

Beverly's writing

In her books, right from the beginning, Beverley employed phantasy as her medium, exploring always the distant and the unknown; using an element of magic to make all things possible, she was able to live out in her stories the situations of her dreams. Her passion for animals, cats in particular, led her into jungles and zoological gardens, and in stories of the 'Puss and Boots' variety in her actual infancy; by the time she had passed her eighth birthday she had need to project herself still further. Then one day she hit upon an idea so brilliant her pen flowed unceasingly as she unravelled skein after skein of her imaginary existence. She simply identifies herself with a black cat called Wendy, who had the most outstanding adventures, unbounded by space or time. I quote the spontaneous beginning of the series of stories which afterwards delighted us all.

Wendy goes to the moon

Wendy is a big black cat. One day she saw a see-saw. She was a very bad cat, so she got on the end of it. No sooner had she done this than a football bounced on the other end of it and up she went. But she did not come down again! Instead she was soaring up, up, up into the sky. Night comes, she was into the stratosphere, and in a few moments more she was in the ionosphere. 'Oh,' she gasped, for she was a few yards now from the moon!

Comment

Sybil Marshall's approach to teaching and learning reflects perfectly the title of this *Guided Reader*. It is based on clear educational principles; it advocates an essentially creative approach to English and all this is brought to a practical level when she relates episodes of teaching and learning in enough detail to show us their character and convince us of their worth. Perhaps the challenge of learning to compose text while paying attention to the many transcriptional tasks is one of the hardest children under eleven have to meet. Often their thoughts and ideas fly much faster and higher than their ability to get them down on the page or on the screen. How often do we find a highly articulate child who seems unable to do themselves justice in the written word.

The impressive thing about Marshall is that her approach to teaching is at heart experimental, one of constantly trying out new ideas to see what actually works in practice. In Chapter 1 of this *Guided Reader* we find risk taking to be one of the characteristics of creative teaching identified by Teresa Cremin. Marshall, in the first of the two short extracts 'The writing books', goes into helpful detail about how she encourages the children to start with an illustration as background to the writing they will do. This, she thinks, gets the imagination into top gear. She considers that thought must precede writing and there is no pretence that it is easy. Not only do these books help children get into the flow of writing without the inhibitions that the prospect of strict marking can bring, they make possible some connection between the happenings and experiences of everyday life and the inner world of the imagination.

Other writing, in a 'Composition' book, is marked objectively, and the essays are read out for other children to appreciate and to offer some supportive and, perhaps, some critical comments. Learning what others have done faced with the same task as yourself is extremely helpful in finding your own voice. In the second brief extract, 'Beverly's writing', Marshall provides a vignette of one young writer's use of the 'free writing' book. Here, a promising young writer has been given her head and risen to the challenge magnificently. Most teachers, during their careers, come across children who create characters and use them in a series of stories, bringing sustained effort to putting the characters into different situations and to working out how they would be likely to react in each one. In Beverly's case, Sybil Marshall judged that her writing offered her 'a magic casement through which she could escape to another world all her own'. The Wendy series included: 'Wendy goes to fairyland', 'Wendy goes to sea' and, intriguingly, 'Wendy goes on honeymoon'. All the children learnt about the importance of having an audience in mind for stories and poems, and the next 'Wendy' adventure was looked forward to by the other children in Beverly's class.

Extract 24

Source

Barrs, M. and Cork, V. (2001) *The Reader in the Writer*. London: Centre for Literacy in Primary Education, 73–4.

It is generally thought that there is likely to be a connection between being a skilful and sensitive reader and becoming an effective writer. But here is an extract from a book which actually demonstrates the truth of this by sharing the results of a year's research, using a case study approach, with 9–10-year-olds in Year 5 classrooms. In the study, reading and writing are brought together in the teaching of literature and literacy. Barrs and Cork conclude that providing certain experiences can indeed promote children's progress in writing. These experiences include hearing teachers read quality literature aloud so that children hear the rhythms of fine writing and exploring character through improvised drama as a prelude to writing in role. The extract takes up one child's response to the invitation to write 'the next chapter' of a story that was being read to the class.

Using texts as models for writing

All the teachers in the project planned writing activities from the texts they had read to their classes. Sometimes texts were used as a basis for children to generate their own ideas – which would obviously lead them away from the text. At other times the texts were offered as a direct model for children to imitate: for instance the task might be to write the next chapter of the story in the style of the author. A good example of this was when Anne, at School B, asked her class to write a follow-on chapter of Dick King-Smith's *Lady Daisy*. This story is about a boy called Ned who discovers a Victorian doll in his grandmother's attic. The doll, Lady Daisy, speaks to Ned and through her he learns about Victorian times. One day a dog runs off with the doll and, just as Ned catches up with her, he bumps into an antique dealer:

'A remarkable specimen,' said the man after a while. 'And the clothes – exquisite. No harm done, it seems – she just needs a wash and brush up. By the way. Let me introduce myself. My name is Mr Merryweather-Jones, and I am an antique dealer.' (From *Lady Daisy*, p. 103.)

Anne (the teacher) invited her class to write the next chapter of the story. Here is an extract from Sophie's chapter:

'Neds's mum went to bed while Ned's dad was reading the newspaper. It wasn't long before the door bell rang. Ned's dad answered it. In came Mr Merryweather-Jones. "I wondered if you had any valuable antiques which are worth a lot of money," said Mr Merryweather-Jones in a normal voice. "Hang on," said Ned's dad as he hurried into Ned's bedroom. He picked up the doll and took it back into the living room …'

Sophie has picked up on the easy but superior manner which characterises the antique dealer and has demonstrated her understanding of his motive and role.

Extract reference

King-Smith, D. (1993) *Lady Daisy*. London: Puffin.

Comment

Barrs and Cork go on to argue that texts offered as models for writing can provide a supportive narrative framework for young writers as well as awakening ideas and showing children the many ways in which language can be used to good effect. Throughout the book the powerful role of the teacher in reading aloud from a variety of texts and promoting discussion is emphasised and supported by strong case study evidence. The example of nine-year-old Sophie's response to 'writing the next chapter' of a book being read aloud to the class shows a child who is able to enrich her own writing with ideas and the language style of an author.

It is pertinent that Sophie is an able young writer who has read widely at home and at school. Some of her favourite authors are: Henrietta Branford, Kevin Crossley-Holland, Jean Ure, Bel Mooney, Enid Blyton, Roald Dahl, Anthony Browne, Michael Morpurgo, Jacqueline Wilson, Lucy Daniels, Michael Coleman and Anne Fine. The extract gives just a glimpse into the riches and wisdom this book provides and it is worth tracking it down and reading it from cover to cover to refine understanding of how reading and writing connect and are mutually supporting.

Extract 25

Source

Horner, C. and Ryf, V. (2007) Writing fiction: A creative approach. In *Creative Teaching: English in the Early Years and Primary Classroom*. Abingdon and New York: Routledge, 94–7.

Horner and Ryf are teaching and writing many years after Sybil Marshall and some years after the publication of *The Reader in the Writer* by Barrs and Cork, but they, too, recommend creative, imagination – stretching approaches to children's writing in English lessons. They have in mind here older primary school children, but many of their suggestions could be adapted for younger ones.

> In order to be creative writers of fiction, children need not only to have their own culture valued, but to have experience of a wide range of texts. Immersion in oral stories and exploration of the characteristics of different writing genres and film through a range of creative activities … must provide the basis for developing children's writing at Key Stage 2.
>
> Equally important is a sense of purpose and audience. When children write non-fiction they are often engaging in functional writing and the audience and purpose is often explicit, for example a thank you letter to a relative. However they may be less aware of the purpose and audience for their creative story writing. In order for children to see themselves as authors who have a story to share, it is important that they know how authors work. Many authors have websites containing online interviews where they share their ways of working including where they get their ideas from. As a result of a visit to school from one local author, the children in my class always carried a notebook where they jotted down ideas that might be useful for a future story. They were encouraged to be observant and look at their surroundings and characters they knew or encountered as possible material …
>
> If children become used to drafting their stories in the compositional stage, they will know that ideas are often rejected, edited out or changed. The process of reviewing, editing and changing the sequence of events should be seen as a response to the needs of an audience.
>
> The use of response partners where children respond and comment on a partner's work is a useful device for helping children to be aware of the needs of the audience. Again, as a teacher it is important to model the process:
>
> 'I understood how angry M felt because you described the way "she clenched her fists". I saw you doing that when you tried to get inside the character through role play.'

Teaching story components creatively

Although it is important that children have the opportunity to produce whole texts for an identified audience, there are strategies we can provide to enable children to provide elements of their writing without resorting to a formulaic approach. For example, children may have thought of a problem they are going to include in their story without having considered the setting. The process of writing a story is not necessarily linear.

The examples below are intended to encourage students and teachers to use a creative approach to teaching and learning that builds upon children's interests in order to develop and extend their language and literacy skills. These components of narrative should not be seen as necessarily sequential.

Scene setting

There are many ways to encourage children to set the scene in their stories and to choose vocabulary and syntax to convey mood and atmosphere for the audience. As teachers we might use music, visual images, taste or smell to suggest words or phrases to convey an atmosphere.

One student teacher I was supervising used a school trip to a stately home to inspire and support children's creative writing. As they soaked up the chill of the atmosphere in the chill of the stairwell and considered the secret lives of the ancestors' portraits that hung on the walls, they were collecting material that would inform their stories when they returned to school. They were authors researching their material.

Characterisation

It is by explaining in detail the range of techniques that an author uses that children learn to use methods other than just direct description of physical or personal characteristics. This is most easily achieved by asking questions of a text that rely on inferential knowledge ...

Problem setting and problem solving

Children are familiar with the dilemmas facing characters in the stories and films they see and the computer games that they play. Improvisation in drama sessions can encourage children to think creatively about the types of problems that may be encountered in a particular genre and different possible solutions. As a teacher you might set a problem for the children to resolve in groups. Children may act out or freeze frame a problem. What actions are required? What contribution do the protagonists make to solve the problem? Groups can set problems or provide solutions for other groups. The stylistic choices that need to be made might then be explored through shared or guided writing.

It is crucial that children have the opportunity to combine the components of narrative that they have been learning about in formal and informal ways to produce their own stories for an audience. This cannot be achieved in a single lesson but will need a longer period of time, if the end result is to be a story they can be proud of.

Comment

Horner and Ryf, like other writers in this section of Chapter 4, emphasise the benefits of reading widely as a way to nourish developing writing abilities. They believe that access to texts at home, including those often referred to as 'popular culture' texts – computer games and cartoons in print and on-screen – help children understand the requirements of different genres. Skilled and imaginative teachers have always looked for interesting experiences to inspire story writing. The example in the extract, drawing on a visit to a stately home with an atmospheric staircase, is a good one.

They consider, too, that young story writers can and should be helped to refine an awareness of their audience and they relate this to the benefit of sometimes researching a setting for their story. This is likely to add to the tale's authenticity and help it ring true. Writing may already have begun when it becomes obvious that some research is needed and so, suggest these authors, writing a story is not always a strictly linear process. This does raise the issue of when an intervention is helpful and when it may not be. Sometimes, when the creative juices are flowing, we might interrupt a young writer's rhythm if we intervene at the wrong time. So, wise teachers use their judgement about when to step in.

How do writers create convincing characters that the reader can 'see'? Horner and Ryf suggest we draw children's attention to ways of doing this other than just giving a straightforward description. I have found these ways might include revelations from what the characters say and do and the remarks about them made by other characters in the story. One of the most important observations these writers make is that time and effort is needed to help children work on their story writing. We might add that listening to each other's stories read out and making constructive comments – such a feature of Sybil Marshall's approach – is well worth making time and space for.

Extract 26

Source

Hughes, T. (2008, 2nd edn) *Poetry in the Making: A Handbook for Writing and Teaching.* London: Faber & Faber, p. 124 'Words and Experience'; p. 23 Note to chapter 1, 'Capturing Animals'.

The last two extracts in this section are to do with helping children to write poems. I begin with insights from Ted Hughes who wrote poetry for both children and adults. His ground-breaking book, which includes his own poems and poems by others, is structured round talks he gave for the BBC's *Listening and Writing* series broadcast in the 1960s. Hughes had in mind children between ten and fourteen years, but his thoughts about poetry and how to encourage young writers are helpful for any age group and anyone wanting to know more about the creative process. This 'creative process' is captured in that part of the extract from 'Words and Experience' and, for me, is the most illuminating and passionate explanation of what poetry can be. Then, the second extract 'Capturing Animals' takes us right into the English classroom. Here, Hughes sets out the stages in an 'exercise' devised to help children gain that intense concentration – be it on an animal, a person or a landscape – needed to create a poem.

Words and Experience

... it is occasionally possible, just for brief moments, to find the words that will unlock the doors of all those many mansions inside the head and express something – perhaps not much, just something – of the crush of information that presses on us from the way a crow flies over and the way a man walks and the look of a street and from what we did one day a dozen years ago. Words that will express something of the deep complexity that makes us precisely the way we are, from the momentary effect of the barometer to the force that created men distinct from trees. Something of the inaudible music that moves us along in our bodies from moment to moment like water in a river. Something of the spirit of the snowflake in the water of the river. Something of the duplicity and the relativity and the merely fleeting quality of all this. Something of the almighty importance of it and something of the utter meaninglessness. And words can manage something of this, and manage it in a moment of time, and in that moment make out of it the vital signature of a human being – not of an atom, or of a geometrical diagram, or of a heap of lenses – but a human being, we call it poetry.

Capturing Animals

Animals are the subject here, but more important is the idea of headlong, concentrated improvisation on a set theme. Once the subject has been chosen, the exercise should be given a set length, say one side of a page, and a set time limit – ten minutes would be an ideal minimum though in practice it varies a good deal with the class. These artificial limits create a crisis, which rouses the brain's resources: the compulsion towards haste overthrows the ordinary precautions, flings everything into top gear, and many things that are usually hidden find themselves rushed into the open, barriers break down, prisoners come out of their cells.

Another artificial help is to give each phrase a fresh line. The result should be a free poem of sorts where grammar, sentence structure, etc. are all sacrificed in an attempt to break fresh and accurate perceptions of words out of the reality of the subject chosen ...

In this ... the chief aim should be to develop the habit of all-out flowing exertion, for a short, concentrated period, in a definite direction.

Comment

I first read Hughes' book many years ago when a young teacher and was startled by the suggestions for exercises included in some of the chapters. It seemed to me then that this was a rather contrived and narrow approach, unlikely to get children's creative juices into top gear. I was wrong, of course: the opportunity to focus attention on one thing for a short period of time, knowing there has to be a final product, can indeed bring about what Hughes calls 'a hit, a moment of truth'. After some exercises of this kind, Hughes believes learners will become able to 'extend associations out from the object in all directions, as widely as possible, keeping the chosen object as the centre and anchor'. He likens the concentration, dedication even, needed to create poems to that required to catch fish. His poem *The Thought Fox* also reveals something important about the intense effort needed to create a poem. The very title of *Poetry in the Making* reinforces the notion of poetry as dynamic and active – something we have to reach for from the depths of our minds, perceptions and memories. The book is also a special anthology of poems which themselves demonstrate the success of Hughes' concept of what quality poetry is. The discussions round poems such as 'Pike' and 'View of a Pig' make this book valuable to anyone wanting to understand how poems come about and especially those who want to strengthen their understanding so they can inspire children.

Extract 27

Source

Wyse, D., Jones, R., Bradford, H. and Wolpert, M.A. (2013, 3rd edn) Poetry. In *Teaching English, Language and Literacy*. Abingdon and New York: Routledge, 52–3.

Wyse and colleagues begin their thoughts on children as readers and writers of poetry by emphasising that enjoyment of patterned language is very much a cross-cultural feature of childhood. Children respond to the rhythm, rhyme and music of nursery rhymes and songs. Young children are exposed to the language, form and content of poetry through advertisements, jingles and song; they also enjoy 'playground games and chants (often rude!) and songs learnt in school'. Like most teachers and scholars who have thought deeply about teaching poetry, Wyse and Jones believe that in the classroom, children benefit from hearing and reading many different kinds of poetry and that this feeds into their writing. But the extract that follows takes up the more controversial issue of how far encouraging children to use poems as 'models' to provide frameworks for their own writing is a helpful strategy.

Using the constructs of particular poetic forms such as the haiku or the cinquain can be interesting starting points for writing poetry. Giving children specific numbers of lines (three in the case of haiku and five for cinquains) and then moving on to the classic syllabic patterns in each line can provide a supportive framework (in a haiku, the syllabic pattern is 5,7,5 and in a cinquain, 2,4,6,8,2). Regular rhyming patterns such as the limerick also provide similar opportunities for children to work within specific poetic structures that are light-hearted and offer reasonably quick returns for their linguistic investment, although like many classic forms this takes time to master. Teachers can also use poems as a model to act as a framework for children to write their own. Examples that are often used are Kit Wright's *The Magic Box* and Miroslav Holub's *Go and Open the Door*. However, while having a framework can be a helpful tool, it should of course be remembered that these are wonderful poems in their own right and that using models for imitation can detract from children's ability to experiment with form and content in order to create new meaning.

If any of the genres of literature were likely to offer the opportunity for children to find their 'voice' and draw on their language resources to express their own feelings, it would be hoped that poetry could do this. Poetry-rich classrooms offer children the chance to exercise real choice between the content and form of their poetry. Finding a balance between form and freedom is a challenge. Whilst models and structures may be helpful to an extent, children should be encouraged to experiment both with form and, importantly, with the development of voice; children need both to know about how working within poetic form requires the poet to adjust and adapt language thought and feeling. This can come about only through extensive reading of poetry. Writing poetry can be a liberating and challenging experience for children and teachers. At its best, it can be vigorous, committed, honest and fascinating and is probably the most personal writing we ask children to do. As such, we also need to respond to their writing with care. Poetry writing should above all be about searching for things that really matter to the writer. As Ted Hughes said 'almost everybody, at some time in their lives, can produce poetry. Perhaps not very great poetry, but still, poetry they are glad to have written' (Hughes, 1967: 33).

Comment

Is using the framework of a particular genre of poetry helpful to young writers? Would Ted Hughes find starting with form and technique dampening to creativity? Perhaps the supreme advocate for using forms and techniques as a starting point for poetry writing is Sandy Brownjohn. In *Does it Have to Rhyme?* and *The Poet's Craft* (Brownjohn, 1994 and 2002) she suggests games and activities to help children understand and use such literary devices as simile and metaphor. 'The Furniture Game' in *The Poet's Craft*, for example, involves children thinking of someone known to the class and asking them to guess who it is by likening them to a piece of furniture, plant or a food. These playful activities seem to Brownjohn a useful prelude to helping children control the technical side of creating poetry. Wyse and associates seem to be suggesting that while some help over form and structure helps young writers, finding a balance in teaching between form and freedom 'is a challenge'.

Questions to discuss with colleagues (Extracts 23–27)

1. Teaching and learning happens now in a very different environment to that experienced by Sybil Marshall. In some countries, including the United Kingdom, much classroom time may be needed to meet statutory requirements. Marshall believed that it was through control over writing (and reading) that a child became able to record their own 'deepest feelings, their own excursions into the realms of thought and imagination'. What might the teacher today take from Marshall's approach to enthusing children's writing in spite of other restraints?

2. An 'English' focus with its emphasis on individual response to events and predicaments can be valuable in other lessons. Sybil Marshall often linked English and history. For example, one year the children in her mixed age class participated in a pageant about the history of their village. Interesting writing resulted: seven-year-old Nicola wrote in role as a bat living in the church when a fire broke out in 1448 and ten-year-old Nina wrote movingly about being left an orphan after the Black Death. Share with the group any experience you may have of links in children's writing between English and another curriculum area. What do you consider might be the benefits or possible disadvantages of this approach?

3. The authors from whose writing the extracts in this section are taken all seem in favour of inviting children to be an audience to their peers' writing. Do you consider this helps develop critical thinking? How would you create an environment in which children would understand that their comments about each other's stories and poems needed to be constructive? Marshall comments that she was surprised by the mature way the children rose to this challenge and the awarding of a star for the best writing became a well-loved weekly ritual. What 'ritual' might you set up to enthuse young writers?

4. The value of involving children in the assessment of their writing is a recommendation in the National Literacy Trust's final report *Transforming Writing* (Rooke, 2013), from which Extract 59 in Chapter 8 of this *Guide* is taken. Interestingly, Rooke and co-workers found that written comments on their work were valued by children, not least teachers' personal comments on how a piece of writing made them feel. How would you go about assessing how useful your written comments on children's writing have been?

5. Horner and Ryf believe that teachers should concentrate on the process of writing a story as well as the finished result. This seems in line with good practice, but do you see any potential downside to requiring a young writer, as a matter of course, to review their story writing at the compositional stage? I'm thinking of some young writers known to me who seemed to need to get a flow of ideas and found interventions sometimes disturbed the rhythm of their writing. How would you cater for individual differences and working preferences when it comes to children's story writing?

6. Multimodal and multimedia kinds of writing and illustrating have rightly found their way into the classroom. However, Horner and Rys remind us that there is still a need for extended writing, for long stories that are nourished by children's

reading of demanding fiction. How would you build this in to the writing programme and encourage young learners to develop writing stamina?

7. Wyse and colleagues point out that pleasures in patterned language 'are a marked
cross-cultural feature of childhood'. How would you nurture this by reading poetry
out loud and encouraging children's own writing of poems?

8. How would you achieve space in your poetry lessons for both helping children to
appreciate and control some of the main poetry genres, while also creating opportunities for the deep reflection and concentration Ted Hughes identifies as necessary for the most successful and meaningful poetry?

Research inquiry

Either:

■ With a small group of four to five-year-olds provide an exciting choice of different colours and sizes of paper, a range of pencils, paints and crayons and items like
sequins and sticky coloured paper. Encourage them to make a picture following a
story you have read or on another topic they prefer. Then when the pictures are
finished, scribe a title or comment for them. Record the comments the children
made about their work and share with colleagues what you think the potential
value of this activity was.

Or:

■ Sybil Marshall used children's art as a prelude to their free writing. Over two or
three sessions with a class or group, help them explore a theme first through artwork
and then through writing a story or poem. How far does doing this lead you to
agree with Marshall that art can be a promising starting point for written creativity?
Choose one young learner's response through painting and writing as a case study to
share with colleagues.

Or:

■ With a group or class, over about two or three lessons, give children a free choice
of topic and format for writing a story or poem. You could begin by looking over
a selection of writing by other children from the anthology in *An Experiment in
Education*, *The Reader in the Writer* or from another book which includes examples
of children's writing. Include writing with illustrations and interesting page design.

When the writing is finished, a screen or visualiser could be used to show the
stories and poems to the class. Invite the children to read their work to the class or
group and encourage a discussion about the feelings generated by the writing as well
as the effect of the choice of form. Ask them if they enjoyed having a free choice
or if they would have preferred to have been given a title or theme or, in the case
of a poem, a particular form or framework. (There may be reasons why particular

children would not wish to have their writing shown on the screen or read out and so some sensitivity should be shown.) Discuss your findings with a colleague.

Or:

■ If you are working with older primary school children, you might like to try using Ted Hughes' suggested exercise as a way into writing a poem (see Extract 26). You could bring, or ask the children to bring in an object – an interesting vase, box or sculpture perhaps – and ask them to concentrate deeply on it and then to write a poem, spending about ten or fifteen minutes. Hughes suggests having a set length, of a side of a page, and that each phrase is written on a new line so that the writing looks like a free verse poem. Ask some of the children if they would read their work aloud and have a constructive discussion about the results. It would also be interesting to have the children's views on whether they found the exercise was helpful. Write an evaluation of the exercise and present your findings to colleagues in a discussion group.

Further reading

Brownjohn, S. (1994) *Does it Have to Rhyme? Teaching Children to Write Poetry*. London: Hodder. Explains an approach to poetry teaching which emphasises forms and techniques.

Brownjohn, S. (2002) *The Poet's Craft: Handbook of Rhyme, Metre and Verse*. London: Hodder. This book, ordered alphabetically, gives comprehensive coverage of the features of different genres of poetry.

Bruce, T. and Spratt, J. (2011, 2nd edn) *Essentials of Literacy 0–7: A Whole-Child Approach to Communication, Language and Literacy*. London: Sage. See chapter 9 for advice on encouraging poetry writing with young children.

Clegg, A. (ed.) (1964) *The Excitement of Writing*. London: Chatto & Windus. Alec Clegg was Chief Education Officer in the Department of Education of the West Riding of Yorkshire. He edited this fine collection of children's writing, mostly about their daily lives in a remote part of the country, which comes with the careful annotation by the children's teachers giving details of the context of the children's work.

Clipson-Boyles, S. (2011) *Teaching Primary English Through Drama: A Practical and Creative Approach*. London: Routledge. Shows how drama can create writing opportunities that have a clear purpose and shows how to help children with script writing.

Cremin, T., Goouch, K., Blakemore, L., Goff, E. and Macdonald, R. (2006) Connecting drama and writing. Seizing the moment to write. *Research in Drama Education*, 11 (3), 273–91. Can improvised drama and role play lead to successful writing? These researchers offer a detailed analysis of the possibilities and suggest that drama can be an immediate impetus into some kinds of writing.

Cremin, T. (ed.) (2015) *Teaching English Creatively*. London and New York: Routledge. See chapter 6 'Developing writers creatively: Early Years' and chapter 7 'Developing writers creatively: Later years', which both place interesting and enjoyable writing activities in a framework of principles based on research.

Dymoke, S., Lambirth, A. and Wilson, A. (2013) *Making Poetry Matter: International Research on Poetry Pedagogy*. London: Bloomsbury Academic. This research-based book offers a comprehensive analysis of the place of poetry in the twenty-first century English curriculum. See chapter 5 for contributions on teaching children's poetry writing. The Afterword is by two leading scholars, Myra Barrs and Morag Styles, who have contributed much to our understanding of the role of poetry in enriching children's language and literacy.

Hughes, T. (2008, 2nd edn) *Poetry in the Making: A Handbook for Writing and Teaching*. London: Faber & Faber. First published in 1967, this is one of the most inspirational books still in print about helping children to write poetry. It takes up themes for poems, for example people, weather and animals. It includes Hughes' own poem 'The Thought Fox', which is about writing, and another of his poems 'View of a Pig' – a devastatingly honest picture of the dead animal and Elizabeth Bishop's 'The Fish'.

Lewis, M. (2011, 3rd edn) Developing children's narrative writing using story structures. In P. Goodwin (ed.) *The Literate Classroom*. Abingdon and New York: Routledge. Maureen Lewis describes and evaluates a term's work with one class and concludes that using story structures to plan and organise their writing helped the children gain confidence in producing coherent stories. The children were in Year 4, but Lewis considers that the approach could be adapted for both younger and older children.

Opie, P. and Opie, I. (2001, new edition with introductions by Iona Opie and Marina Warner) *The Language and Lore of School Children*. Oxford: University Press. First published in 1959 by the Opies, who were folklorists and anthologists, this new edition keeps alive their insights into the rhymes, songs, jokes and games that are so important in the social world of children.

Vernon, J. (2003) As red as a turkey's wattles: The poetry of everyday language. In M. Barrs (ed.) *The Best of Language Matters*. London: Centre for Literacy in Primary Education. The approach suggested here is an experimental one. It suggests that we help children to have their 'poetical antennae' alert for memorable words that come up in everyday language and familiar rhymes.

Section 4: Writing to plan and set out an argument

Extract 28

Source

Mallett, M. (2012, 4th edn) Persuasive genre. In *The Primary English Encyclopedia*. London and New York: Routledge, 315–16.

English lessons offer children the time, space and atmosphere to integrate the knowledge, ideas and feelings important to them as growing and developing human beings. Children often feel passionate about issues such as those to do with the environment, threatened species, children's rights and local concerns. So there is an important place for informational kinds of language in the English programme. This kind of language and thinking is addressed and explored in several chapters.

In Section 4 of Chapter 2, 'Speaking and listening in English lessons', we find children planning presentations, analysing their improvisations and using a 'dialogic space' to comment on their own writing and that of their peers. The analysis in Section 5 of Chapter 3, 'Reading and responding to texts in English Lessons', explores non-fiction kinds of reading in different media and suggests ways of sharpening children's critical analysis of persuasive texts like advertisements and newspaper reports. A traditional and strong context for a range of children's non-fiction writing is the school newspaper or class magazine. Here we find 'recounts' about personal experiences, 'reports' on school concerts and sports events, 'procedural writing' in, for example, the form of favourite recipes and 'explanatory' writing comes to the fore in such areas as helping show how new school equipment works.

But when young writers take up the role of journalists and news reporters they have an interesting and challenging opportunity to write in the genre we call 'argument'. The first extract in this section (Extract 28) considers two kinds of language in the argument category, persuasion and discussion, and suggests that developing children's ability to use these is an important part of literacy development in lessons across the curriculum and in English. Then the issues round providing a supporting structure for writing, often known as 'writing frames' are considered in Extract 29.

Persuasive kinds of language present the case for one viewpoint and include advertisements and political propaganda. Visual texts can be powerful in pressing one way of looking at things. In the UK the now abandoned *Framework* (2006) made a distinction between 'persuasive' texts which present one side of a case and 'discussion' texts which set out more than one viewpoint. Both of these kinds of writing involve argument, and we tend to consider that children cope better with such challenging texts after the age of ten. This reflects a general assumption that developmentally narrative precedes argument and that 'recounts' will be the main kind of non-fiction writing before about nine years.

There have been some convincing challenges to this view. Mallett and Doyle found five-year-olds were alert to the environmental issues when learning about whales. The picturebook *The Whales' Song* by Sheldon and Blyth contrasts the view of Uncle Fred that whales are valuable for their blubber and oil with the belief of Lucy and her Grandmother that whales are unique and beautiful creatures which should be protected. It is never too soon to discuss issues! (Mallett, 1999: 164). Riley and Reedy also used a picturebook, Anthony Browne's *Zoo* in this case, to help children organise their arguments for and against keeping animals in captivity. They conclude that there are good reasons for including 'argument' in our teaching from the earliest years. The kind of thinking used in spoken and written forms of argument and persuasion seem to develop much earlier than was once thought. Where children are deeply interested in a topic their enthusiasm can be harnessed to acquiring a form to express it (Riley and Reedy, 2000: Chapter 8). There are some things to bear in mind in developing this kind of thinking, discussing and writing throughout the primary years. First of all we need to plan the work round something likely to engage the children's interest and arouse strong feelings. Riley and Reedy's work came about within a bigger theme – 'living things'. Some kind of new experience can awaken a line of thinking – a letter, a picture or a story. In the Riley and Reedy case study, a picturebook was the trigger to thinking about some rather troubling issues. In Browne's book the mother thinks the lion looks 'sad'. And children begin to reflect on why this may be so. The second thing to consider is how we support children's writing, how we direct all the excitement and feeling into an appropriate written form. Class or group discussion helps children consider the arguments and counter arguments of the issue.

(Persuasive language presents one viewpoint but we do need to be aware of possible counter arguments in presenting the case powerfully.) Wilkinson got seven-year-olds to talk about the case for and against having playtime before asking them to write. The children were particularly encouraged to make a point and then elaborate it, and this structure was taken through to their written accounts later on (Wilkinson, 1990). Sometimes it is helpful to put a structure on discussion by linking it to headings on a board or flip-chart. In Riley and Reedy's 'zoo' case study the teacher organised the children's discussion under two headings on a flip-chart: 'good for animals' and 'bad for animals'. Of course we must remember that much early writing is transitional and we do not want to press young children too quickly into mature forms (Barrs, 1987; Mallett, 2010). The gentle shaping of thinking before writing used in the 'zoo' case study seems appropriate.

Are there some ways of helping older primary children to come closer to controlling the conventional ways of presenting argument? They still benefit from discussing the arguments first. When it comes to writing, they may need some help in creating a structure. Some children find the writing frames developed by Wray and Lewis helpful. These frames suggest that persuasive accounts setting out an argument begin with an opening statement defining the issue, go on to state the arguments using point and elaboration and end with a summary. A slightly different structure is suggested for discussion texts. They begin with a statement of the issues and also a brief preview of the main arguments. Then the arguments for the case are set out with supporting evidence, next the counter arguments get the same treatment and the writing concludes with a summary and recommendations (Wray and Lewis, 1997: 119).

The teaching challenge is, of course, to make sure the excitement and interest survives the writing tasks. It is well worth spending time on persuasive talking and writing, not least because understanding the controversial aspects of a topic takes children forward in becoming critical readers and writers.

Extract references

Barrs, M. (1987) Mapping the world. *English in Education* (NATE), 21 (3).

Browne, A. (1994) *Zoo*. London: Red Fox.

Department for Education and Skills (DfES) (2006) *Primary Framework for Literacy and Mathematics*. London: HMSO.

Mallett, M. (1999) *Young Researchers: Informational Reading and Writing in the Early and Primary Years*. London: Routledge (see chapter 6, 164).

Mallett, M. (2010) *Choosing and Using Fiction and Non-fiction 3–11*. London and New York: Routledge (see chapter 32, 'Argument').

Riley, J. and Reedy, D. (2000) *Developing Writing for Different Purposes*. London: Paul Chapman (see chapter 8, 'Developing control of the argument/persuasive genre').

Sheldon, D. and Blyth, G. (illustrator) (1993) *The Whales' Song*. London: Red Fox.

Wilkinson, A. (1990) Argument as a primary act of mind. *English in Education* (NATE), 24 (1).

Wray, D. and Lewis, M. (1997) *Extending Literacy: Children Reading and Writing Non-Fiction*. London: Routledge.

Comment

Although the UK *Framework* (2006) has ended, teachers still often think of its six genres when planning children's non-fiction writing. Mallett concentrates here on 'persuasion'. It is undoubtedly one of the more challenging genres but it is argued that even very young children can have strong feelings about issues and their talk and improvisation about them can lead to writing with the teacher as scribe. The teacher in the 'Whales' case study had read stories and factual accounts about whales to her class of four-year-olds. Books and film were brought in to help answer the children's questions. One was about 'animals at risk', including whales. One child said that if all the whales were killed 'children like us will not be able to see them'. The children were eager for the teacher to scribe annotations to their pictures. These dictated comments showed that the children were thinking about the issues of endangered species. Opal asked the teacher to write 'The whale is dying, a man killed him with a knife' at the bottom of her detailed picture. This approach gives children an early start in realising that books do not just give 'the facts'; not only are 'the facts' not always clear cut, but they raise issues about which people have different opinions. The children in this case study were helped to understand this when the teacher read them *The Whales' Song* in which Uncle Fred and Lucy have very different views about whales and how they should be treated.

Mallett goes on to consider how older children can be supported as they make progress in controlling an argument. Talk is still, for older children, a good preliminary way of ordering thinking. Lively debate can be an excellent preliminary to writing. This could lead to a more formal debate, with a panel of four, with two children speaking on one side of an issue and the other two on the other side. The teacher could demonstrate the pattern of argument that involves making a point, elaborating it and then moving on to the next point. The rest of the class could join in after the speakers have made their cases and comments and questions are taken from the floor. As well as being enjoyable and valuable for its own sake the discussion and debating prepares the way for a structured written response.

Extract 29

Source

Wilson, A. and Scanlon, J. (2011, 4th edn) Writing frames. In *Language Knowledge for Primary Teachers*. Abingdon and New York: Routledge, 39.

When we set out to discuss an issue with a group of friends, the textual cohesion we spoke about above is not such an important matter. We expect talk to range to and fro. We can backtrack easily, by inserting into the conversation something we meant to say earlier. As we talk, we are likely to think of more ideas, and to be prompted by the others to remember things we had forgotten. Someone may take on the role of chair and attempt to keep order, but on many occasions talk will be a free-for-all, and may indeed become very incoherent.

Constructing written texts can be a much more lonely business, and the demands to organise what we have to say can be much greater. One's gran may be so pleased to get a letter that she doesn't mind what order the points come in, but other readers will be less forgiving. The more formal and abstract the types of text to be constructed, the greater the demands – especially on an experienced writer. Response partners are invaluable in this situation but there will still be many occasions when a class may be faced with getting on with a piece of writing without immediate help being available. Wray and Lewis (1997) suggest offering children an outline structure in the form of a writing frame to support them in the six most frequently occurring non-fiction written forms. The writing frame would suggest to children those stages in the construction of the text that we have already referred to, and might offer some starting phrases, or phrases for linking one stage of the text to the next: 'on the one hand …' or 'nevertheless …' or 'I would like to begin by …' As Wray and Lewis point out there are many possible writing frames for the six broad purposes for writing, and it is important that any frame suggested to children stays flexible and does not become a rigid form. It could be said that a frame should also be regarded like a pair of water wings, with all the dangers of over-dependence that they can produce, and every effort should be made to dispense with its use as quickly as possible. We have seen story frames in various formats used quite frequently, but in fact it is probably with the more complex structures of non-narrative texts that some children need help.

Extract reference

Wray, D. and Lewis, M. (1997) *Extending Literacy: Children Reading and Writing Non-Fiction.* London: Routledge.

Comment

As part of their work on the EXEL Project at Exeter University Wray and Lewis devised writing frames for the six non-fiction text types identified in the 2006 *Framework*, but always pointing out that they should be used flexibly and that they should not be used as exercises to teach the different genres. It is argued in the extract that the 'starting' and 'linking' phrases that make up the frame can be helpful in providing a structure for less confident writers. Wilson and Scanlon's metaphor of the frames as 'water wings' is a good one, suggesting as it does that the frame is a prop or support which can be abandoned as the writer gains more confidence and competence.

Questions to discuss with colleagues (Extracts 28 and 29)

It would be helpful to bring to the discussion texts that you think might be a good starting point for discussing different viewpoints about an issue. These texts might include picturebooks, short stories, information texts, novels, newspaper articles, material on internet sites and 'popular culture' texts.

1. Two short case studies referred to in Extract 28 suggest that picturebooks (those mentioned are *The Whales' Song* and *Zoo*) can inspire young children's thinking, talking and writing about issues that matter to them. Bring to the discussion your own ideas for picturebooks and explain the reasons for your choices. Promising titles include John Burningham's book *Oi! Get off this Train* (Red Fox, 1991) about endangered species, Patrick George's wordless picturebook *Animal Rescue* (Patrick George publishers, 2015), David Daywaite and Oliver Jeffer's book *The Day the Crayons Quit* (HarperCollins, 2014) about finding a way to bring conflict to an end, and Quentin Blake's *The Five of Us* (Tate Publishing, 2014) about focusing on what you can do – with the help of friends.

2. Suggest some picturebooks you consider would appeal to older primary children as a starting point for discussing and writing about topics they feel strongly about, including some with a controversial element and give rise to different points of view. Some suggestions include: Anthony Browne's books *The Tunnel* (Walker Books, 2008) and *The Piggybook* (Walker Books, 2008), which can lead to conversation about sibling relationships and gender issues; Quentin Blake's *The Clown* (Red Fox, 2001, which tells a story about finding happiness after disaster by encouraging people to be kind; Shaun Tann's picturebooks, for example the graphic wordless book *The Arrival* (Hodder, 2007) about adventure and about loneliness in a new environment, and *The Lost Thing* (Hodder, 2010) – all about the things that we notice and which shape our thinking. The importance of creating an environment with growing, living greenery as opposed to relentless urban development might arise from reading and reflecting on *The Promise* by Nicola Davies (Walker Books, 2014).

3. Share some of your own suggestions for information texts in print or online which you think would help children understand, discuss and write about different viewpoints on particular issues. Suggestions for younger children might include: Lauren Child's *Charlie and Lola: Look After Your Planet* (Puffin, 2011); Jan Hughes' *What Happened to the Dinosaurs?* (William Morrow, 2001) and Kate Knighton's *Why Shouldn't I Eat Junk Food?* (Usborne, 2008). For older children some suggestions are: David Smith's *If the World Were a Village* (A&C Black, 2004); Dorling Kindersley's *Titanic, Eyewitness* (DK, 2014) and David McCandless's *Information is Beautiful* (Collins, 2009).

4. What do you consider is the contribution of learning to write texts in the persuasion and discussion genres to children's intellectual development?

5. How would you explain the advantages and possible disadvantages of using writing frames to structure non-narrative kinds of writing to an older child or to a parent who has inquired about them?

6. Bearing in mind the views of Wilson and Scanlon, in what contexts would you consider using a 'frame' for a child's writing, either one devised by Wray and Lewis or one you have constructed yourself?

Research inquiry

The kinds of writing that are to do with argument benefit from being set in a context children find meaningful and interesting. Both these suggestions use dramatic improvisation – that great provider of contexts for writing – to help children find a 'voice'.

Either:

■ Set up an improvised drama with younger children by reading an 'information story', for example Lauren Child's *Charlie and Lola: Look After Your Planet* or an information book raising an issue, for example Kate Knighton's *Why Shouldn't I Eat Junk Food?* Another option would be to use information about the environment from an educational website, for example www.bbc.co.uk/schools. Over several sessions, encourage the children to refine and talk about their drama. Then bring in a persuasive writing task in context. For example, the children might make a notice entitled 'Please reuse plastic bags' with reasons or make an illustrated booklet on 'Why you should eat fruit and vegetables' and integrate these items into the improvisation. This could lead to the children showing their work to another class or group or making it part of an assembly. Some groups or classes many need your support as 'teacher in role'.

Or:

■ With a group or class of older primary children, create an idea for exploring an issue through drama, an issue that you think will create an interesting context for persuasive writing. You may have an idea of your own to develop or choose to work on, change or modify the suggestion that follows.

The people who live in a small town in the countryside awake to find a notice at the entrance to a large field on the outskirts of the town looking over a fine landscape. The notice informs them that the space is to be sold and a large hypermarket built. The people gathered round the notice have two different viewpoints. One group think that the loss of the view will compromise the enjoyment of living in a town in a beautiful setting. They also believe that the increased flow of traffic the hypermarket will attract will cause considerable congestion and inconvenience. The other group are attracted by the thought of the many jobs that the hypermarket will create. They also feel that the increase in visitors will bring life and energy to what has been rather a quiet town. One of the people viewing the notice is a councillor and she suggests that they organise a meeting in the town hall to discuss the issues and produce a plan of action.

The meeting is chaired by the councillor who says she will remain neutral. The other members of the panel are:

☐ On the pro-development side – the developer who wants to buy the site and a resident who says she wants the jobs the development will bring for her grown-up children and other young people in the town.

- On the anti-development side – a local writer (or artist?) who wants to pre-serve the existing character of the town and a mother/father of young children who does not want the fumes of extra traffic and much prefers the idea of making the space into a park with swings for children.

The rest of the group or class could be residents or journalists writing notes for a newspaper article on the issues. You might choose to help structure the improvisation as 'teacher in role' – perhaps as the councillor leading the meeting.

Children could think of names for the town and for the members of the panel. Writing tasks could include:

- newspaper article by 'journalist' (with illustrations) for the local newspaper;
- letters from members of the public taking up different viewpoints for the letter page of the local newspaper (one child could act as Editor);
- lyrical letter from the local writer/artist saying what the town has meant to him/her and what will be lost if the development goes ahead;
- letters from people who have ideas for a development that they would prefer to the hypermarket.

The drama could end with a display of writing and drawing and a presentation to another class. Or, after the meeting, 'residents' could vote for or against the develop-ment and more drama about the reactions to the result of the people of the town could follow. I have seen children and teachers working with different variations on this theme and similar ones which have the potential to provide an enjoyable and meaning-ful context for the challenge of persuasive kinds of writing.

Further reading

(See also Extract references.)

Barrs, M. (1991/2) Genre theory – what's it all about? *Language Matters*, 1. London: Centre for Literacy in Primary Education (CLPE). While children are entitled to learn about the kinds of reading and writing valued in their society, we must remember that these are dynamic and ever-changing and not static. Barrs argues against teaching genres directly to young children.

Cremin, T., Goouch, K., Blakemore, I., Goff, E. and Macdonald, R. (2006) Connecting drama and writing: Seizing the moment to write. *Research In Drama Education*, 11 (3). Makes the case for improvised drama as an important context for all kinds of writing, not least journalistic and persuasive kinds.

Doyle, K. and Mallett, M. (1994) Were dinosaurs bigger than whales? Four year olds make sense of different kinds of text. *Early Years Journal of TACTYC*, 14 (2). Very young children begin to understand that people have different viewpoints on important issues. The programme was enriched by museum visits, artwork, discussion, film of whales in their natural environments and books of all kinds from picturebooks to information books.

Farmer, D. (2012) *Learning Through Drama*. London: Drama Resources. This practical book, which draws on the work of Dorothy Heathcote and Gavin Bolton, has sections on 'Drama and writing' (p. 4) and 'Teacher in role' (p. 17).

Glen, P. (1982) *Mr Togs the Tailor: A Context for Writing*. Scottish Curriculum Development Service, ERIC Number: ED267404. A teacher and her class of six- to seven-year-olds spent a term talking, improvising, writing and drawing about Mr Togs, a tailor's dummy given to the school by a parent and set up in a 'shop' in the classroom. Mr Togs had many experiences – some pleasant like a birthday and a holiday – and some more alarming – a burglary and his illness. The persuasive kind of writing came in when the children thought about the benefits of having a burglar alarm. The children became deeply involved in Mr Togs' triumphs and troubles and a range of lively writing resulted: greeting cards, postcards, shop security advice and recipes. One former pupil, now a teacher, comments 'Even now at nearly 40 I vividly remember doing this project … Mr Togs took we little people on a voyage of discovery. I still remember feeling sad when he retired and closed his shop' (books.google.co.uk/books/about/Mr-Togs-the-tailor.html, accessed 17 March 2015). Many others have been inspired by this project to create opportunities for contextualised writing using their own and the children's ideas for characters and situations.

Horner, C. and Ryf, V. (2007) *Creative Teaching: English in the Early Years and Primary Classroom.* Abingdon and New York: Routledge. See 'Creative approaches to writing non-fiction in the early years', pages 128–37. Included are examples of picturebooks linked to non-fiction activities they could inspire. For example, *Peepo!* by Allan and Janet Ahlberg (Puffin) could lead to role play in a baby clinic, perhaps with lists nudging parents towards things best for baby. Following Horner and Ryf's analysis, it occurred to me that making the cases for and against giving babies dummies might be a good issue for discussion.

Mallett, M. (2010) Argument: Discussion and persuasion texts. In M. Mallett (ed.) *Choosing and Using Fiction and Non-Fiction 3–11.* Abingdon and New York: Routledge. This book looks at the features of texts that have a logical rather than a chronological organisation and suggests a range of books and resources to help children read, talk about and write about different viewpoints about issues.

Roche, M. (2015) *Critical Thinking Through Picturebooks: A Guide for Primary and Early Years Students and Teachers.* London: Trentham Books. The argument for using picturebooks for dialogic conversation is made with many suggestions for a school's picturebook collection.

Rothery, J. and Callaghan, M. (1988) *Teaching Factual Writing: A Genre Based Approach.* Report of the DSP Literacy Project, Metropolitan East Region, Sydney, NSW Department of Education. These Australian authors were part of a project that found that primary schools tended to favour narrative kinds of writing – for example news and stories in a time sequence. They were among those who drew attention to the non-narrative kinds of text which have an important place in the world outside the classroom and therefore, they argued, should be brought into the classroom and taught in school. The British researchers, David Wray and Maureen Lewis, drew on this work in their Nuffield-funded EXEL Project at Exeter University and their classification of non-fiction texts informed several versions of the National Curriculum English programmes and the *Framework* (2006). Teachers still find it useful to think about non-fiction writing with reference to the six non-fiction text types: recount, report, procedural, explanation, persuasion and discussion.

Wray, D. and Lewis, M. *An Approach to Scaffolding Children's Non-Fiction Writing: The Use of Writing Frames.* Available at: www.learning.wales.gov.uk/docs/learning wales/publication/writing frames (accessed 14 March 2015).

Section 5: Some other important issues – young bilingual writers; special writing needs; gender and writing; writing multimodal, multimedia and 'popular culture' texts

This final section gives space and attention to issues to do with writing that are of continuing importance to teachers of Early Years and primary age groups. Extract 30 looks at the needs of young bilingual learners when it comes to writing in their additional language.

Young learners who have special educational needs often find writing particularly challenging and so Extract 31 examines strategies to help them. Forward young writers need encouragement too, and to be provided with sufficient challenge and opportunity.

Writing is also to the fore when we consider gender differences in children's use of language and Extract 32 looks at the research studies into the writing of small boys designed by Julie Cigman, while Extract 33 sets out the conclusions to a study about creating the right conditions for the writing of older boys to flourish.

Multimodality in children's language work in English and across the curriculum is of great importance and interest and Extract 34 considers helpful ways of thinking about the issues and offers ideas for the classroom.

Finally, Extract 35 homes in on a small-scale study which suggests that children's choices about what they write about matter, and concludes that some of the multimedia and 'popular culture' texts that are a vibrant part of children's home experience of reading and writing also have a place in school.

5.1 Young bilingual writers

There is a growing number of children who use English as an additional language in our schools. The results of research studies have led to changes in teachers' approaches to helping these young learners. When it comes to writing, many of their needs are now thought to be similar to those of first language writers. In Extract 30 Kimberley Safford reinforces what has been learnt from a number of studies, for instance that knowing about home literacy helps teachers make important links between this and the kinds of writing done in school.

Good practice has also come to reflect the observation that children who are literate in a language other than English do not need to start learning to write in their new language by simply being taught de-contextualised skills. Rather, they benefit by being helped to develop their writing abilities in mainstream lessons as soon as possible. And the opportunity to write for real purposes and real audiences is valuable for all young learners. Safford goes on to point out that there are benefits associated with giving children the opportunity to write, sometimes, in their first language at school.

Extract 30

Source

Safford, K. (2010, 3rd edn) Multilingual writers. In J. Graham and A. Kelly (eds) *Writing Under Control*. Abingdon and New York: Routledge, 36–8.

Bilingual and multilingual children will be at various stages of English language learning: some may be new to English, whilst others may be UK-born and live in families where other languages are used. They may be familiar with a range of writing for traditional, cultural, community or religious purposes, such as wedding lyrics, Eid cards or email …

The cognitive benefits of multilingualism and how bilingual learners are able to make useful connections between languages and cultures is well researched (see CILT, 2006, for example). There are many practical steps you can take to draw upon the language knowledge of your pupils (see Safford and Collins, 2006). In her study of multilingual children in a nursery setting, Kenner (1999) documented how providing texts in community languages (such as video posters, calendars, recipes, letters, alphabet charts, newspapers, magazines and books) for writing activities encouraged young children to recognise and develop their literacy skills … Kenner found that bilingual nursery children showed a strong motivation to make use of community language texts to generate their own writing, and that they showed increasing understanding of the purposes and symbols (scripts) of these texts. In KS1 and KS2 you can plan opportunities for children to write in their first or home languages, particularly for children whose receptive understanding may be ahead of their ability to produce oral and written English.

When I was teaching Year 5, I read my class the novel 'Bill's New Frock' by Anne Fine. After the first few chapters, children were instructed to write in the role of Bill and how he felt waking up as a girl. I had a new arrival, a boy from Spain. He understood the story, but he asked if he could write about it in Spanish. As he had very little English, I agreed. But then other children began to ask, 'Can I write it in my language?' I had to be fair, so I agreed that they could. We had writing in Twi, Cantonese, Arabic, Tamil and Portuguese as well as Spanish and English. From then on I planned that once a week all the children could write in their languages. They really enjoyed doing it, and they enjoyed reading their writing aloud and comparing different scripts, words and sentences in different languages. They learned a lot from each other, and I learned a lot too. (Roehampton English Education tutor.)

In planning routines where children discuss their writing, you can be alert to the ways in which children's first and home languages influence their written English. Nona Shah-Onwukwe, a newly-qualified Year 4 teacher, notices this in children's writing:

Sometimes when I'm reading their work I can tell how they are thinking … making literal translations … 'Do you brush' instead of 'Brush your teeth', and 'Close the light'. (Roehampton English Education interview, 2008) …

These kinds of observations will help you to identify patterns in the written English of children learning EAL so that you can support them more effectively. This is important even for advanced learners of English. Cameron and Besser (2004) analysed the texts of KS2 bilingual pupils who had high levels of English fluency and found that these children continued to develop errors in written English, these included:

- Formulaic phrases and collations, e.g. 'They waited for long', 'For a lot of time', 'After some couple of weeks', 'She burst into happiness';
- 'small' words and prepositions, e.g. 'Help on reading', 'Regret of what they did';
- subject–verb agreements, e.g. 'There are so much traffic', 'Everyone else are looking'.

Cameron and Besser advise that the moment to teach collocations and grammar explicitly is when you observe children attempting to use them orally and in writing.

You can support multilingual pupils by correcting their errors sensitively and consistently, by modelling written English through texts and reading aloud, and in the focused teaching elements of written genres.

Extract references

Cameron, L. and Besser, S. (2004) *Writing in English as an Additional Language at Key Stage 2* and *Could They Do Better? The Writing of Advanced Bilingual Learners at KS2: HMI Survey of Good Practice*. London: OFSTED.

CILT (2006) *Positively Plurilingual: The Contribution of Community Languages to UK Education and Society*. London: The National Centre for Languages.

Kenner, C. (1999) Children's understandings of text in a multilingual nursery. *Language and Education*, 13 (1), 1–16.

Safford, K. and Collins, F. (2006) *EAL and English: Subjects and Language Across the Curriculum*. Available at: www.naldic.org.uk/ITTSEAL/teaching/English.cfm (accessed 8 November 2008 and 26 March 2015).

Comment

This is a positive and well-informed contribution to our understanding of how to support children learning to read and write English in a language different to their mother tongue. What comes across is the belief of the authors that operating in more than one language has considerable intellectual, social, cultural and linguistic advantages. But more than this, the presence of bilingual children in the classroom is also a huge potential resource for all the children. An enthusiastic and well-informed teacher can encourage an interest in language and in language and cultural differences. Alongside supporting children's progress in their new language the authors suggest that encouragement to bring their home language into school is helpful. In the extract, one teacher reserves a time each week for all the children to do some writing in their mother tongue.

Questions to discuss with colleagues

1. What kinds of knowledge and understanding do you think teachers of classes where there are young bilingual children need to achieve best practice in helping the children enjoy learning to read and write in English?
2. Safford and Collins believe that all the children in a class can have an interest in language energised by the presence of bilingual children. How would you set about encouraging this (a) with early years children, and (b) with older primary school children?
3. In the extract, the authors give examples of the errors even advanced learners whose first language is not English make in written English. How would you go about helping these young writers in a sensitive and encouraging way?

Further reading

Baker, C. (2014, 4th edn) *A Parents' and Teachers' Guide to Bilingualism*. Clevedon: Multilingal Matters. This is a book which manages to be both scholarly and accessible. It has a helpful question-based approach, for example 'How important is it that my child's two languages are practised and supported outside the home?' The book presents a detailed account of the advantages of bilingualism including those under the headings – social, cultural, cognitive and linguistic. A comprehensive glossary adds to the usefulness of the book.

Gregory, E. (2008 edn) *Learning to Read in a New Language: Making Sense of Words and World*. London: Paul Chapman. This second expanded edition of an influential book recommends the kind of classroom practice that helps young bilingual children feel part of a community of readers and writers. While being research based and scholarly, it has many helpful recommendations for supporting children who are learning to become literate in a language different from their mother tongue.

Issa, T. and Ozturk, A. (2008) *Practical Bilingual Strategies for Multilingual Classrooms*. Leicester: UKLA Minibook 27. The importance of young bilinguals continuing to practise and make progress in their home language is a strong recommendation in this book. Children's needs at different stages in the Early and Primary Years are brought to a practical level by case studies of good practice.

Kelly, C. (2010) *Hidden Worlds: Young Children Learning Literacy in Multicultural Contexts*. Stoke-on-Trent, UK and Sterling, USA: Trentham Books. This is one of those human books in which the children 'come alive on the page' and it is, therefore, a pleasure to read. It is built round six case studies of young children from different cultural backgrounds attending the same nursery school. Clare Kelly finds that children draw on their home experiences to make sense of what is offered to them. Writing and drawing accompanied role play, talk and book-making. What is needed is informed, sensitive and skilled support and intervention by adults to help the children to make connections.

Whitehead, M. (2010, 4th edn) *Language and Literacy in the Early Years*. London: Sage. See 'Multilingualism' (pages 36–43) for definitions of bilingualism and helpful discussion and teaching suggestions.

Wyse, D., Jones, R., Bradford, H. and Wolpert, M.A. (2013, 3rd edn) *Teaching English, Language and Literacy*. Abingdon and New York: Routledge. See chapter 26 'Supporting black and multilingual learners'. This chapter includes advice on promising classroom approaches to help young learners of English as an additional language.

5.2 Special writing needs

Every class is made up of young learners at very different stages in learning to write. The teacher's challenge is to support widely differing needs. Judith Graham, an inspirational scholar, researcher and writer about children's literature and children's writing, suggests how these differing needs can be met by planning whole-class writing activities that have interest and appeal to all the children, from those still struggling to those that are already gifted writers.

Extract 31

Source

Graham, J. (2010, 3rd edn) Children who claim that they hate writing and do the bare minimum or nothing at all. In J. Graham and A. Kelly, A. (eds) *Writing Under Control*. London and New York: Routledge, 206–9.

'Once upon a time there was a dinosaur and' (Neil, aged 7)

Most scraps of writing like this end up in the waste paper basket. Thrown there after 30 minutes of a wasted lesson by an angry despondent child or found by the teacher when she retrieves the tightly screwed up ball from under the desk. It is a situation familiar to most teachers and very worrying. Usually these children will add a word or two if you are sitting beside them but once you leave they will dry up again. The reasons for this behaviour fall into two categories: anxiety about getting it wrong and a shortage of ideas ...

In truth what is good practice for all your class is good practice for these children too. Obviously there would be no need, for instance, to scribe for a fluent writer but that child, in her time, may have benefited enormously from such a practice. Regard your inexperienced writer as just that – inexperienced – and do not attribute errors to carelessness, reluctance or laziness. It is more complicated than that. One of the advantages of the old Literacy Hour – in the sense of a predictable classroom routine that will provide structure and regularity – is that it is the less secure children in your classroom who will appreciate consistency and continuity. Try to provide as much writing time as possible for your children with difficulties, especially of extended pieces. You will also want to encourage writing at home.

Gifted and talented writers

You will notice that able children are very quick to experiment with and put into their writing whatever models you have been sharing with them. Their private reading also influences their writing as does evidence of the written word that they see around them in a print-saturated environment. The conventions, tone, vocabulary and style of new genres seem to be effortlessly absorbed by them and no sooner have they mastered a form than they will begin to play with it, perhaps subverting its conventions to amusing effect. At a sentence level too, you may find that a taught session on, for example the use of subordinate clauses, will see gifted writers experimenting with how many subordinate clauses they can add to a main clause before the sentence becomes unwieldy. New terminology delights them and will turn up immediately in their writing.

Some able children arrive at school writing accurately, fluently and enthusiastically. It is through the tasks you devise for your gifted writers that you will be able to cater for this deftness ...

Many written activities can be devised that suit the whole class, irrespective of ability. These tasks are of the open-ended type so that a gifted writer can write more, write with more depth and more originality, but essentially on the same subject. Let us suppose a Year 5 class has been reading novels by 'a significant author', perhaps Dick King-Smith, and has begun with *Martin's Mice*, which is the story of a cat, Martin, who wishes not to eat mice but to keep them as pets. A written activity that asks children to rewrite an incident as a play scene might lead to opportunities for the gifted writer to write his or her scene with a detailed set of directions to a film director and/or camera crew. You may find the child turns the whole text into a play script, word processes it and insists that the class perform it!

Equally, you might devise a writing frame for most of the class to marshal their thoughts about the serious message of the novel: the rights of animals to be free and not kept as pets. Class discussion will precede this activity but the gifted writer will not need the writing frame and may turn in something that is balanced and logically structured, and could stand as an editorial in a newspaper. Few children will go on to read Dick King-Smith's more challenging novels (*The Crowstarver* and *Godhanger*, for instance) but able children will, and can then be given tasks tailored to this wider reading. They can bring their reading of the author's novels together, perhaps in answer to a question such as, 'You have been asked to recommend a Dick King-Smith novel for a children's radio programme. Say why you would elect one rather than another.'

Extract references

King-Smith, D. (1999) *The Crowstarver*. London: Corgi (imprint of Random House).
King-Smith, D. (2004) *Martin's Mice*. London: Puffin.
King-Smith, D. (2012 edn) *Godhanger*. London: Corgi (imprint of Random House).

Comment

The importance of helping children feel inspired or motivated to write is a theme throughout this chapter. Writing is hard for most of us whatever our age and to be successful we have to be interested in the topic or storyline we are creating and have a meaningful purpose and understanding of our audience. In Extract 31, Judith Graham suggests that the problem for many children with special writing needs is to do with lack of motivation. She prefers to describe this group as 'inexperienced writers' and she suggests that interesting writing tasks can be used to help these young learners.

Further, she believes that teachers can differentiate writing tasks within a lesson with the whole class, whatever the writing ability of different learners. Interesting stories, for example, can be a promising starting point for all children's writing. Reading or listening to the teacher reading a range of texts gives children an understanding of the choices open to them as writers. So it is not surprising that gifted young writers tend to be avid readers. They are also often willing to experiment with different styles and forms of writing, and encouragement to the more reluctant writers to do this might well inspire their interest and creativity.

Questions to discuss with colleagues

1. How would you help very young children to find learning to write satisfying and enjoyable?
2. What might be the advantages of making links between home and school writing?
3. What steps would you take to make your classroom an inviting writing environment for children of different abilities?
4. Judith Graham suggests that reading an interesting story can be an appealing starting point for writing. She mentions Dick King-Smith's book *Martin's Mice* as being a book that could give rise to writing tasks to suit children of different abilities. Share with colleagues your ideas for other texts which you think might give rise to interesting writing responses. Suggest how you would go about differentiating the writing tasks to suit the less confident as well as the gifted writers in the class.

Further reading

Graham, S. (2010) Facilitating writing development. In D. Wyse, R. Andrews and J. Hoffman, J. (eds) *The Routledge International Handbook of English, Language and Literacy Teaching*. London and New York: Routledge. This research-based account sets out clearly some implications for practice in the teaching of writing.

Riley, J. and Reedy, D. (2000) *Developing Writing for Different Purposes: Teaching About Genre in the Early Years*. London: Paul Chapman. Even though written some years ago, this is still one of the best books about supporting young children's writing development in all genres. It includes a detailed account of a well-known and inspirational case study of children's thinking and writing round Anthony Browne's picturebook, *Zoo*.

5.3 Gender and writing

Very generally, more boys than girls seem to have difficulty in learning to write. The differences in attainment seem to be particularly noticeable when it comes to doing exercises and formal tests. On the other hand, some girls may need more encouragement than boys to gain control over reading and writing ICT texts and can be less comfortable with computer activities. Some girls find reading and writing certain kinds of non-fiction, especially those with a non-narrative organisation, unappealing (Myers and Burnett, 2004).

In the first of two extracts on 'Gender and writing', Extract 32, Julie Cigman, an Early Years teacher and researcher, shares the aims and results of a series of 'Boys' writing projects' focused on boys in the Early Years. She designed and supported the classroom-based inquires in which funding was targeted at improving the writing attainment of boys as they fell behind girls, as measured by scores in the Early Years Foundation Profile. At the beginning of the projects, practitioners observed that many children of both genders were not given enough opportunity to express 'their natural exuberance and creativity' or to have enough time to ask questions and explore their world. Observations of boys, in particular, led to them being described as 'noisy' and 'unable to sit still', and these early judgements tended to affect children's perceptions of themselves as learners in a negative way. The participating practitioners noted this and decided to focus and build on more positive things, such things as 'he loves climbing trees', 'he likes being involved in things' and 'he prefers to lie down when he writes'. This way of regarding young pupils is very much in line with that of Mary Anne Drummond, see Extract 58 in Chapter 8. Drummond recommends that we use careful observation to understand and act on the richness of children's potential as learners. Extract 32 explains the principles on which the projects were based and particularly the role of the Early Years teacher as observer and creator of rich enabling environments for young learners.

The team at the Centre for Literacy in Primary Education set up a series of classroom-based research studies in the first decade of the twenty-first century which are of continuing relevance to teachers eager to employ strategies to encourage boys' progress in and enjoyments of writing. Extract 33 sets out some research conclusions at the end of one of these studies, *Boys on the Margin*, which was principally funded by the Esmee Fairburn Foundation. Building on an earlier study, *Boys and Writing*, this study involved teachers of ten- to eleven-year-olds in trying out some of the promising strategies suggested, including using interactive ICT, improvisation and discussion.

Extract 32

Source

Cigman, J. (2014) Introduction. In *Supporting Boys' Writing in the Early Years: Becoming a Writer in Leaps and Bounds*. Abingdon and New York: Routledge, xxi–xxii.

The boys' writing projects set out to research: 'How can we improve boys' confidence, motivation and attainment as writers?' They were designed round the following principles:

Principle 1. Effective literacy learning and teaching is rooted in research into how young children develop and learn.

It acknowledges that boys are as competent as girls but that they often learn in different ways and at a different pace. The role of the Early Years practitioner incorporates a range of complex skills needed to facilitate children's active construction of meaning and to teach children the way they learn – through play. The skilled adult has a good understanding of how young children learn typically, how boys and girls learn differently and how individual children learn best. They have a good understanding of how children learn good language and literacy skills and aptitudes. They are able to support the process of learning through child-initiated play and adult-led teaching: planning and identifying opportunities for learning, providing suitable and stimulating resources, engaging in play and modelling reasons to write. They make learning enjoyable and motivating for children and help them build 'learning power' (Claxton, 2005).

At the centre of the role of Early Years practitioners is the ability to observe children in their play and to use observation to set up enabling environments.

Principle 2. Enabling environments for young writers offer flexible non-prescriptive and responsive learning spaces, indoors and outdoors, that allow for active and energetic learning styles displayed by many boys.

An enabling learning environment is stimulating and purposeful, and is appropriate for the learning styles and stages of development of all children. As part of an enabling environment, practitioners create sustained time for child-initiated learning. They provide accessible challenging, open-ended resources that can be used playfully, creatively and imaginatively, supporting the characteristics of effective learning that underpin writing development as well as all other areas of learning (DfE, 2012) …

The writing projects showed that when practitioners moved away from making simple 'tick-list' observations for their assessments and started to make open observations of the boys and their self-directed play, they got to know the boys better and they learnt about the things that fascinated them such as rocket man, blog stations, sinking sand and other things that sat outside the experiences of most Early Years practitioners! The power of implementing such an approach was noted by one practitioner after one week: 'It's already paying off – there has been increased emphasis on observing all children's interests closely.'

Extract reference

Department for Education (DfE) (2012) *Statutory Framework for The Early Years Foundation Stage.* London: DfE.

Comment

Three things press on me after reflecting on this research. First, here is a classroom-based study whose findings situate success in learning to write in overall good Early Years practice. This is practice which combines 'child-initiated play and adult-led teaching' and creates rich resources and 'enabling environments'. Equally important in encouraging children's progress in writing, and more generally, is skilful and constructive observation of the young learners. Second, the 'action research' classroom-based nature of the research made it possible for teachers to put positive findings into immediate practice. One teacher noted that her observations led her to energise the children's role play and writing by the imaginative use of outdoor as well as indoor environments. Role play round dens, 'garages' and round 'superhero' adventures proved particularly successful. Third, while Cigman's conclusion is perhaps not surprising, it is certainly interesting and encouraging that: 'the lessons that we learnt – the practitioners and myself as the consultant who designed and supported these projects – were relevant for all children and all areas of learning'. The embedding of writing in exciting and meaningful activities benefited the girls as well as the boys.

Extract 33

Source

Safford, K., O'Sullivan, O. and Barrs, M. (2005) *Boys on the Margin: Promoting Literacy at Key Stage 2.* London: Centre for Literacy in Primary Education, (a) 2, (b) 105–6.

Part a: Foreword

The education of the emotions goes hand in hand with literacy education. In order to become more thoughtful readers and writers we must also learn to empathise and imagine. This kind of view challenges a consensus over recent years in discussion of boys and literacy, a consensus which has been described as 'keep it short, keep it sharp, keep it finite' (Daly, 2002). This idea that boys take to literacy learning more readily if it is presented to them in 'bite-sized chunks' did not correspond to our findings in the project. Nor did the idea that boys prefer non-fiction texts seem to fit the facts. On the contrary, it was only when teachers allowed more time to explore really involving texts, and time to develop writing, that the boys we were observing began to make visible progress ...

Part b: Interaction of the major factors – the big shapes of an inclusive pedagogy for boys

In classrooms where targeted boys improved within whole class improvements, all children had opportunities to

- develop ideas and language for writing through extensive, open-ended discussions;
- enact texts through forms of drama and role play;
- write at length over days and weeks in a range of collaborative and independent formats;
- write in different voices around the same text and bring these together for a whole class purpose or performance;
- collaborate for support and for enjoyment;
- regularly access ICT for discussion, independent and collaborative writing, and ownership of the writing and editing process;
- perform and publish their texts;
- 'play' at writing.

Extract reference

Daly, C. (2002) *Literature Search on Improving Boys' Writing.* London: OFSTED.

Comment

In the short extract from the foreword of their book, Safford and colleagues challenge the commonly expressed view that boys prefer non-fiction and that this might lead to them missing out on the appeal to the feelings and imagination evoked by fiction and poetry. But perhaps some kinds of non-fiction can appeal to both the feelings and the imagination. Here I am thinking of, for example, the intriguing mystery of the fate of The Princes in the Tower, the plight of endangered species and the wonders of space. Most of these strategies, found successful in making reluctant writers into much keener and more successful ones, are based on activity and on social approaches to literacy learning.

These findings are compatible with those of the Cigman research with very young children from which Extract 32 is taken and seem recommendable as good practice for writing progress with all age groups and including girls and boys. The project from which Extract 33 is taken focused on boys who did not have major literacy difficulties but who were making little progress because, compared with their peers, they did not engage enthusiastically with reading and writing and remained 'on the margin' and were in danger of being overlooked.

This *Reader* encourages teachers and students to carry out small-scale action research studies. The strength of this kind of research is shown in the studies from which Extract 32 and Extract 33 are taken. Teachers are a major part of the research teams and, in both cases, strategies tried out and found to be successful are immediately incorporated into the cycle of planning, teaching, learning and assessing.

Questions to discuss with colleagues (Extracts 32 and 33)

1. In Extract 32, Cigman and the practitioners involved in research into the writing of very young boys found that contexts need to be created for the kind of writing boys can understand and enjoy. What kinds of contexts do you consider would be most interesting and meaningful for boys aged seven years and under? And how far do you consider that small girls would also find these contexts inspiring?

2. What do you think teachers of children over seven years might learn about creating 'enabling environments' for both girls' and boys' writing from good Early Years practice?

3. Safford and associates consider that the education of the emotions goes 'hand in hand with literacy education'. Share with colleagues details about texts in print or online that you feel would be helpful (a) for younger boys and girls, and (b) for older boys and girls. Include in your discussion some thoughts about which of the books would appeal to a particular gender.

4. In Extract 32 it is implied that non-fiction texts are less likely than fiction to encourage young readers and writers 'to empathise and imagine'. This may be true in general, but can you suggest non-fiction texts which do tap into feeling and inspire reflection?

5. Discussion, drama and interactive ICT dominate the list of promising approaches in Extract 33. Have you either carried out or observed practice leading to successful writing from both boys and girls using one or more of these approaches? If so, consider how this success might be applied across the school.

Further reading

Barrs, M. and Pidgeon, S. (2002) *Boys and Writing*. London: Centre for Literacy in Primary Education (CLPE). This book brings together articles by members of a CLPE project on boys and writing, the results of which have had a considerable impact on teachers' thinking and practice. A particularly interesting and useful feature of this study is that it spans age groups. So there is Sue Hirschheimer's 'Tuning into boys' interests in the early years', Mary Jo McPherson's 'A story telling project', showing the benefits linking story-telling with story writing with nine-year-olds and Elisabeth Baker's 'An aversion to writing', presenting case studies of reluctant male writers in the secondary school.

Browne, A. (2009) *Developing Language and Literacy 3–8*. London: Paul Chapman. In chapter 7, 'Language, literacy and gender', Browne emphasises that the reading material Early Years teachers provide, if rich and wide, helps both boys and girls to broaden the kinds of writing they do.

Carrington, V. and Robinson, M. (2009) *Digital Literacies: Social Learning and Classroom Practice*. London: Sage, with UKLA. These authors and researchers share helpful teaching approaches to support the developing digital literacy of both boys and girls.

Mallett, M. (2012) Girls' literacy. In *The Primary English Encyclopedia*. London and New York: Routledge, 182–5. Here it is pointed out that although some girls seemed to need more support than boys when reading and writing digital texts, at a time when the digital age had just got underway, they seem to be catching up and enjoy the more social digital activities – texting, Facebook and blogs for example (see also, in the same volume, 'Boys' literacy', pp. 45–8).

Myers, J. and Burnett, C. (2004) *Teaching English 3–13*. London and New York: Continuum International. In chapter 12, in the section on 'Gender and literacy', (p. 127), these authors find narratives about such things as animal life cycles and journeys, and non-fiction which evokes an affective as well as an intellectual response, a more inviting introduction to reading and writing non-fiction than those with a non-narrative organisation.

Palmer, S. (2004) Primary review. *Times Educational Supplement*, 18 October. Sue Palmer points out that small boys are often simply not ready to 'sit still, listen for individual sounds in language, relate these to abstract symbols, and then manipulate a pencil to draw the symbols'.

Terlecki, M. and Newcombe, N. (2005) How important is the digital divide? The relation of computer and videogame usage to gender differences in mental rotation ability. *Sex Roles, Journal of Research*, 53 (5–6). These researchers found some gender differences linked to a gender gap in spatial ability to the disadvantage of girls and women.

5.4 Writing multimodal, multimedia and 'popular culture' texts

Interest in children's learning from visual texts and multimodal and multimedia texts has intensified in the twenty-first century (see also Extracts 18 and 20 in Chapter 3). Becoming literate now involves being comfortable with an ever-changing array of texts and with new ways of thinking, reading and writing. Teachers are constantly working to find the best ways of helping children become confident readers and writers in different modes and media. In this section some of the issues round supporting children as writers and creators of multimodal and multimedia texts are addressed. Children's writing draws on their reading and it follows that they need to have read a range of texts and to have reflected on them with their teacher and peers to become able to write in particular genres.

In Extract 34 Eve Bearne argues that teaching writing now includes teaching about multimodality and that this means children need to be introduced to a wide range of reading material. She gives suggestions for exploring story in different modes and media and ponders on, for example, what a print picturebook offers as compared with a film and how each format can be used to the best effect. These things need to be understood, she argues, to promote successful writing. In the past multimodal and multimedia texts, particularly of the 'popular culture' kind have been enjoyed in children's leisure time but, increasingly, popular culture is used in school as part of the literacy programme.

Extract 35, taken from an article by Jill Dunn and her colleagues, shares the results of a study investigating the views of young children on popular culture. These researchers consider that children's views on popular culture are important as a matter of children's rights and urge teachers to give children a choice over what they write. This article is well worth reading in its entirety, not least because of its focus on children's views and preferences.

Extract 34

Source

Bearne, E. (2004) Multimodal texts: What they are and how children use them. In J. Evans (ed.) *Literacy Moves On.* London: David Fulton, 27–8 from 'In rethinking literacy' to 'ideas in each mode or medium'.

Eve Bearne is one of a number of researchers who have led the way towards making the reading and writing of multimodal and visual texts part of children's school experience. This extract has been chosen as it remains one of the best analyses of how teachers can put in place practical ideas to help children's multimodal and visual literacy in the Early Years and primary classroom.

> In rethinking literacy, it is necessary to take into account the dimensions of children's text experience and the ways that new types of text might shape children's thinking. If their experiences are to be genuinely recognised in the classroom, then it is important to discover just what children know about the texts they encounter inside and outside the school and the many ways they might represent their ideas. The pace and nature of technological change have had an impact on just what 'reading' and 'writing' have come to mean so that being visually literate in the twenty-first century will be as important as verbal literacy was in the twentieth century. Literacy teaching now means teaching about multimodality, involving:
>
> ■ understanding how texts and modes work;
> ■ demonstrating this understanding in the classroom;

- encouraging children to use multimodal representation to shape and communicate their ideas;
- helping children to develop a repertoire of approaches and then to be selective in matching mode with purpose and in making appropriate choices.

Rethinking literacy requires deliberate consideration of how children can be helped to extend and practise their control in many different modes by making explicit to themselves – and their teachers – what they know about multidimensional texts and how they work. However, the task is not only to engage in dialogues which will help children recognise the different representational demands made by different texts. It is equally important to develop a community of professional experience – a bank of professional capital – about multimodality. If we are to help learners to move readily between modes, we need a descriptive vocabulary for the several dimensions of texts, including the movement, the sound, the dynamic, implicit in print texts – both visual and verbal. We also need a language of gestural texts and moving image. This raises further questions about how we can develop ways of describing what children know about texts and what progress in multimodality might look like. Perhaps the greatest demand, however, is to imagine a curriculum that helps children to draw on their knowledge of different ways to represent and communicate ideas and that acknowledges and builds teachers' expertise – a curriculum for the twenty first century.

In tackling issues of the different affordance of texts, children and adults perhaps need to be helped to identify for example, what a film offers that a book does not or what a picturebook allows the reader to do in relation to a video. Take, for example, Raymond Briggs' *The Snowman* or *The Bear*; both are produced in picturebook and video form and Briggs was involved in making the video for each, which helps perhaps in making comparisons. Careful reading and watching reveal interesting differences: the video of *The Bear* includes a 'prequel' to the picturebook narrative. It is worth considering why the prequel was included. It may be related to the possibilities for revisiting a picturebook text by flicking the pages backwards and forwards compared with the relatively greater difficulty of revisiting DVD text. There are, of course, rewind and scene selection buttons but does that afford the same kind of rereading opportunities that the picturebook does? There are also video versions of nearly every Roald Dahl story: *James and the Giant Peach*, *Danny, Champion of the World*, *Matilda*, *The BFG*. Using these or realistic novels like *Holes* by Louis Sacher allows discussion about the affordances of words and moving images plus sound and colour. Taking an episode of the video and book text allows consideration of how each text creates atmosphere, depicts character or structures the unfolding narrative ...

It is all very well to recognise children's experience in multimodal communication. It is clear that children draw on multimodal models of texts as they shape their own. However, the issue remains about those children who fail to make a transfer between their inner text experience and the demands of writing. Translating from one mode to another does not necessarily come easily. Helping children to make the transition from inner to outer experience might be considered from various directions: from sound to writing; from (moving) image to writing; from writing to image. While information about the detail of children's thinking might be revealed by, for example, reading a passage aloud and asking the class to draw what they hear, the shift from sound to image should not stop here. It is necessary to make explicit how the two modes relate to each other, to consider with the class what is needed for clear communication in each mode, to talk with them about their choices, asking them to explain their decisions about layout, colour, close-up or distance images. This approach could be used with both narrative and non narrative pieces to see what the differences might be. Translating a piece of video into written form might mean asking the class to retell the action, describe the atmosphere or character. Discussing the choices they made and the implications of moving between modes and media means an explicit recognition of the different affordances of texts and the accommodations that have to be made when representing ideas in each mode or medium.

Comment

The book from which this extract is taken was published back in 2004 and so we find that things have moved on – DVDs have taken over from video films and technology develops and changes constantly, requiring new vocabulary to describe new concepts. There are, however, some things that remain constant and which are central to the argument in the extract. Teachers will always need to modify their practice to keep pace with new ways of conceiving literacy and with the development of new kinds of text – some perhaps unexpected or beyond imagination. Eve Bearne's four bullet points at the beginning of the extract remain a useful checklist for students and beginning teachers helping children to read and write multimodal texts.

Extract 35

Source

Dunn, J., Niens, U. and McMillan, D. (2014) 'Cos he's my favourite character!' A children's rights approach to the use of popular culture in teaching literacy. *Literacy*, 48 (1), 27.

The researchers in this small-scale study asked six- to seven-year-old children from two classes in two primary schools in Northern Ireland what they would like to write about and found that popular culture featured strongly. In fact, the children showed considerable knowledge and enjoyment of a wide range of popular culture. Dunn and co-workers consider that their findings support the view that the potential of popular culture texts to energise the literacy programme should be exploited in the continuous quest 'for a meaningful curriculum for contemporary children, which will ultimately raise standards in literacy'. The key research questions were to do with children's views on the use of popular culture in the teaching of writing and gender differences when considering these views.

The research included a number of activities: children were first asked for suggestions for popular culture texts to use in writing lessons. Then a series of lessons took place using different genres and popular culture texts (for example, a showing of part of *Toy Story 3* was used to focus on writing character studies – of Woody, for example). A most unusual and valuable aspect of the study was that a representative group of children were actually involved in designing it and assessing the findings. Children were asked to show their favourite writing topic by drawing something that they liked from the lessons. The extract takes up the story after the drawings were completed.

When the children were asked why they had chosen to draw particular characters from popular culture or why they had chosen to photograph or sort pictures of popular culture characters as topics they would like to write about, there were some recurring themes. These were having favourite characters, liking the popular culture artefacts, liking aspects of the stories they came from and having fun.

Some of the children's comments were the following: 'cos he was my favourite character'; 'because I like writing about my favourite character'; 'because I like Mario Kart and I used to have Mario Kart on my Nintendo DS and it was really fun and I won a couple of medals on it'; 'cos I like Jessie and I like the Aliens and I like Mr Potato Head and I like Buzz as well'; 'because I like the bit where he goes into the nursery and all the babies keep on wrecking him'; 'because it's fun'.

Marsh and Millard (2000: 191) assert that 'popular culture imparts untold pleasures as children weave their dreams and aspirations into a rich tapestry of interlocking threads'. Similarly Kenway and Bullen (2001) recognise that pleasure has to do with fantasy and escapism from the everyday controlled world (Seiter, 1995). It is this pleasure that Dyson (2000) acknowledges that is in opposition to the prescriptive frameworks of the curriculum and that may motivate children to engage with writing and in turn raise literacy achievement. Motivation is recognised as one of the key ingredients in becoming a competent or skilled writer (Graham, 2010). Boscolo (2009) argues that research indicates that for children to be motivated to write, they need authentic writing experiences with collaborative dimensions. The unique experiences that children have with regard to popular culture and their insider knowledge provide common ground and an opportunity to bond with peers, and in this study the children constructed their writing collaboratively: discussing their ideas as they worked, engaging in conversations about popular culture and asking their peers questions about their work.

Extract references

Boscolo, P. (2009) Engaging and motivating children to write. In R. Beard, D. Myhill, J. Riley and Nystrand, M. (eds) *The Sage Handbook of Writing Development*. London: Sage, 300–12.

Dyson, A.H. (2000) On reframing children's words: The perils, promises and pleasures of writing children. *Research in the Teaching of Reading*, 34 (3), 352–67.

Graham, S. (2010) Facilitating writing development. In R. Beard, D. Myhill, J. Riley and M. Nystrand (eds) *The Routledge International Handbook of English, Language and Literacy Teaching*. London: Routledge, 125–36.

Kenway, J. and Bullen, E. (2001) *Consuming Children: Education – Entertainment – Advertising.* Buckingham: Open University Press.

Marsh, J. and Millard, E. (2000) *Literacy and Popular Culture: Using Children's Culture in the Classroom.* London: Paul Chapman.

Seiter, E. (1995) *Sold Separately: Children and Parents in Consumer Culture.* New Brunswick, NJ: Rutgers University Press.

Comment

Just because you are young does not mean you have nothing to say – this is a key message to be gleaned from this study. Dunn and associates take as their starting point the message in Article 12 of the United Nations Convention on the Rights of the Child, which states that every child has the right 'to say what they think in all matters affecting them, and to have their views taken seriously'. These researchers put in place an innovative strategy in their research on using popular culture as a basis for children's writing, a strategy which was very much in the spirit of Article 12: the appointment of some of the children to a Children's Research Advisory Group which not only contributed to devising research methods but also to interpreting the findings. The data strongly suggest that children are inspired to write with enthusiasm when given a choice about what to write about. Their choices will sometimes reflect their affective response to popular culture, and their shared experience of and liking for this makes meaningful peer collaboration over writing more likely.

In their analysis beyond the extract Dunn and colleagues discuss their finding on gender differences and conclude that there was no apparent difference in boys' and girls' enjoyment of popular culture. There were, however, some perhaps predictable gender differences in reasons for choices. For example, boys tended to like Mario because Mario's friends are 'nearly all boys' and Mario was popular with girls 'because it has Princess Peach'. The researchers point out the potential this shows for teachers to challenge the gendered messages in some kinds of popular culture.

Questions to discuss with colleagues

It would be helpful to bring any examples you may have of children's multimodal, visual texts or film to this discussion.

1. Eve Bearne, in Extract 34, sets out what is involved in literacy teaching as we move through the twenty-first century. One requirement is that teachers help children understand how different texts and modes work. This has implications for teachers' knowledge about language and texts. How would you go about teaching children how multimodal texts work and how would you support children as they attempt their own?

2. The huge commercial dominance of popular culture texts and artefacts with all the accompanying issues round financial profit and vested interest is often commented on. Yet children today have considerable knowledge about and liking for these

and the best are just as valuable and as imagination stretching as more traditional classroom texts. What principles do you consider that teachers might use in their selection of popular culture writing tasks for (a) the under-sevens, and (b) the eight to elevens?

3. Share with colleagues your experience (through your own teaching or that of others you have observed) of children's written response to popular culture texts. What have you found to be favourite characters and stories with children of different ages and genders?

4. How far do you agree with Dunn and co-workers (Extract 35) that children should be able to choose what they wish to write about? If you do agree with the proposition, how would you convince a sceptical parent or friend or the school of its value?

Further reading

Bearne, E., Ellis, S., Grahams, L., Hulme, P., Merchant, G. and Mills, C. (2004) *More Than Words: Multimodal Texts in the Classroom*. London: QCA/UKLA. This text is a helpful introduction to the value of multimodality and contains interesting examples of children's multimodal work.

Bearne, E. and Wolstencroft, H. (2007) *Visual Approaches to Teaching Writing*. London: Paul Chapman. These authors investigate how we help children read and write multimodal and visual texts. It includes a CD with examples of children's multimodal work.

Bus, A. and Neuman, S. (eds) (2014) *Multimedia and Literacy Development: Improving Achievement in Young Learners*. London: Routledge. Valuable practical advice is given to teachers supporting the encounters of young readers and writers with multimedia texts, for example stories on the internet and DVDs.

Dowdall, C., Vasudevan, L. and Mackey, M. (2014) Editorial: Popular culture and the curriculum. *Literacy*, 48 (1). Provides an invitation to the articles in this Special Issue and an overview of the development of research and thinking.

Marsh, J. and Millard, E. (eds) (2006) *Popular Literacies, Childhood and Schooling*. London: Routledge. This collection contains articles by such well-known contributors to knowledge about popular cultures as Guy Merchant, Gemma Moss and Colin Lankshear; there is a foreword, 'Why popular literacies matter' by A.H. Dyson, pp. xvii–xxii.

Vincent, J. (2006) Children writing: Multimodality and assessment in the writing classroom. *Literacy*, 40 (1), 51–7. This article considers the issues round the assessment of multimodal texts with their combination of design, pictures and writing.

Wyse, D., Andrews, R. and Hoffman, J. (2010) Introduction. In D. Wyse, R. Andrews and J. Hoffman (eds) *The Routledge International Handbook of English, Language and Literacy Teaching*. London: Routledge, 1–8. These authors pinpoint the main challenge for the teacher when encouraging young writers: a balance needs to be achieved between the need to control transcriptional aspects of writing as well as those to do with composition while maintaining children's engagement and interest.

Knowledge about language

Grammar, spelling, punctuation and handwriting

Introduction

There always has been and probably always will be public and professional debate about how and when children should be taught the various aspects of knowledge about language. At times, the debate has become so passionate that the feelings generated have been referred to as 'the simmering volcano' (Mallett, 2012: 270). This chapter examines some views about what children and what teachers need to know about language as a system and about those aspects of writing which are often termed transcriptional or secretarial. Some countries have statutory requirements about how these aspects of language are taught: in parts of the United Kingdom there has been, for some time, both statutory guidance and advice which has included, for example, the requirement that primary children are helped to incorporate into their writing some characteristics of the various forms, like parts of speech, and to use grammatical constructions that are characteristic of spoken and written standard English.

Angela Wilson and Julie Scanlon are among those who have thought deeply about the language knowledge that teachers need and the ways in which they can teach such knowledge to young children. In Extract 36 they share some thoughts on approaches to teaching children about language as a system. They caution against too direct and mechanistic an approach to incorporating examples of the parts of speech children have been learning about into their writing. And yet there should be a relationship between learning about language and children's own writing and their own reading.

Following the principles that Deborah Myhill and her team at Exeter University drew out during their research on contextualised grammar teaching at Exeter University, Melanie Hendy, in Extract 37, shares some case studies of teachers and children integrating their learning about grammar in their own writing and appreciation of the books they were reading. I was drawn to Hendy's article as it is in the spirit of a strong theme in the present book: that theory and classroom practice should relate to one another seamlessly. Intellectual rigour does not need to be a stranger to application in school.

The scholars and researchers from whose work extracts are taken in Sections 2, 3 and 4 all argue that what have been thought of as transcriptional, secretarial or presentational aspects of language are in fact important in children's thinking and composing. Section 2 on 'Spelling' shows its links with reading and thinking and handwriting fluency. In Section 3 on 'Punctuation', Lynn Truss shows the link between good use of punctuation and the clear communication of meaning while Henrietta Dombey and her team, in Extract 42, examine what the evidence says about promising approaches to teaching it.

Finally, in Section 4, recent research and thinking about handwriting is explored, and particularly Wray and Medwell's argument that acquiring good handwriting automaticity helps children compose. Perhaps we have expected that those aspects of language sometimes termed 'secretarial' are less interesting than those to do with composing. But the writers whose work is drawn on here have thought deeply about the issues and write about their thinking and research in a way that taps into the everyday decisions of classroom teachers.

Section 1: Grammar

Extract 36

Source

Wilson, A. and Scanlon, J. (2011, 4th edn) Language as process; language as product. In *Language Knowledge for Primary Teachers*. London and New York: Routledge, (a) 3, (b) 6–7.

Children learn a great deal about language by interacting with others in their everyday life. Wilson and Scanlon believe teachers will draw on all this richness and extend it through talking, listening, reading and writing in the classroom. But the subject of the extract and the book from which it is taken is those things that children need to learn about language as a system. To help here, teachers themselves need to have a secure knowledge base about the structures and functions of language. What approaches to teaching these things seem most effective? These authors reject the idea of dull routines and urge teachers to ensure that what children learn will increase their competence and enjoyment as language users.

Part a

We all acquire language knowledge as part of living our lives; we listen and we talk; we read and we write. Some of us do these things more than others, and the kinds of speaking, listening, reading and writing we do will vary enormously. But what specific kinds of language knowledge do we need to become successful primary teachers? ...

Part b

If you can get this right you will have a classroom in which children are using language to understand the world better, including the world of reading and the media, and are finding in language ways to explore their own feelings and attitudes towards what these worlds portray. In response to their thinking and feeling, these children will create a range of texts, both written and spoken, that will bring pleasure and delight to themselves, their teachers, their parents and others. The talking, reading and writing will flow out, across the whole curriculum and beyond it.

But this is not the whole story ... It is clear that at the same time you should gradually be making children more familiar with language as a system, or a series of systems. Children are not reinventing the language wheel; they are inheriting ways of doing things with language that have evolved and are evolving constantly within the cultures and social groups that each child is a member of ... Most importantly the children need to learn about the systems of language in such a way that their own uses of language are genuinely enriched and enhanced.

Learning about language and developing language knowledge is not like learning how to make a sponge cake. In that case, as soon as you've read about how to do it, or watched someone else, you set about making one. Language knowledge, on the other hand, can be stored in the mind in a number of ways. For example, a group of Year 6 children★ we worked with had thoroughly enjoyed discussing conjunctions. They'd found examples in the text they were reading and made a poster for the classroom wall. They could remember a lot of examples and they knew that the teacher wanted them to make use of them. However, a scrutiny of their English books revealed few of them had actually done so. Yet their written work was lively and interesting. Sadly, because many of them had been given a target 'use more conjunctions', in the short term they seem destined for a feeling of failure. If they had tried to drag conjunctions into their writing 'willy-nilly' the results would probably have been disastrous ... We still need more sensitive understanding of what it means to acquire and use language knowledge, particularly in the area of developing children's writing.

★ Children aged 10–11 years old

Comment

Wilson and Scanlon pinpoint two aspects of English teaching. First of all, primary teachers strive to help children on the journey to becoming successful users of language who enjoy and feel confident about talking and listening and reading and writing. The second aspect is to do with children's explicit understanding of language as a system or systems. This involves, for example, knowing about how sounds build into words, how we combine words in line with the rules of grammar and mastering spelling and punctuation conventions. These teachers and scholars use a short but powerful classroom example to show the challenge combining these two aspects of English teaching presents.

Extract 37

Source

Hendy, M. (2013) Improving writing through teaching grammar in context: A silver lining to every cloud! *English 4–11*, 49 (autumn 2013), 11–13.

This presentation of creative approaches to teaching grammar, by embedding it in children's reading of literature and their own writing, is a good example of research findings being applied fruitfully in the classroom. Melanie Hendy shows how teachers, informed by the findings of the 'Research in writing' project directed by Deborah Myhill at the University of Exeter, put into practice contextualised grammar teaching.

The approach we are using comes from research carried out at Exeter University by Debra Myhill and her team who focused on teaching grammar to Year 7 pupils within the context of a unit of work. They found that embedding grammar into the teaching of reading and writing had a positive impact on the quality of learners' writing. The greatest improvements were made by more confident writers, who were taught by teachers with good grammatical subject knowledge. During the research, the grammar activities used to support students were 'engaging, focused and motivating and … explicit in highlighting how different aspects of grammar can inform the making of choices in writing' (Myhill *et al.*, 2012a).

The teaching was built upon key principles in *Grammar for Writing Schemes of Work* (Myhill *et al.*, 2012b):

- grammatical metalanguage is used, but it is always explained through examples and patterns;
- links are always made between the feature introduced and how it might enhance the writing being tackled;
- discussion is fundamental in encouraging critical conversations about language and effects;
- the use of 'imitation' offers model patterns for students to play with and then use in their own writing;
- the use of authentic examples from authentic texts links writers to the broader community of writers;
- activities should support students in making choices and being designers of writing;
- language play, experimentation, risk-taking and games should be actively encouraged.

Following attendance at a training session, a group of positive and enthusiastic teachers have been working to build these principles into their classroom practice. The following examples show how primary children have been engaged in investigating language, through the use of quality texts with strong grammatical features, which can be imitated and developed.

Becky Bond, Year 6, Queensmead Academy, Leicester

Context

We were reading *Stormbreaker* by Anthony Horowitz (2005). I wanted the children to write in role as the main character, Alex Rider. The emphasis was on enabling the reader to empathise with Alex's thought and feelings through his actions and speech. The children needed to develop their use of interesting and imaginative vocabulary, in both written and oral language, so it was really important that we explored this before they wrote.

Teaching strategies

We began by looking at effective verbs and adjectives. I provided the children with paper bags of vocabulary, some taken from *Stormbreaker*. The children were looking at how they could use the language of Horowitz to enhance their own vocabulary. In pairs, they began by picking out individual words. They arranged them into a large grid identifying which words they believed were effective or mundane. They were encouraged to use a dictionary to find out what unfamiliar vocabulary meant and then discuss how they could use them in order to clarify meaning in context. This generated considerable partner talk about why words were effective and whether they were appropriate or not for the context of the narrative we were reading.

Stormbreaker – Anthony Horowitz vocabulary sorting grid	
EFFECTIVE ADJECTIVES	metallic, sleek and silver, unnatural, hellish, rusty, pure white, ice-cold
VERBS How do we know what the character is doing? How do the verbs give us a clue?	glowed, silhouetted, rasping, leapt
ADVERBS How?	suspiciously, soundlessly, immediately
Phrases or sentences that create an image for the reader	half hidden in the shadow; moonlight spilled onto; sucked into the darkness
Anything else from Horowitz's writing that I can look at to help me with my writing	short sentences to emphasise the character's viewpoint and add pace to the story

Figure 5.1 *Stormbreaker* – Anthony Horowitz vocabulary sorting grid.

The children then wrote down their definitions for the new verbs/adjectives and pinned them onto our working wall so everybody could share the vocabulary, which now included 'child speak' definitions. Each pair was left with a grid containing effective verbs and adjectives linked to the context of the text that they could use in their writing. (see Figure 5.1 showing one pair's grid.)

During a shared writing session we discussed how we could use this language to bring Alex's character to life and the effects the language had on the reader. Through modelled writing, I demonstrated how to use some of the vocabulary before children wrote their own first-person accounts. Their writing demonstrated how to use some of the vocabulary before children wrote their own first-person accounts. Their writing demonstrated that they had a good understanding and command of the new language and were using it in a more precise manner to impact on the reader.

An example of Year 6 writing in role as the character Alex Rider:

'Gloomy shadows covered the walls. Alex quickly turned his torch on and the mine immediately lit up. He could smell wet and damp and he heard dripping water. He took a deep breath and then put one foot into the dark tunnel. Alex was shaking with fear.'

By M.

Kaye Wilson, Year 6, Holy Cross Catholic Primary School, Leicester

I always try to base my English units of work on quality texts. I use the teaching sequence to link all aspects: speaking and listening; reading and writing and I scaffold the learning round the chosen text. Punctuation and grammar is taught throughout the teaching sequence and linked to the book we are reading.

As part of a unit of work based on David Almond's *Skellig* (2009), we focused on embedding correct punctuation of dialogue and the use of effective speech verbs. Following shared reading, the pupils worked in pairs to discuss what they had noticed, identifying how David Almond's dialogue – language usage, layout and punctuation – adds to the meaning. I had taken a moment in the narrative when Mina first saw Skellig for herself. It is a tense passage in the book: Michael is worried that Mina will not see the creature that he has discovered. The children spent time discussing how she might react and engaged in role play and speaking in the style of Almond using simple and precise language. Their lively conversations, posture and facial expressions created a wealth of ideas and inspired their independent composition.

Short, shared writing activities enabled children to try out new techniques and punctuation, imitating the author's style. Following this, I encouraged my class to write longer, independent texts applying these skills.

Two examples of Year 6 writing continuing a chapter in the style of David Almond:

'Hand in hand, we went into the garage. I was engulfed in darkness, then a click. My eyes seared from the light.

"Where is it?" Mina said.

"Over here."

Mina followed me towards the tea chests.

"There's nothing there," Mina whispered.

"What?"

"Nothing," Mina said.'

By T.

'Confidently Mina crouched down and began to study him. Suddenly the man's eyes snapped open. Mina jumped but was not fazed.

"Hello" said Mina.

"Who are you?" squeaked the man.

"Mina," spoke Mina.

"Get out," snapped the man.'

By G.

Jenny Brierley, Year 3, Avenue Primary School, Leicester

Jenny used *Leon and the Place Between* by Graham Baker–Smith to embed grammar teaching into a fantasy unit of work. The text is set in a circus tent and time was spent exploring Baker-Smith's use of nouns in the description of the setting. They asked: why use 'lantern' and 'glow' instead of 'light'? What images do these words create in our minds? How do they add to the build up of tension? The pupils greatly enjoyed altering nouns in their own sentences in order to sharpen meaning.

Opportunities were provided in shared and independent writing sessions for the pupils to imitate the author's use of language. After exploring the impact of noun phrases in *Leon and the Place Between* (Baker-Smith and McAllister, 2009), the children composed their own to describe features of circus artists, including their expertise, costume, equipment and the venue in which they performed. The children focused on application of these skills when describing the setting for their fantasy story.

'Soaring rockets left a trail of smoke. The colourful carousel started to play a wonderful magical tune … a golden unicorn appeared from no-where and flew in front of the spinning carousel. A roaring tiger ran across the dark stage.' By Aaron.

Further discussion of techniques and their impact, combined with opportunities to imitate and play with language patterns impacted on the children's understanding of fantasy narratives and enjoyment of *Leon and the Place Between*.

Ed Toone, Year 2, Forest Lodge Primary School, Leicester

Ed found that the combination of clever illustrations and a great storyline in *Biscuit Bear* (Grey, 2005) inspired pupils to improve their use of grammar and punctuation when writing stories with a familiar setting. Responding to a challenge from Biscuit Bear himself, the children embarked on a mission to design a new biscuit friend and write an exciting adventure in which he would star. Biscuit Bear advised them to read the text carefully, looking for ideas and vocabulary that they could use in their writing. Once they had 'magpied' adjectives and effective verbs from the text, the children were given the opportunity to explore a range of cake decoration materials and use their senses to collect verbs and adjectives that describe how the ingredients looked, felt and tasted. Using shared writing sessions to build on the descriptions in the text the children were able to use their language to write their own detailed character descriptions, including effective adjectives, verbs and commas in lists.

These examples demonstrate how teachers are using quality texts to teach grammar within meaningful reading and writing activities. They are allowing children opportunities to discuss and play with language, which is enabling them to apply grammatical techniques effectively in their writing … Our challenge as professionals is to continue to embed effective teaching of grammar to aid meaning, and foster a love of writing as a process of choice built on a repertoire of grammatical techniques.

Extract references

Myhill, D., Jones, S.M., Lines, H. and Watson, A. (2012a) Re-thinking grammar: The impact of embedded grammar teaching on students' metalinguistic understanding. *Research Papers in Education*, 27 (2), 139–66.

Myhill, D., Jones, S.M., Lines, H. and Watson, A. (2012b) *Grammar for Writing Schemes of Work*. National Association for the Teaching of English (NATE).

Children's books in the extract

Almond, D. (2009) *Skellig*. London: Hodder Children's Books.

Baker-Smith, G. and McAllister, A. (2009) *Leon and the Place Between*. Dorking, Surrey: Templar.

Grey, M. (2005) *Biscuit Bear*. London: Red Fox Picture Books.

Horowitz, A. (2005) *Stormbreaker*. London: Walker Books Ltd.

Comment

Hendy notes that, in their research, Deborah Myhill and her team found that able children whose teachers had good grammatical subject knowledge achieved the greatest improvements in their writing. This fits with Wilson and Scanlon's belief in making primary school teachers experts in language subject study. The teachers in

Extract 37 showed skill in creating imaginative activities round books and writing, and their work was clearly underpinned by their own sound knowledge of language as a system. In Extract 36, Wilson and Scanlon did not support making children add adjectives or other parts of speech 'willy nilly'. In the examples of the Leicester teacher's work children are engaged with the language and illustrations of the authors of the quality books they are studying. But they made their own selections of vocabulary in their writing.

Interestingly, the principles on which these teachers and thinkers about language study base their work are similar to the basic ideas behind the Language in the National Curriculum (LINC) materials which were rejected by the government of the day (see Carter's book in the 'Further reading' section).

These four principles can be summarised as follows.

1. Teaching about language should build on children's implicit knowledge – on the rich linguistic resources they bring to the classroom.
2. Children use language before they analyse it in school and they can be helped to use appropriate terminology about how language is used and feed this knowledge into their own use of language.
3. Language is best analysed in purposeful settings rather than out of context.
4. Teaching children about attitudes to language, its uses and misuses, can help children see how it is used to communicate people's underlying attitudes and beliefs (Cox, 1995).

Questions to discuss with colleagues

1. How did you acquire knowledge about language as a system? Were you taught in a formal and systematic way?
2. When you write, do you draw consciously on this knowledge?
3. How useful do you feel it is for teachers and children to use a metalanguage to talk about such things as 'sentence', 'tense' and parts of speech like 'verb', 'noun' and 'conjunction'?
4. Consider some approaches to language study suitable for children in the Early Years.
5. Would you supplement the approach of the teachers in Extract 37 with some exercises to cement knowledge about, for example, parts of speech?
6. How would you assess children's developing knowledge about language?

Research inquiry

Drawing on the ideas in Extract 37, design a lesson/lessons for your age range around a chosen children's book and show how learning about language as a system is embedded in your teaching and the children's learning.

Further reading

Bain, R. and Bridgewood, M. (1998) *The Primary Grammar Book: Finding Patterns, Making Sense.* Sheffield: National Association for the Teaching of English (NATE). Do not be put off by the date of publication! This resource book is still hugely helpful to teachers as it brings grammar to a practical level with interesting language activities. For example, there are ideas for games and drama to help children learn about the functions of nouns and verbs in a sentence.

Carter, R. (ed.) (1991) *Knowledge about Language and the Curriculum: The LINC Reader.* London: Hodder Arnold/Hodder & Stoughton. The LINC materials were a government-funded, in-service resource to help implement language study programmes produced by Professor Carter and his team. Then one of the most dramatic decisions in the history of English was made – the Government of the day refused to publish the materials. Why? The official censorship arose from the Government's traditional view of grammar as a prescriptive rather than a descriptive study, which was at odds with the views of many teachers, most linguists and educationists, who considered the materials were based on a balanced view of teaching about language.

Cox, B. (1995) *Cox on the Battle for the English Curriculum.* London: Hodder & Stoughton. Brian Cox sets out the drama of the abandonment of the LINC materials with insight and passion.

Crystal, D. (2010, 3rd edn) *The Cambridge Encyclopedia of Language.* Cambridge: Cambridge University Press. This is one of many books by David Crystal which have helped teachers and others refine their knowledge about language. His breadth of knowledge and understanding and his ability to interest the reader in debates makes this and his other books well worth seeking out. One of the key insights running through his books is that language study should be descriptive rather than prescriptive. This is pertinent to the conflict about the LINC materials.

Mallett, M. (2012) *The Primary English Encyclopedia: The Heart of the Curriculum.* Abingdon and New York: Routledge. Teaching about grammar is covered on pp. 185–7.

Petty, K. and Maizels, J. (illustrator) (1996) *The Great Grammar Book.* London: The Bodley Head. This is an interactive teaching resource to help enthuse children from about age seven years about grammar and language. Wheels, flaps and pull-outs teach about parts of speech and the concept of a sentence.

Reedy, D. and Bearne, E. (2013) *Teaching Grammar Effectively in Primary Schools.* Leicester: United Kingdom Literacy Association (UKLA). Does using more adjectives and adverbs make for better writing? These writers and researchers doubt that this is the case. They believe that language learning is a cumulative process and that explicit teaching of grammar should take place in a context using real texts to explore the authors' use of syntax and of language. While the book is linked to UK national curriculum expectations, the framework it provides and the helpful case studies set out make it useful to anyone teaching grammar to the primary school age group.

Whitehead, M.R. (2010, 4th edn) *Language and Literacy in the Early Years.* London: Sage. This author knows how to present complex ideas clearly, as her chapter on 'Language and learning' shows. Linguistics, grammar, systems and signs are covered. She has in mind practitioners working in Early Years settings, but she provides valuable insights about the role of language in children's development that would be helpful to teachers of any age group.

Wilson, A. and Scanlon, J. (2011, 4th edn) *Language Knowledge for Primary Teachers.* London and New York: Routledge. One of the clearest and most engaging accounts known to me about the knowledge and understanding that teachers of young children need to acquire. One of the chapters on grammar is called 'What big teeth you have, grammar' because so many people think grammar is 'a set of rules waiting to catch them out'.

Section 2: Spelling

Extract 38

Source

Kelly, A. (2009) Transcription: Spelling, punctuation and handwriting. In J. Graham and A. Kelly (eds) *Writing Under Control*. Abingdon: David Fulton, (a) 132, (b) 138–41.

In this extract Alison Kelly considers some of the difficulties which children encounter when they are learning to spell. Some of these difficulties arise from complexities in the origins of the English language. She goes on to examine developmental and 'emergent writing' approaches which have influenced Early Years practice in teaching children to write and spell. The thinking which has led to the notion that there are stages in learning to spell is set out. She offers a summary of Richard Gentry's well-known spelling stages and makes some critical comments.

Part a

There are 26 letters in the alphabet but at least 44 single sounds (phonemes) that those letters have to represent and … some of them have to work overtime! One difficulty lies with the alphabet used for English, which was not one that was intended to fit English sounds. Its history can be traced back over thousands of years and thousands of miles to 1700 BC in the Middle East, where a North Semitic language, like Hebrew, was spoken. This alphabet was passed from the Phoenicians to the Greeks, whose model influenced the Etruscans, who, in turn, influenced the Romans. Christian missionaries arrived in this country in the sixth century and brought the Roman alphabet with them (Crystal, 1995) … Our language has also been influenced by the different groups of people who have settled here over the centuries all bringing with them their own languages. All this makes for a rich but sometimes bewildering potpourri and one where fewer than half of common English words have regular sound–symbol correspondence.

Part b

Concerns about the teaching of spelling

Early approaches to writing focussed exclusively on transcriptional aspects at the expense of composition. Rote learning and copying were the order of the day. By the 1960s, the pendulum had swung back with the 'creative writing' movement, where all the focus seemed to be on the production of imaginative writing. A teacher then was quoted as saying that 'spelling is learned naturally by the children and, from the reading, punctuation becomes increasingly familiar' (quoted in Clegg, 1964: 40). This idea that, for some children, spelling can be learned 'naturally' is one that recurs from time to time and Margaret Peters' research into spelling (first published in 1967, revised edition 1985) gave us a neat sound bite for this with the title of her book *Spelling Caught or Taught?* Peters cites evidence of challenges (and counter-challenges) to the systematic teaching of spelling from the beginnings of this century, and the more recent writing 'process' movement and 'developmental' or 'emergent' approaches to writing have been criticised for marginalising the teaching of the presentational skills of writing.

Writing process approaches

... The writing process movement which drew teachers' attention to the composition/transcription distinction suggested it was necessary for children to be clear about that separation too. A teacher's prompting that children should, in the first instance, concentrate on getting the ideas down without worrying about spellings is indeed a worrying one if that was all that was going on. But for many, such advice was seen only as the first step in the process of writing and the children would go on to 'edit' their work paying proper attention to the spelling and other surface skills of writing. It could be that the separation of composition and transcription, with the apparent relegation of transcription to second place, led to some misunderstandings about the importance teachers were placing on it. This may have been the case for some teachers, but many carefully attended to the teaching of spelling and handwriting.

Developmental / emergent approaches

The tension between composition and transcription is possibly most visible for a very young writer when the strain of writing letters and spelling words can seriously inhibit the fluency of writing ... Research into children's early moves into literacy revealed how they can make active and creative hypotheses about ways in which all of the writing system works. It became clear that encouraging children to make unaided spelling guesses not only showed teachers what the children knew and understood about writing but it also freed children from the transcriptional strain of 'getting it right' at the first attempt. They were enabled to focus on what they wanted to say. So the suggestion that children should 'have-a-go' at their spellings stems from a concern to 'free up' composition.

At about the same time, interesting research was being published about the nature of the children's invented spellings. For instance the work of Ferreiro and Teberosky (1979), two researchers who were influenced by Piaget's work, suggested that children go through stages in their writing and that it is possible to describe a developmental progression. *The Beginnings of Writing* (Temple *et al.*, 1982) was read by many teachers and reinforced the idea of spelling stages ... The danger with labels like 'developmental' and 'emergent' is that they might suggest that the teacher can simply let it all happen and does not need to do any specific teaching. The notion of stages also suggests a rigidity and uniformity in children's learning and that all children will pass through the same stages in the same way. Teachers know that this is not the case! ...

One commonly used model of spelling development comes from Richard Gentry (1982) who identifies five possible stages. His work is based on a case study of a single child (Bissex, 1980), which means we do have to approach it with some caution! The labels he uses for the different stages describe what the child is doing, not the teacher ... Here is a brief summary of the features of Gentry's stages:

1. Pre-communicative

    ■ knows that symbols can be used to say something;
    ■ uses a range of symbols (invented, numbers, letters – upper and lower case);
    ■ does not make sound–symbol connections.

2. Semi-phonetic

    ■ is beginning to make sound–symbol connections;
    ■ knows about word boundaries, how writing is arranged on a page;
    ■ may shorten some words.

3. Phonetic

    ■ uses sound–symbol connections consistently;
    ■ uses known words (sight vocabulary).

4. Transitional

    ■ uses visual strategies;
    ■ uses most conventions of the spelling system.

5. Correct

    ■ has basic knowledge of the spelling system and rules;
    ■ knows about word structure (morphology);
    ■ has a large sight vocabulary.

Extract references

Bissex, G. (1980) *GNYS AT WRK: A Child Learns to Read and Write*. Cambridge MA: Harvard University Press.

Clegg. A. (ed.) (1964) *The Excitement of Writing*. London: Chatto.

Crystal, D. (1995) *The Cambridge Encyclopaedia of the English Language*. Cambridge: Cambridge University Press.

Ferreiro, E. and Teberosky, A. (1979) *Literacy Before Schooling*. London: Heinemann.

Gentry, R. (1982) An analysis of developmental spelling in *GNYS AT WRK*. *The Reading Teacher*, 36 (2).

Peters, M.L. (1985 edn) *Spelling: Caught or Taught – a New Look*. London: Routledge & Kegan Paul.

Temple, C., Nathan, R. and Burris, N. (1982) *The Beginnings of Writing*. Massachusetts: Allyn and Bacon.

Comment

Alison Kelly gives a helpful overview of the challenge learning to spell presents for young children. Fewer than half of common English words have regular sound–symbol correspondence, which suggests that visual as well as 'sound' aspects of words must be an important aspect of learning to spell. She points out that compositional aspects of writing can be restrained by the sheer strain felt by young children struggling to form letters and to combine them to spell words. Her measured assessment of developmental and 'emergent writing' approaches, which aimed to reduce the tension between compositional and transcriptional aspects of writing, led her to recognise the danger of giving the impression that a child would 'catch' spelling without careful, appropriate direct teaching. She keeps on her critical hat also in looking at the notion of stages in children's development of spelling ability. She argues that teachers best take up a flexible attitude as not all children will pass through the stages in the same way or according to the same time scale. One of the best known models of spelling stages was set out by Richard Gentry in 1980. Kelly points out that it must be borne in mind that Gentry's scheme of development was based on the work of one child as described by Glenda Bissex in *GNYS AT WRK* (1980).

Extract 39

Source

Peters, M.L. (1985) Attention and perception. In *Spelling: Caught or Taught: A New Look*. London: Routledge & Kegan Paul, 25–6.

Children just beginning to write will try to create their own version of a word. But they will soon need help in learning conventional spelling. Over many years, Margaret Peters researched and wrote about children's growing competences as spellers and how teachers could provide the support and direction needed. Her 'Look, cover, write and check' approach became a mantra that informed the practice of hundreds of teachers. She did not believe that good spelling was 'caught' by children from their reading; readers tend not look at every letter or at letter sequences. Nor is listening likely to help children pick it up. Here, she builds up her case that spelling involves acquired visual abilities including the habit of 'looking with intent'.

> Spelling is not … 'caught' just through reading. It is certainly not through listening since the English spelling system can have more than one spelling for any one

sound, e.g. cup, done, does, blood, tough, and more than one sound for any one spelling, e.g. does, goes, canoe. It is almost certainly 'caught' in the early years through looking but ... looking in a specially intent way. It is 'caught' through the child's developing forms of imagery and serial reconstructions and, as a consequence of this, becoming accustomed to the probability of letter sequences occurring. The children who have 'caught' spelling are familiar with these sequences in the world around them. They are, as we have said, sensitised to the coding of English and this is in a benign social context where parents and teachers are reviewing, commenting on and predicting events in the child's day, e.g. shared activities which are regulated by the child in speaking and writing.

The task of the teacher is, therefore, to put those children who have not caught the skill into the way of looking with intent, and collecting a bank of letter sequences (or 'letter strings' or as the children call them 'letter patterns') from which they can generalise, to the new words they need to write. She also teaches well-formed handwriting and uses opportunities (not wasting them) to pursue joint activities, conversations and correspondences with individual children as well as with groups.

Attention and perception

On every hand we are beset with stimuli, sight, sounds, smells, the feel of things, tastes, etc., and from all these competing attractions we select for our attention only one bit of output. We only perceive that bit to which we attend and, of course, we tend to remember what we have perceived. But it is the first element of all this that is important, the selection of what to perceive. This is where the caring and concerned mother or teacher takes over when she actively and deliberately *points out* what seems to be important in the environment for the child to select and attend to. The 'environment' would be a pale and bland world without the perceiving mind of the adult. 'Oh, look at this furry caterpillar!' 'Can you see that girl with the skipping rope?' 'Listen, I can hear a cuckoo, can you?'

We know, only too well, something pointed out very strikingly by Wells (1981) when he shows that it is the child's own directing and initiating that engenders more and better conversation. This does not occur except within a warm and inviting parent/child or teacher/child relationship and it certainly stems in the very beginning from the time when the mother 'points out' things in the world around to the very small baby in his pram and when she demands responsive cooing by fixating him with eye-to-eye contact, talking to him and then *waiting* for seconds at a time till he responds. As the baby learns what kinds of things bring about these kinds of responses, he is learning to behave intentionally (McShane, 1980) ...

Now we do not 'look with intent' unless we have a reason for doing so. In the case of spelling this is to reproduce a word. Hence, this involves an intention on the part of the mother and/or teacher that the child should look closely at the name before writing it. To show an intention, it is necessary to state it for only in that way can the meaning of the intention be made clear to the child. At a very early age, the child can be reinforced in his intention to write his name by the mother or teacher pointing out the interesting features and expecting him to be able to reproduce this without copying.

The teacher lets the children give out named books and boxes, so that the children become familiar with Christian names that are characteristic of the spelling patterns of their own language structure. Children, too, are constantly requesting words to be put in their finger-tracing file or their personal dictionary, and here they are learning the possibility of spelling patterns as the teacher points out interesting features within the words they ask for. More systematic observation of word structure is important, however …

Parents' knowledge of the spelling system

If the parent or teacher is to be in a position to point out likenesses within words, she must herself be aware of these. The difficulty is that though she knows how to spell, that is to say she has a model of the spelling process, which some call a phonic map and some a mental lexicon to refer to, she may not know what that model or map or mental lexicon looks like. She may learn what it is like by playing games like Scrabble or doing crosswords or just by being interested in word structure. This pointing out of letter patterns to children, however, does imply that she is aware of these. Further, the fact that she is aware of them and interested in them will motivate her to direct the children's attention to them …

A visual skill? How do we know?

If we need to be convinced about the fact that spelling is a visual skill, we only have to look at ourselves as adults. When we are uncertain about how to spell a word we *write it down to see if it looks right*. In other words, we check visually and, because we can read, because we have looked again and again at letter sequences in English, we see at once that the word is spelled correctly. We are completely secure when we see that a word *looks right*.

Extract references

McShane, J. (1980) *Learning to Talk*. Cambridge: Cambridge University Press.
Wells, G. (1981) *Learning Through Interaction: The Study of Language Development*. Cambridge: Cambridge University Press.

Comment

Some children seem to 'catch' spelling early on. This extract is concerned with arriving at the best ways of helping the great majority of children who need well-directed teaching. These ways include, Peter argues, help from teacher or parent directing a child's attention to letter strings. The words 'stream', 'strap' and 'strong' all have the letter string 'str'. But, above all, she considers that a child needs careful support in achieving what she describes as 'imaging': this involves looking at a word, covering it, writing it down and checking that it is spelt correctly. The mnemonic is, of course, 'Look, cover, write, check' and this approach has been followed by many teachers in the years following Peter's influential work and especially her book *Spelling: Caught or Taught*.

While there are great linguistic and intellectual benefits associated with early fluent reading, Peters argues that this in itself does not seem to help children with spelling. Nor is listening the complete answer as less than half of common words have regular sound–symbol correspondence. However, as well as focused teaching, Peters also considers good spelling is encouraged by adults fostering a general interest in language and particularly word structure. Language play with parents and Early Years teachers helps considerably from the earliest years. Does she consider it important that teachers have good knowledge of language structure and function? Certainly, as they can then respond in an informed way to children's developing concepts about word structures and patterns.

Extract 40

Source

O'Sullivan, O. (2011) Teaching and learning spelling. In P. Goodwin (ed.) *The Literate Classroom*. London and New York: Routledge, 60.

There are an increasing number of spelling programs and websites providing resources and activities to help children's spelling development. In the following extract, Olivia O'Sullivan suggests how the computer can be a valuable aid to teaching and learning about spelling.

Computers can be used in a variety of ways to support the teaching of spelling. All aspects of writing, spelling and editing can be demonstrated by the teacher on a large screen or whiteboard – however there is a strong reason for maintaining the use of the flip chart for many aspects of writing – to show how handwriting 'goes'. Children should also have the opportunity to work in pairs or individually. Computers can also be used to create word banks, posters and lists of words with similar patterns, meanings and structures. The use of computers encourages reluctant writers through increasing the amount of writing they do (Safford *et al.*, 2004). Children who are less successful spellers also find it easier to detect misspellings on screen than in their handwritten texts, and find the use of the keyboard easier than handwriting. With older children the use of the spellchecker can be introduced.

Computer programs directed to teaching the alphabet or a range of spelling competences can be helpful for a wide range of children, particularly if supported by a teaching assistant. Practice of this kind is often more helpful when carried out in a pair or small group where discussion of word features can take place.

Extract reference

Safford, K., O'Sullivan, O. and Barrs, M. (2004) *Boys on the Margin*. London: Centre for Literacy in Primary Education (CLPE).

Comment

O'Sullivan considers the role of the computer in providing ways in which children can develop their spelling abilities through activities on screen. While spelling programs benefit all children, they seem to help motivate the more reluctant young writer and speller.

Interestingly, she thinks the flip chart still has a role in showing how 'writing goes'.

Questions to discuss with colleagues (Extracts 38–40)

1. How do you think teachers can encourage children to create their own early versions of written language while also helping them towards conventional spelling?
2. How helpful are schemes of spelling stages, like Gentry's, to the Early Years/Primary Years teacher? Do you agree with Alison Kelly that some flexibility is needed in considering spelling stages?
3. Margaret Peters, the supreme advocate of the importance of visual approaches to teaching spelling, developed the 'Look, cover, write, check' approach. Would you, following those who believe there is also a sound element in learning to spell, add 'say' after 'cover'?
4. A main plank in Margaret Peter's spelling research is the recognition that good spelling depends considerably on visual references and so, as she mentions in her revised version of *Spelling Caught or Taught* (1985), computer spelling programs have considerable potential here. What would you look for in selecting a good quality computer spelling program for either the fives and under or the seven to elevens?
5. Margaret Peters believes that achieving good spelling and well-formed handwriting free a child to compose and improve a young learner's self-image as a writer. Share in your discussion any experience you have had where a young learner's writing confidence has improved alongside increased control over spelling.
6. What would you look for in selecting on-screen programs and activities to help with spelling?
7. How were you taught to spell? Was it effective?
8. Are there formative ways of assessing spelling progress?

Research inquiry

Choose a child in your specialist age range and carry out a case study of their progress in spelling over some weeks. Write up your study and include one or more of the following:

- a transcript of a discussion with the child about their progress, helping them use some metalingual terms like 'syllable', 'vowel' and 'consonant'. Look at Gentry's stages set out in Extract 38 and judge how useful or otherwise they are in helping you assess the child's progress;
- samples from the child's personal spelling dictionary. How helpful is the dictionary in informing the child's spelling checks when writing?;
- comments on whether Peters' 'Look, cover, write and check' strategy works well for this young learner;
- some observations of the role of phonics in learning to spell;
- samples of the child's writing with some annotation and analysis;
- comments on using a spelling game (perhaps one you have invented) to nurture an interest in word patterns;
- an evaluation of a computer program or on-screen spelling activity;
- an analysis of two dictionaries and two thesauruses (in print or on-screen) and the child's views on these aids.

Further reading

Mudd, N. (1994) *Effective Spelling: A Practical Guide for Teachers*. London: Hodder & Stoughton, in association with UKRA (now UKLA). As well as a history of how words are spelt, Mudd looks at the different approaches there have been and offers some suggestions for spelling activities in the classroom. While accepting Peters' view on the importance of visual factors in learning to spell she points to the role of auditory factors, particularly in the early stages, and recommends we see spelling progress in the context of learning to write as a whole.

Waugh, D., Warner, G. and Waugh, R. (2013) *Teaching Grammar, Punctuation and Spelling in Primary Schools*. London: Learning Matters/Sage. The spelling chapters, like those on grammar and punctuation, set classroom teaching and learning in the framework of academic research. We need, say these authors, teaching about spelling and not just testing.

Section 3: Punctuation

'A cat has claws at the ends of its paws.
A comma's a pause at the end of a clause.'
(Quotation from a Greek dramatist living about 2,000 years ago; see Lynne Truss, 2006.)

Extract 41

Source

Truss, L. (2003) *Eats, Shoots & Leaves: The Zero Tolerance Approach to Punctuation*. London: Profile Books, 26–7.

Lynne Truss challenges and entertains with her views that in some matters of punctuation there are clear rights and wrongs, but sometimes this is not the case. So we need often to be 'staunch' and also know when to be 'flexible'.

When he wrote *Mind the Stop*, G.V. Carey gave just one paragraph to the apostrophe, because there was so little to say about it. 'If only all marks were so easy,' he sighed. But this was in an age when people had been taught the difference between 'Am I looking at my dinner or the dog's?' and 'Am I looking at my dinner or the dogs?' What I hope will become clear from this book is that one can usefully combine a descriptive and prescriptive approach to what is happening to this single aspect of the language. The descriptive sort of linguist tends to observe change in the language, note it, analyse it and manage not to wake up screaming every night. He will opine that if (say) the apostrophe is turning up in words such as 'Books', then that's a sure sign nobody knows how to use it any more; that it has outlasted its usefulness; it is like Tinkerbell with her little light fading, sustained only by elicited applause; it will ultimately fade, extinguish and die. This is an entirely sane and healthy point of view, of course – if a little emotionally cool. Meanwhile, at the other end of the spectrum, severely prescriptive grammarians would argue that, since they were taught in 1943 that you must never start a sentence with 'And' or 'But', the modern world is benighted by ignorance and folly, and most of modern literature should be burned.

Somewhere between these positions is where I want us to end up: staunch because we understand the advantages of being staunch; flexible because we understand the rational and historical necessity to be flexible. In *Mind the Stop* Carey defines punctuation as being governed 'two-thirds by rule and one-third by personal taste'. My own position is simple: in some matters of punctuation there are simple rights and wrongs; in others, one must apply a good ear to good sense. I want the greatest clarity from punctuation, which means, supremely, that I want apostrophes where they should be, and I will not cease from mental flight nor shall my sword sleep in my hand (hang on, didn't 'Jerusalem' begin with an 'And'?) until everyone knows the difference between 'its' and 'it's'.

Extract reference

Carey, G.V. (1939) *Mind the Stop: A Brief Guide to Punctuation with a Note on Proof-Correction.* Cambridge: Cambridge University Press.

Comment

At a time when children text and email, and the more subtle conventions of punctuation seem much less in evidence, Lynne Truss argues for accurate and conventional use. Good punctuation plays a major role in making meaning crystal clear and avoiding ambiguity in written language. The different punctuation points each have a role which we should help children to understand, she argues. The different functions of the colon and the semi-colon can be explained clearly and improve clarity in writing. If a piece of writing is becoming too peppered with commas it is permissible to use dashes to separate phrases or mark out when something is an aside. I am personally very glad this is the case!

But is she really in favour of 'zero tolerance', as the title of the book from which the extract is taken proclaims? She seems to be arguing that the mature punctuator will have come to know when to be strictly conventional and when to show flexibility. Here, developing a good ear in aid of meaning seems crucial. Encouraging children to read aloud, discuss and think about the role of punctuation in their writing would all follow from Truss's analysis. This is not conventional academic writing, but it makes helpful points to inform and possibly refine our own punctuation as part of our knowledge base of language knowledge as well as our work in the classroom. As she says, in the introduction on page 7, it is helpful to think of 'punctuation as the basting that holds the fabric of language in shape'.

Extract 42

Source

Dombey, H. (2013) *Teaching Writing: What the Evidence Says.* Leicester: United Kingdom Literacy Association (UKLA), 29, section 6.20.

Professor Henrietta Dombey has made an outstanding contribution to our understanding of how children's literacy develops and what are the most effective teaching approaches to support it. Extract 42 is taken from her study for the UKLA, with the assistance of colleagues, of best practice in teaching all aspects of children's writing. What is reproduced here shares a concern with making progress in punctuation.

Calkins (1980) found that in classrooms where writing was purposeful and attention was focussed on the reader, 8 to 9-year-olds used a wider variety of marks and did so more than their age mates in classrooms where writing was more regulated and punctuation learned by the rules. Hall's research (2001) with 5 and 6-year-olds tells a similar story. He found that meaningful understanding of punctuation results from a combination of the following: meaningful reading and writing activities; talk about punctuation emphasising the effect it produces; encouragement of an experimental approach; and a well-punctuated classroom environment. An important contribution was also made by the teacher's self discipline in limiting herself to one type of explanation for punctuation – either elocutionary (how the text should be read aloud), grammatical (how punctuation indicates syntactic divisions and relationships) or semantic (how it shows meaning). Skill in using punctuation is also supported by children's experience of a range of text forms, and a classroom ethos in which talk about learning is ongoing and interest in punctuation marks is encouraged.

However, the children Hall observed to make most progress in their use of punctuation were given very little explanation by the teacher. The principle criterion they used in deciding on whether to use a particular mark was semantic – what the mark would make the words mean.

Extract references

Calkins, I. (1990) When children want to punctuate: Basic skills belong in context. *Language Arts*, 57, 567–73; (1994) *The Art of Teaching Writing*. Portsmouth, NH: Heinemann.

Hall, N. (2001) Developing understanding of punctuation with young readers and writers. In J. Evans (ed.) *The Writing Classroom: Aspects of Writing and the Primary Child 3–11*. London: David Fulton.

Comment

Dombey notes that Nigel Hall, one of the most influential researchers into punctuation of recent times, found that young children who made most progress were given little direct explanation of punctuation rules by the teacher. However, teachers of these children were found to use some strategies. They were successful in creating a classroom environment that encouraged children to experiment and to talk about the effect punctuation produces on meaning.

Questions to discuss with colleagues

1. How would you help children understand those differences between speech and writing that make punctuation necessary in the written forms of language?
2. Lynne Truss believes that we must sometimes be 'staunch' and sometimes 'flexible' in our use of punctuation. Where would you be 'staunch' and where would you be inclined to show flexibility?
3. How far do you think children in pairs might help each other edit their writing, particularly when it comes to punctuation amends? What kind of teacher support would be helpful? (See Waugh, Warner and Waugh, 2013.)
4. How is teaching about punctuation informed by its link with understanding of grammar and particularly sentence structure?
5. In Extract 42 Dombey noted that Hall (2001) found some kinds of direct teaching of the rules of punctuation was not of great help to young writers. How might reading and looking at a picture or storybook help children make progress in using punctuation in their own writing?
6. What would you keep in mind when planning a broad framework for teaching punctuation to children from the Reception class up to Year 6? You might like to make a chart showing which punctuation points might be placed in each year.

Research inquiries

Either:

- After working with one or more young writers in your specialist age group over a few weeks, write up a case study including analysis of two of the following.

  - How far you found helping children to place full stops conventionally in their writing seems to be linked with acquiring the concept of a sentence.

  - How far direct teaching about the use of full stop substitutes, denoting questions and exclamations for example, is effective. How else might you support children's developing understanding of this?

  - In the case of older primary children, how would you help them learn how to use apostrophes – for example the correct use of 'its' and 'it's'?

  - Again with older children, how would you teach about the correct use of colons and semi-colons.

Or:

- Choose a picturebook of interest to your age group and use it to discuss how the author's use of punctuation adds meaning to the story.

Further reading

Hall, D. and Robinson, A. (eds) (1996) *Learning about Punctuation*. Clevedon, Philadelphia, Adelaide: Multilingual Learning Matters.

Hall, N. (1999) Young children's use of graphic punctuation. *Language and Education*, 3. This is a two-year classroom study of a group of young children's first efforts at punctuating their writing. The main conclusion is that it is graphic rather than linguistic principles that seem to influence early use of punctuation. Teacher language about punctuation and models of punctuation in children's books are two of the helpful intervening factors.

Hutchinson, D. (1987) Developing concepts of sentence structure and punctuation. *Curriculum*, 8 (3), 13–16. This researcher carried out a case study with one child who had written his own version of the story told in John Burningham's picturebook *Come Away from the Water, Shirley* (1977). At first, Danny wrote as he would speak, without putting in punctuation marks. But when redrafting the piece, he added full stops. Hutchinson notes that children may spontaneously add punctuation when editing their work.

Truss, L. and Timmons, B. (illustrator) (2006) *Eats, Shoots & Leaves: Why Commas Really Do Make a Difference*. London: Profile Books. A picturebook that teaches about the use of commas using hilarious illustrations showing how a misused or missing comma can confuse. For example, 'Eat a huge hot dog' has a very different meaning to 'Eat a huge hot-dog'. This sort of thing makes children chuckle and understand that learning about language can be fun.

Waugh, D., Warner, C. and Waugh, R. (2013) *Teaching Grammar, Punctuation and Spelling*. London: Learning Matters. Chapters 6 and 7 help secure teachers' own knowledge of punctuation use and suggest how learning about and teaching about punctuation in the classroom can be creative.

Section 4: Handwriting

Extract 43

Source

Wyse, D., Jones, R., Bradford, H. and Wolpert, M.A. (2013, 3rd edn) Handwriting. In *Teaching English, Language and Literacy*. Abingdon: Routledge, 245–8.

These authors introduce the main issues to keep in mind when teaching children handwriting. They cover such practical things as appropriate grip, setting and posture and go on to set out technical terms that can be used to talk about handwriting. The work of Rosemary Sassoon is described, including her belief in the wisdom of teaching letters in 'families'. They introduce Margaret Peters' argument that fluent handwriting is linked to good spelling. Wyse and colleagues argue powerfully that the early mastery of motor skills provides the foundation for clear, fluent writing.

Handwriting has always been taught; in England, for example, it has been a significant feature of the curriculum since the introduction of the 1870 Education Act. Increasingly, children have access to means of producing print without having to hand-write, which suggests that children should be taught how to use keyboards in the most efficient way. However, the teaching of handwriting is still an important part of the early years and primary curriculum. It is thought that the kinaesthetic movements that are part of forming letters help with visual memory of letter shapes. Also … there is research showing that handwriting is linked with comprehension. Finally, it is interesting to note that there are a considerable number of professional writers, particularly of narrative and poetry, who find handwriting a better way to express themselves than the keyboard.

Learning to form the individual letters of the alphabet and produce legible handwriting at a reasonable speed, involves a complex perceptuo-motor skill. The goal of handwriting teaching is a legible, fluent and comfortable style. Legibility will have different levels according to the purpose of the writing. Sassoon (1990) points out that children cannot be expected to produce their neatest writing all the time, so she advocates different levels of handwriting. While schools should have a handwriting policy in place which is shared with parents and which is adhered to when modelling writing and marking children's work, it is also important to acknowledge that handwriting needs to be fit for purpose. A calligraphic standard for special occasions, for example, might require a careful, deliberate approach which will be more time-consuming than a legible everyday hand. There will also be times when pupils are drafting text or making notes that they alone will read where a lower standard of legibility is appropriate. Fluency is particularly important in tests and exams when time pressures are present.

A comfortable style requires an appropriate grip, appropriate seating and good posture. Posture and working space are important elements of handwriting ... Left-handers can be helped by ensuring that they sit to the left of a right-hander so that their elbows are not competing for space. Whatever your own writing orientation, you will need to ensure that these issues are made explicit and discussed when you model handwriting ...

Basic handwriting concepts

Sassoon (1990) puts forward the concepts behind our writing system. Direction, movement and height are all crucial: left to right and top to bottom; the fact that letters have prescribed flowing movements with specific starting and exit points; the necessity to ensure that letters have particular height differences. In addition, the variance between upper and lower case must be recognised and the correct spacing consistently applied. She also stresses the importance of taking particular care when teaching certain letters that have mirror images of each other, such as *b–d, m–w, n–u* and *p–q* to avoid confusion for young learners.

There are a small number of technical terms that are useful when talking about handwriting. *Ascenders* are the vertical lines that rise above the mid-line (or x-line) on letters like 'd'; *descenders* are the vertical lines that hang below the baseline on letters like 'g'. Letters have an *entry stroke* called a *crossbar* and the height of the letter should only be three-quarters. This means that the top of the letter finishes between the mid-line and the ascender line. There are four important horizontal lines: the *descender line*, the *baseline*, the *mid-line* and the *ascender line* ... Children need to understand these concepts if they are to have legible and fluent handwriting.

Jarman (1989), like Sassoon, suggests that letters can be taught in families that are related by their patterns of movement. There are slight differences between their approaches, but both underline the importance of the idea of letter families.

Handwriting and writing

Peters (1985) discussed perceptuo–motor ability and argued that carefulness in handwriting goes hand in hand with swift handwriting, which in turn influences spelling ability. Children who can fluently write letter-strings such as *-ing, -able, -est, -tion* and *-ous* are more likely to remember how to spell words containing these strings. It was also Peters' view that the teaching of 'joined up' or cursive writing, should begin long before the junior school, that is to say Key Stage 1 rather than 2 ...

More recent research has begun to show the importance of automaticity in handwriting in order to benefit composing processes. Medwell and Wray (2007) argue that handwriting has been taught in mainstream schooling based on the link between correct spelling and the use of fluent, joined-up handwriting and its impact on compositional skills. In Scheuer *et al.*'s (2006) study, children aged nine gave reflective accounts of learning to write. Their views represented writing as a developmental process which moves from early mark making to producing and understanding conventional writing over a relatively extended period of time.

Such research suggests that when teaching handwriting, we should focus on developing children's fine motor skills so that they are first and foremost able to hold a writing implement comfortably, and hand–eye coordination to support the 'uniform' formation of letters. Development of these early skills will support automaticity and fluency in handwriting which will impact on their future success as writers.

Extract references

Jarman, C. (1989) *The Development of Handwriting Skills: A Resource Book for Teachers*. Oxford: Basil Blackwell.

Medwell, J. and Wray, D. (2007) Handwriting: What we know and what do we need to know? *Literacy*, 41 (1), 10–15.

Peters, M.L. (1985) *Spelling Caught or Taught: A New Look*. London: Routledge & Kegan Paul.

Sassoon, R. (1990) *Handwriting: A New Perspective*. Leckhampton: Stanley Thornes.

Scheuer, N., de la Cruz., M., Pozo, J. and Neira, S. (2006) Children's autobiographies of learning to write. *British Journal of Educational Psychology*, 76, 709–25.

Comment

In the first of the two extracts in this section, Wyse and associates set out the key features of the processes engaged when writing by hand. They believe that if these processes are understood and applied, a child's handwriting will become both legible and more fluent in execution. These understandings would helpfully inform any school's handwriting policy. Drawing on the work of Rosemary Sassoon (1990), they argue that children need skilled help and regular practise in forming the individual letters of the alphabet. This involves acquiring complex perceptuo-motor skills and learning about the direction, movement and height conventions of our writing system. They need to control the prescribed flowing movements with specific starting and exit points and the height differences between letters. These writers believe that, whatever particular handwriting style is chosen, children can be helped to become fluent by holding the writing implement correctly, developing good posture and practising the formation of letters. They set out a number of terms that can be used to discuss handwriting – 'ascenders', 'descenders', 'entry strokes' and 'exit strokes'.

So the suggestion is that teachers need to have metalingual conversations to help children achieve fluency and legibility. Issues like at what age children best start to use 'joined up' writing and the benefits of teaching letters in families related to their patterns of movement are considered. As these writers note, Peters, writing in the 1980s, was of the view that swift writing of letter strings like 'ing', 'able' and 'tion' could help improve children's spelling. Wyse and co-workers also refer to more recent research which suggests and explores a possible crucial connection between automaticity in handwriting and children's developing compositional abilities. The second extract, from an article by Medwell and Wray (2014) takes up this connection in more detail.

Extract 44

Source

Medwell, J. and Wray, D. (2014) Handwriting automaticity: The search for performance thresholds. *Language and Education*, 28 (1), 34–51. Extract from pp. 35-6.

Drawing on international research these authors build the case for recognising a connection between handwriting automaticity and children's writing composition.

Handwriting is a language act

... A US programme of research (e.g. Berninger and Graham, 1998; Berninger *et al.*, 2006) developed the insight that handwriting is not simply a motor act. Berninger and Graham (1998) stress that it is 'language by hand' and their research suggests that orthographic and memory processes (the ability to recall letter shapes) contribute more to handwriting than do motor skills (Berninger and Amtmann, 2004). Handwriting does not merely involve training the hand; it involves training the memory and hand to work together to generate the correct mental codes for production of letters and translate these into motor patterns of letters – automatically and without effort! If this is the case, then handwriting is important in writing as a language act, rather than just a motor act used to record writing. It may, therefore, be that focusing teaching and assessment exclusively on letter formation and neatness, and even speed, can address only a small part of the importance of handwriting in writing.

Understanding how different writing processes (translation, planning, reviewing) are accomplished using the same, limited, working memory space seems to be particularly important for understanding the development of children's composition. Gathercole *et al.* (2004) note that working memory is particularly associated with the literacy scores of younger children. If young writers have to devote large amounts of working memory to the control of lower-level processes such as handwriting, they may have little working memory capacity left for higher-level processes such as idea generation, vocabulary selection, monitoring the progress of mental plans and revising text against these plans. Indeed, in contrast to skilled writers, developing writers engage in little explicit planning and revision (Bereiter and Scardamalia, 1987). It may be that handwriting can 'crowd out' composing processes. One way of managing limited working memory capacity is to automate some processes, such as handwriting, so that they can be done without the need for cognitive attention (La Berge and Samuels, 1974). This frees up cognitive resources to deal with higher-level processes. The development of skill in writing may require the automatisation of lower-level skills so that they use less of the available working memory resources ... Some studies have suggested that automatic letter writing is the single best predictor of length and quality of written composition in the primary years (Graham *et al.*, 1997) ... However, we do not know when handwriting typically becomes automatic for children, in terms of age or rate of letter production. English national testing does not currently assess handwriting automaticity. It seems likely that we are currently failing to assess an important aspect of writing even though researchers such as Connelly *et al*. (2006) have offered convincing evidence that, for many children, handwriting continues to be a demanding activity into the secondary years and beyond.

A number of children experience difficulties with handwriting throughout their schooling, but estimates of how many children are affected vary enormously, as do the basis of the estimates, which range from as high as 44% (Rubin and Henderson, 1982; Alston, 1985) to as low as 12–22% (Graham and Weintraub, 1996). These figures suggest that lack of handwriting automaticity may affect a significant number of primary and secondary aged children, although the question of how far that automaticity may relate to the generation or production of letter codes and movements may be an issue for graphonomics research, involving the use of tablets to measure acceleration in writing movements (Tucha, Ticha and Lange, 2008). Such research has identified the importance of 'in air time', that is, pauses during writing.

Extract references

Alston, J. (1985) The handwriting of seven to nine year olds. *British Journal of Special Educational Needs*, 12, 68–72.

Bereiter, C. and Scardamalia, M. (1987). *The Psychology of Written Composition*. Hillsdale, NJ: Lawrence Erlbaum.

Berninger, V.W. and Graham, S. (1998) Language by hand: A synthesis of a decade of research on handwriting. *Handwriting Review*, 12, 11–25.

Berninger, V.W. and Amtmann, D. (2004) Preventing written expression disabilities through early and continuing assessment and intervention for handwriting and/or spelling problems: Research into practice. In L. Swanson, K. Harris and S. Graham (eds) *Handbook of Research on Learning Disabilities*. New York: Guilford Press.

Berninger, V.W., Abbott, R.D., Jones, J., Wolf, B., Gould, L., Anderson-Youngstrom, M., Shimada, S. and Apel, K. (2006) Early development of language by hand: Composing, reading, listening and speaking connections; three letter writing modes; and fast mapping in spelling. *Developmental Neuropsychology*, 29 (1), 61–92.

Connelly, V., Campbell, S., MacLean, M. and Barnes, J. (2006) Contribution of lower order skills to the written composition of college students with and without dyslexia. *Developmental Neuropsychology*, 29, 175–96.

Gathercole, S.E., Pickering, S.J., Knight, C. and Stegmann, Z. (2004) Working memory skills and educational attainment: Evidence from National Curriculum Assessments at 7 and 14 years of age. *Applied Cognitive Psychology*, 18, 1–16.

Graham, S. and Weintraub, N. (1996) A review of handwriting research: Progress and prospects from 1980–1994. *Educational Psychology Review*, 8, 7–87.

Graham, S., Berninger, V., Abbott, R., Abbott, S. and Whitaker, D. (1997) The role of mechanics in composing of elementary school students: A new methodological approach. *Journal of Educational Psychology*, 89 (1), 170–82.

La Berge, D. and Samuels, S.J. (1974) Towards a theory of automatic information processing. *Cognitive Psychology*, 6, 283–323.

Rubin, N. and Henderson, S.E. (1982) Two sides of the same coin: Variation in teaching methods and failure to write. *Special Education: Forward Trends*, 9, 17–24.

Tucha, O., Ticha, L. and Lange, K. (2008) Graphonomics, automaticity and handwriting assessment. *Literacy*, 42 (3), 145–55.

Comment

Medwell and Wray are among those scholars exploring, with persistence and rigour, a possible connection between automaticity and children's composition. If this link between children's fluency in handwriting and their success in creating text can be convincingly shown, there would be considerable implication for the status of handwriting and how it is taught. So, interestingly, just as typing and word processing seems to be gaining favour as a way of children being able to create text, evidence is accumulating which shows handwriting to be much more than a presentational aspect of language. How convincingly do these researchers set out the case for a relationship between writing fluency, described technically as 'orthographic-motor integration', and writing composition?

Drawing on international research (for example that of Berninger *et al.*, 2006), they believe that they have demonstrated such a relationship and that this relationship may be more significant than realised. The argument goes something like this. Given that handwriting is challenging for young children, the physical act of letter generation is likely to take up what these researchers term 'working memory capacity'. This might well reduce a child's energy for dealing with higher level composing tasks, which include processes like planning and reviewing. So some of the strategies suggested in the first extract in this section – teaching about 'letter families' and 'letter strings', helping children understand and practise the formation of the letters of the alphabet and acquiring the conventions of direction, movement and height – in fact anything that encourages handwriting fluency is well worth a place in a handwriting policy that informs classroom teaching. Much of the research and writing about the relationship between handwriting automaticity and successful composition has been done in Australia, France and the United States.

Later in their article, beyond the account in the extract, Medwell and Wray attempt to see how far the findings of these scholars can be generalised to Britain where children often learn a writing script which is simpler than that favoured in some other countries. They describe their pioneering attempt to establish thresholds for handwriting automaticity, below which children's compositional abilities might be at risk. They do this by combining the results of two empirical studies with different age groups. In their conclusion, Medwell and Wray argue that their research studies do indeed indicate that a high proportion of variance in composition for the children included does relate to their handwriting. This was particularly evident in children's ability to generate letters automatically, as measured by the Alphabet Task used in the studies. More tentatively, they suggest thresholds for handwriting automaticity that might help predict composition ability for children of various ages.

Questions to discuss with colleagues (Extracts 43 and 44)

1. Do you agree with Sassoon (1990, referred to in Extract 43) that different levels of handwriting legibility and accuracy should be acceptable according to the task? How would you build this principle into a school handwriting policy?

2. Wyse and associates, in Extract 43, suggest that teachers and children should share a metalingual vocabulary to discuss handwriting techniques and progress. With reference to your age range, do you consider this to be feasible and, if so, how would you introduce such terms?

3. How far do you agree with those who recommend an early start to 'joined up' writing? What arguments would you offer for or against such a recommendation?

4. In Extract 44, Medwell and Wray comment that in England automaticity is not assessed. Should it be?

5. How were you taught to handwrite? What have you learnt through your own experience and that of others about the challenge that acquiring handwriting that is fluent and legible presents?

6. The authors of each of these two extracts do not recommend a particular handwriting style. Based on your personal experience and your experience as a teacher, what would you look for in choosing a handwriting style for a school?

7. How might school and parents work together to carry through the school's handwriting policy?

Research inquiry

Either:

■ Write a report on one school's approach to handwriting, suggesting its strengths and possible weaknesses.

Or:

■ Observe a teacher's lessons on handwriting with your specialist age group over a number of weeks. Chart the progress of one or two young learners and in your account discuss how far they have made progress in:

☐ forming the individual letters of the alphabet;
☐ achieving the best posture and way of holding the writing implement;
☐ using metalingual terms like 'ascender' and 'descender';
☐ achieving fluency/automaticity.

■ Mention the ways you or the class teacher intervened to help and include some samples of children's writing and children's comments.

Further reading

See the texts listed in the extracts.

The rich landscape of children's literature

Introduction

Fiction is at the heart of English teaching at all ages. It is through reading, hearing, viewing and talking about fiction that children enrich that inner world of the imagination, first created through play, an important theme explored in the extracts in Chapter 1. Stories in all their different forms show us how others live and feel, allow us to share in adventures, to live other lives vicariously and to integrate all this to discover what it is to be a human being. Year by year the treasure store of children's fiction grows, especially now that graphic, screen-based and interactive texts have joined those published in traditional print form. But rather than nudging print texts aside, use of the new technology has enhanced many print texts, adding variety and visual power. This is particularly true of picturebooks which have become ever more imaginative and ever more interactive in design.

What are the implications for teachers as they survey this richness and reflect on the place of fiction in the English lesson? Chapter 3, on reading, considers how children learn to read and respond to fiction. This chapter concentrates on the features and the value of genres of fiction important for the under-elevens. What are the implications for teachers' subject knowledge about fiction texts of all kinds as they find themselves faced by all this richness and variety? It is an important question because teachers have a great influence on the value children give to reading, their enthusiasm for fiction, the choices they make and their developing literacy. Enjoyment of fiction also shows them the possibilities open to them as writers, including as writers of creative texts. Here, it is worth looking at the United Kingdom Literacy Association's 'Teachers as readers: Building communities of readers' project which aimed to enrich and extend teachers' knowledge of the canon of children's literature and their understanding of how they could help children read for pleasure (Cremin *et al.*, 2008; see www.ukla. org/downloaded/teachers-as-readers.pdf).

Type 'children's literature' or 'children's literature studies' into your search engine and a bewilderingly large number of sites appear. This is not surprising because the academic study of children's literature ranges widely, covering for example: the history of children's books, analytical and critical studies of texts as well as works on its social, cultural, international and educational aspects. It is also the case that children's publishing is a huge international industry from which a vast number of texts, paper and electronic, constantly flow. Those who spend much of their time reading and reviewing books and working with students and children find it a challenge to keep up with the rich stream of new texts for children. Even so, we have to keep a critical eye open – not everything written for children is of high quality.

As I worked on this chapter, the second edition of Peter Hunt's large two-volume work *International Companion Encyclopedia of Children's Literature* (2004) was a handy tome to keep by my side. There are chapters in the *Companion* covering theory and critical approaches, forms and genres, publishing and reviewing and use of texts in the classroom. Another excellent resource is the second edition of *The Oxford Companion to Children's Literature*, a classic book by Humphrey Carpenter and Mari Prichard first published in 1984, updated by Daniel Hahn in 2015. Out of all the bewildering bounty in Hunt and elsewhere I posed the question: what are the priorities for a new teacher coming into an Early Years or primary classroom? In answering this question it seemed to me that, more than anything else, what they needed most was to be able to look over the landscape of children's literature and understand its shapes and forms, that is to say, they needed a way into being able to reflect on the nature and value of some of the most important genres.

The chapter begins, in Section 1, with poetry and with an extract from Morag Styles' essay in Hunt (2004). It offers an historical perspective – looking at how poetry for children reflects beliefs about childhood and morality at particular times. She then considers the choices of poem open to teachers and children in the twenty-first century, noting that these choices can take in all the popular forms of the past as well as the work of contemporary poets.

Section 2 turns to picturebooks: texts that combine the verbal and the visual in interesting, playful and often thought-provoking ways, and which have become an important cultural form. Some of the best have qualities that make them a hugely enjoyable and valuable resource for learning to read and for encouraging independent reading. Many are narratives and give children their first taste of the things fiction has to offer: the opportunity to wonder and to predict what might come next. Extract 46, from the writing of David Lewis, illuminates how young readers learn to make meaning from picturebooks by moving back and forth from pictures and text. It is the reference to specific texts, texts which have become favourites in the Early Years and primary classroom, that makes his account so interesting and helpful.

Extract 47 in Section 3 from Elizabeth Cook's pioneering book *The Ordinary and the Fabulous* tells us something about the history of telling aloud and reading traditional tales and assesses their appeal and value.

Short stories, covered in Section 4 with Extract 48 from an unpublished lecture by Eve Bearne, have not always received the critical attention they deserve. And yet, not only are the best exciting and often innovative in theme and style, they can also serve as helpful bridging books. This 'bridge' is one that helps young children learn to manage stories which have helpful illustrations but carry their main message through written text. Here, Bearne sets out some key landmarks in the history of the form and recommends texts for the classroom.

The extracts in Section 5 examine the different kinds of novel that children might read or have read to them. First, in Extract 49, Mallett looks at some of the genre features recognised by narrotologists – the 'story structure' or 'story grammar' of longer stories and novels. Then, in Extract 50 from *Teaching Dickens in the Primary School*, Eve Bearne argues that the under-elevens can be helped to make a critical as well as an emotional and moral response to some great novels, which have sometimes been thought of as mostly suitable for older children and adults. These days, children often first encounter Charles Dickens' stories through musicals and plays, television films and DVDs, coming to reading the books later. These media, audio and graphic versions of the stories may well be the best way into these powerful stories by Dickens and other writers of classics for some children. Children today also bring to their reading and viewing of challenging material like classic novels their experience of popular television serials. This engagement with an aspect of 'popular culture', Eve Bearne argues, often energises children's discussion of plot, characters and themes and their cogitating on moral dilemmas carries through to enjoyment of films and books of great novels.

There is more about 'popular culture' texts – which are sometimes multimodal, graphic or in comic book format in print or on-screen in Section 6. These cross genre boundaries and are often highly motivating in the classroom and at home. Extract 51 homes in on comics – long both multimodal and multimedia – and explains how they have shown great resilience and an ability to reinvent themselves so that they continue to appeal to children and adults in many parts of the world. Extract 52, from the work of a children's librarian, draws attention to the new kinds of visual story-telling in comics children under eleven enjoy at home and helps us reflect on how they can be used in the classroom. The number of children's books on the market in each category covered in this chapter is so great that those in the lists towards the end of the sections are only a small selection.

Section 1: Poetry

Extract 45

Source

Styles, M. (2004, 2nd edn) Poetry. In P. Hunt (ed.) *International Companion Encyclopedia of Children's Literature*, vol. 1. London and New York: Routledge, 396–9.

Poetry deserves an important place in the literature programme. It is the perfect medium for the expression of some ideas, observations and feelings. Indeed, poems can bring thinking and feeling into harmony. There are many poetic forms beginning for many young children with playful, rhyming, rhythmic nursery rhymes. The brevity of verses and songs for the very young makes them easy to remember and the strong rhythms encourage singing and dancing. In the playground, children continue to enjoy sound and rhyme in verses that are sometimes subversive. How many versions of Happy Birthday do you know? As they get older children become ready to appreciate other poetic forms: ballads, epic poems, haiku, limericks, sonnets and free verse.

Morag Styles, Emeritus Professor of Children's Poetry at Cambridge Institute of Education, has long had an interest in the scholarly study of poetry, has contributed to international conferences, researched and written in the field and worked intensively to bring poetry into classrooms in a meaningful way. In Extract 45 she begins by reflecting on the question: what is poetry for children? She goes on to discuss poetry anthologies, which she regards as 'gatekeepers of the cannon'. The choices anthologists have made through the years have been, to a great extent, a function of the views about childhood and how children should be socialised commonly held in their time. The preferences of what she terms 'elite groups of academically educated men', who tended to be the poetry anthologists in the past, seem to have led to certain groups – women and black and Asian poets for example – being under-represented. Knowing something about the 'big shapes' in the history of the ways in which poetry was offered to children is likely to be helpful background for teachers today choosing poems to introduce to their class. Are there some universal themes which are explored by each generation of poets who write for children? Professor Styles considers what sort of poems children themselves actually choose and enjoy today.

Anthologists – the gatekeepers of the canon

I am tempted to say that there is no such thing as poetry for children. There is poetry *about* children and some of the best poetry ever written is about *childhood*. In addition, a significant proportion of the so-called 'canon' of children's verse was never intended for the young at all, but was poetry for adults which was considered suitable for children. The gatekeepers of the canon are the anthologists.

Of course, many poets have written specifically for children, some choosing to divide their time between different audiences (Robert Louis Stevenson, Christina Rossetti, Ted Hughes, Charles Causley, Roger McGough, Carol Ann Duffy, Jackie Kay to name but a few); others specialise in poetry for the young (for example Michael Rosen, Allan Ahlberg, Tony Mitton). Both groups have, however, been marginalised by influential editors ...

Look at prestigious anthologies of the nineteenth and twentieth century and consider the omissions. Where are the poets writing for children? Where are the women? And, until very recently, where are the black and Asian poets? Many anthologies of the past are testimonies to the preferences of the elite groups of academically educated men.

The tension between the improving instincts of adults and what children choose to read is nowhere more keenly demonstrated than in the anthologising of verse for the young. A large body of the poetry actually favoured by children (so the evidence would suggest) has been ignored by anthologists. On a more positive note, some of the poetry for adults which has an established place in the children's canon appears to have been adopted by the young readers themselves, a healthy trend which shows the powerful drive children have to shape their own literature. Kaye Webb's *I Like This Poem* (1979), a collection of declared favourite poems of children (although, perhaps, a privileged group), includes much that was written before the twentieth century. Traditionalists do not have much to worry about; children today seem simply to like a varied diet. See, for example, Michael Rosen's video, *Count to Five and Say I'm Alive* (1995), where children from a wide range of ethnic groups in schools all over the British Isles perform raps and gutsy playground rhymes in standard English, various dialects and other languages; read poems they have written themselves; enjoy performances by published poets; and recite from memory their favourite poems by Shakespeare, Shelley, Keats, Tagore *et al.*

Poetry about childhood

Some of the most popular themes for children remain fairly constant: nature, magic, weather, the sea, school and family life, adventure – and anything that makes them laugh. However, one of the most powerful topics has always been the exploration of childhood itself. It seems probable that many poets write for children partly because they want to understand the 'child within themselves', looking back with some longing at their own youth and coming-of-age. At worst, this can be self-indulgent and nostalgic; at best, it reaches the gentle self-scrutiny of Stevenson; Causley's occasional, but revealing, unsentimental allusions to his parents' lives and his own changing view of time as he gets older; Duffy's moving exploration of childhood from the vantage point of a mother loving a young daughter; or Rosen's funny and unpretentious accounts of everyday life based on observation of his children, as well as reflection on his own past. Adults will always view children through the 'distorting lens' of their own dreams, hopes, memories and prejudices: this has led to some of the most tender, deep and rewarding poetry ever written.

Changes over time

Until the beginning of the nineteenth century, most poetry (indeed, most literature) for children was didactic and severe, expressed through lessons, fables, improving verse and hymns, although the latter included some of the most lyrical literature available to the young. To those who could get their hands on it, what a contrast the rude, crude and sensational literature (including verse) available in the chapbooks to the widest possible audience must have made.

By the early nineteenth century, significant numbers of poets writing for children aspired to entertain rather than simply educate young readers. Harsh moral tales in verse began to develop into the extravagances of cautionary verse; light-hearted poems about the imaginary doings of insects, birds and small animals became popular; nonsense verse began to flourish and the first child-centred poetry began to emerge. A sea-change occurred in the 1970s when poetry for children moved into the city, and the earlier gentle and often rural lyricism turned into something more earthy, harking back, perhaps, to the bawdiness of the chapbooks. Gone are the descriptions of neat nurseries, rolling countryside and sweet fancies. Nature may still be central, but it is more likely to come in the shape of muscular poetry about animals by poets like Hughes, or hard-hitting descriptions about how humans have destroyed the environment. Humour is widespread, but serious concerns are not neglected. John Rowe Townsend called it 'urchin verse'. 'Here is family life in the raw, with its backchat, fury and muddle, and instead of woods and meadows are disused railway lines, building sites and junk heaps' (Townsend, 1987: 303).

As for content, there are few unmentionables left. The twenty-first century's attitude to childhood in poetry is refreshingly robust – too much so for some tastes. Iona Opie's work (for example, *The People in the Playground*, 1992), should convince more tender-hearted commentators that children are by and large hardy and resilient and require a literature that takes account of that fact. Contemporary poetry for children also favours the vernacular and tends to be informal. All the popular forms of the past are still evident; but children's poetry also features raps, song lyrics, dub poetry, haiku, concrete verse, dialect poetry, dramatic monologues and realistic conversation poems, as well as other more traditional verse forms with regular rhyme and metre.

Another recent development is the recognition of children's own writing. Contemporary poetry is accessible to children and encouraged by teachers, poets, community events and competitions. Publication of this poetry demonstrates the high standards that can be achieved, despite the limited stamina and developing skills of the writers.

Poetry for children, then, is defined by the age: contemporary poetry emphasises the need to love, value, amuse and protect the young, and has a liberal tolerance of their private brand of humour, whereas poetry of the Puritan age believed its function was to save the souls of children by admonishing them to virtue, godliness and obedience. Romantic ideas led to a welcome shift in perspectives on childhood, some of which are still with us today. At best, it encouraged adults to value childhood, lightened some of the worst excesses of moralistic literature for children and ushered in new ways of thinking and writing about children; at worst, there lingers still a desire to idealise childhood and equate it with innocence which can lead to unhealthy and unrealistic expectations of the young.

Extract references

Opie, P. and Opie, I. (1992) *The People in the Playground.* Oxford: Oxford University Press.
Rosen, M. (1995) *Count to Five and Say I'm Alive.* London: Team Video Productions.
Townsend, J.R. (1987, 3rd edn) *Written for Children.* London: Penguin.
Webb, K. and Maitland, A. (illustrator) (1979) *I Like This Poem.* Harmondsworth: Penguin.

Comment

Professor Styles gives us here a helpful historical review of how poetry for children developed through the ages. Poetry for the young, she points out, is 'defined by the age' and has moved from poetry with 'an improving purpose' of earlier times to poetry with themes and about things that chime with children's true interests and preferences. So poetry for children can reveal how childhood was understood and regarded at a particular time. But her analysis is much more than an historical review, as her reflections are helpful to anyone wishing to know more about the value and pleasure of reading poetry today. Her finding that children like a varied diet of poems written at different times is of great help to the practitioner making a collection for their class. Children still like traditional poetry about nature – but seem to prefer more robust treatment of the topic, as in some of Ted Hughes' poems. But there has been a move to include poetry about the city and the street – often expressed in modern forms like rap, conversation poems and song lyrics. She also mentions that there is more encouragement for children to express their opinions about poems and to write their own. There is more about children as writers of poetry in Chapter 4 on writing.

Those who wish to delve more deeply into the history of poetry for children and who track down the whole article from which the extract is taken, will find that Professor Styles goes on to attend in greater detail to poetry for young people throughout the centuries. So she looks at the poetry of the eighteenth and nineteenth centuries: William Blake, the romantic poetry of Wordsworth and Coleridge and at Victorian nonsense verse as well as the timeless poetry of Walter de la Mare – 'The Listeners' for example. Her analysis of twentieth-century poetry for children takes in poetry for children internationally and Caribbean-British poetry on which she is a leading expert.

Questions to discuss with colleagues

It would be helpful for participants to bring to the discussion some poems used successfully with children and perhaps some questions and puzzles to share and talk about.

1. Styles argues that children are 'by and large hardy and resilient and need a literature to reflect that fact'. If you agree, how would this affect your choice of poetry for your age group?
2. 'Contemporary poetry favours the vernacular and tends to be informal.' Bearing in mind Style's comment, share with the group some contemporary poems for children that you favour. Include in your selection poems by writers from different parts of the world.

Figure 6.1 Front cover of *You Tell Me!* by Roger McGough and Michael Rosen. Cover illustration ©
2015 by Korky Paul. Reproduced with the permission of the publishers, Frances Lincoln
74–77 White Lion Street, London N1 9PF.

3. Childhood has always been a favourite theme explored by poets. Do you agree
   with those who consider this is because poets want to keep alive 'the child within
   themselves'?
4. Share with the group some of your own favourite traditional poems. What qualities
   do you consider make a poem stand the test of time?
5. Bring to the discussion group poems suitable for children by different poets about
   a particular topic – nature, magic, weather, school or family life – and compare the
   different treatments.
6. How would you justify – perhaps to the unconvinced – making poetry a central
   part of the literature programme for children in your specialist age range?
7. What do you consider might be the advantages of children learning by heart some
   of the poetry they enjoy? Explain how you would carry out a programme of readings by children – perhaps for another class or assembly.

Research inquiry

Either:

- Evaluate some poetry or nursery rhyme anthologies for two of the following age groups:

  - [ ] zero to five years;
  - [ ] five to seven years;
  - [ ] eight to eleven years.

Read some of the poems with your chosen age range and share with colleagues what you found were favourite themes and forms of poem.

- Choose a living, or recently living, poet who writes for children with whom you are not very familiar – perhaps Carol Ann Duffy, Ted Hughes, John Agard, John Hegley, Valerie Bloom or Debjani Chatterjee. Prepare a short paper to present to colleagues on the poet and their poems and how you have used/would use them in the classroom.

Or:

- After a series of poetry lessons with a group or class, ask each child to choose a poem, to write it out by hand and set out the reasons why they have chosen it. Select a small editorial team to anthologise the children's choices in a class book. You may find it helpful to read parts of K. Webb's book *I Like This Poem* to the children. Write a short paper explaining what you have learnt about children's preferences and attitudes and share the children's class book and your findings with colleagues.

Further reading

Mallett, M. (2010) Poetry: An introduction. In *Choosing and Using Fiction and Non-Fiction 3–11*, chapter 15. Abingdon and New York: Routledge. Chapters 16–19 go on to cover the features of the main poetry genres for children and some ways of approaching poems in the classroom.

Opie, I. (2004) Playground rhymes and the oral tradition. In P. Hunt (ed.) *International Companion Encyclopedia of Children's Literature*. London and New York: Routledge. This article updates some of the Opies' previous writing about playground rhymes by considering more recent approaches to studying children's folklore, including the role of increasingly sophisticated audio visual technology in recording chants and rhymes.

Opie, P. and Opie, I. (2000, new edition with introductions by Iona Opie and Marina Warner) *The Lore and Language of School Children*. Oxford: Oxford University Press. First published in 1957, this is a boundary-breaking collection of playground rhymes showing children's capacity for humour, subversive playfulness and urge to invent rhyme.

Potter, N. (2015) Interview with Michael Rosen. In the 'Author interview' series online, the English Association's Children's Literature Special Interest Group. Available at: engassoc@le.ac.uk.

Styles, M. (1998) *From the Garden to the Street: Three Hundred Years of Poetry for Children*. London: Continuum. Perhaps the most comprehensive and important contribution to our understanding of the history of children's poetry; it shows how each form developed over time – for example the move from Bunyan's country rhymes up to contemporary football chants.

Watson, V. (ed.) (2001) *The Cambridge Guide to Children's Books in English*. Cambridge: Cambridge University Press. See 'Playground rhymes' pages 569–71 for an analysis of the form and function of rhymes and chants which are partly simply to do with 'survival in the school playground'.

Wilson, A. and Scanlon, J. (2011, 4th edn) *Language Knowledge for Primary Teachers*. London and New York: Routledge. See pages 97–8 and pages 109–12 if you would welcome help and inspiration when working with children to grasp a poem's meaning. Wilson and Scanlon explore Kit Wright's poem 'The Frozen Man', which has an interesting layout so that the text works visually as well as verbally.

Zaghini, E. and Halford, D. (2006) *Universal Verse: Poetry for Children*. London: Barn Owl Books. Contains articles, for example by John Foster, Janette Otter-Barry and Morag Styles, and reviews of over 200 poetry books to help teachers select the best for their class.

Poetry anthologies for children

Cookson. P. (selector) (2010, 10th anniversary edn) *The Works*. Basingstoke and Oxford: Macmillan. Helpful in the classroom as it is a large tome with poems in different genres, both traditional and contemporary.

Duffy, C.A. and Stevenson, A. (illustrator) (2014) *New and Collected Poems for Children*. London: Faber. Taken largely from four previous volumes of poetry for children, this book has over 100 poems, some of them new. They are thought provoking and imaginative and probably best for children of age nine and over. 'Meeting Midnight' is full of lovely but quite sophisticated images and 'Late', about a child falling into a grave on her way home, is unsettling to say the least.

Fine, A. (2002) *A Shame to Miss*. London: Corgi. In volumes 1–3 for seven- to eleven-year-olds and with poems both traditional and new including some by Debjani Chatterjee, Brian Patten and Diana Hendry. It has a helpful introduction addressed to the young readers and useful annotation of the poems – with a light touch.

Foster, J. (compiler) (2000, 2009) *Twinkle Twinkle Chocolate Bar*. Oxford: Oxford University Press. An entertaining collection about childhood experiences compiled by an anthologist who understands what children like and with the work of such favourites as Michael Rosen, Wendy Cope, Brian Moses and Judith Nicholls. This collection is a good bridge between nursery verses and more demanding poems and includes 'Danger Game', John Walsh's poem, about Jessica playing on the escalator:

> 'When suddenly she tripped
> And the escalator ate her.'

Lines, K. and Jones, H. (illustrator) (2004) *Lavender's Blue: A Book of Nursery Rhymes*. Oxford: Oxford University Press. This facsimile edition of a 'timeless classic' is a comprehensive collection with some of the original eighteenth- and nineteenth-century woodcarving illustrations.

Rosen, M., McGough, R. and Paul, K. (illustrator) (2015, new edn) *You Tell Me!* London: Frances Lincoln. Contains some of the best poems of each poet.

Webb, K. and Maitland, A. (illustrator) (1979) *I Like This Poem: A Collection of Best-loved Poems Chosen by Children for Other Children in Aid of the International Year of the Child*. London: Puffin.

There are poems by William Wordsworth and Christina Rossetti as well as newer ones by Michael Rosen and Roald Dahl. Reasons for choosing a poem are included: Ursula likes to imagine 'the animals doing the things' in Edward Lear's poem 'The Owl and the Pussycat'. Michael Morpurgo comments that the selected poems 'sing to your soul'.

Wright, D. (compiler), Moriuchi, M. (illustrator) and Rosen, M. (introduction) (2015, 2nd edn) *My Village: Rhymes from Around the World*. London: Frances Lincoln. A lively selection for young children, including both amusing and thoughtful poems.

Section 2: Picturebooks

Extract 46

Source

Lewis, D. (2001) Describing the interaction between word and image. In *Reading Contemporary Picturebooks: Picturing Text*. London and New York: Routledge, 31–3.

'Picturebooks' are not just books with illustrations, but a recognised art form that combines the verbal and the visual in innovative and often intriguing ways. They flourished in the final decades of the twentieth century and remain a major part of contemporary children's literature. Every imaginable topic and theme is covered from the joyful to the tragic and the illustrations are created in an exciting range of media. Traditional oil and watercolour techniques have been joined by crayon, pastel, pen and ink, collage and digital media. Paper engineering has become even more adventurous with ever more elaborate pop-ups, wheels, pull-outs, carefully cropped pages to entertain and often to enhance the story. Their multi-layered nature makes them capable of being appreciated by children of different ages. Anthony Browne's *The Tunnel*, for instance, is used by teachers of children from age seven to eleven. Creators of picturebooks use a combination of design, illustrations and written text and so this section connects with Section 6 of this chapter on multimodality in comics and graphic books.

Few scholars have done more to enlighten us about the significance of the picturebook as an important cultural and artistic form than David Lewis. In the following extract he draws on a lifetime of research and teaching in exploring some of the ways in which word and image in picturebooks interact to create meaning.

> 'The big truth about picturebooks ... is that they are an interweaving of word and pictures. You don't have to tell the story in the words. You can come out of the words and into the pictures and you get this nice kind of antiphonal fugue effect' (Allan Ahlberg cited in Moss, 1990: 21).

> The picturebook began to be taken seriously as an object of academic study during the latter years of the twentieth century. The first major works in English

to address the form and nature, for example, *Ways of the Illustrator* by Joseph Schwarcz and *Words About Pictures* by Perry Nodelman were published in the 1980s (Schwarcz, 1982; Nodelman, 1988) and since then there has been a steady increase in the flow of articles, conference papers and book chapters dedicated to the study, criticism and analysis of the picturebook. There has been a gathering sophistication in the attempts to understand its properties, but I believe we are still some way off understanding many of the picturebook's most significant features. Even though we are experienced readers of verbal texts we are still learning how to read the picturebook, both in the sense of reading individual books, and in the sense of understanding how they work ...

Describing the interaction of word and image

When we read picturebooks we look at the pictures and we read the words and our eyes go back and forth between the two as we piece together the meaning of the text. In *Have You Seen Who Has Just Moved in Next Door to Us?* (see page 11) the rhyme at the top of each page directs our attention to characters and events, one or two at a time, represented in the street scene below. The scene itself, however, always overflows whatever the words say about it and our eyes are tempted to wander around, roving up and down the street, inspecting the houses and their occupants, reading the captions and speech balloons, grasping (or missing) the jokes and the puns. In *So Much*, the pictures show us a family at play. The words give us the sounds and rhythms and intonations of their speech so we watch what the aunties, cousins and grans do with the baby and 'hear' their exclamations of delight and declarations of affection. In *Drop Dead*, much of the verbal text is in the form of captions to preposterous pictures so that when we read of Gran and Grandad that '(They) forget things!' we look to the picture to see what has been forgotten and smile at the old man's missing trousers and the polka-dot boxer shorts.

Children reading picturebooks must also find routes through the text that connect words and images. Here six-year-old Jane reads to me from *Time to Get Out of the Bath, Shirley* by John Burningham. As she reads, she moves from the words to the pictures below the words and across the gutter to the scene on the right-hand page (words in capital letters represent book text read aloud).

J: HAVE YOU BEEN USING THIS TOWEL SHIRLEY OR WAS IT YOUR FATHER? ... (*looking at picture below*) probably her father 'cos it's got big hands.

DL: Hmm.

J: (*examining the picture to the right of the gutter*) She's gone on the back of the horse ... is that an owl or a bat? ... bat!

DL: Don't know ... could be.

J: Oh look, there's a witch.

Time to Get Out of the Bath, Shirley, and its sister text, *Come Away from the Water, Shirley* are justly famous for their teasing quality, the way words and pictures do not seem to fully match. In the former story, Shirley is taking a bath while her mother potters about the bathroom uttering banal remarks like the one in the extract above. At each page-opening the pictures beneath the words show mother at the moment of speaking while those to the right of the gutter show Shirley to be involved in an adventure involving storybook knights and kings and queens which we may suppose is taking place in her imagination. The words act as a prompt for further investigation of the page, for on their own they simply do not tell us enough about what is going on. Jane actively scans and interrogates both pictures, searching for semantic links that will help her piece together the story. Picturebook text is thus usually composite, an 'interweaving of words and pictures' as Allan Ahlberg puts it. The metaphor of weaving is useful for not only does it pick out for us the sensation we have when reading a picturebook of shuttling between one medium and another, but it is also related, through sense and meaning to the term *text* which is itself etymologically and semantically close to *textile*. A text in this sense is something woven together, a cohesive patter of inter-related strands that adds up to more than a mere accumulation of individual parts. For this interweaving to proceed, however, we need to have the images and the words displayed before us in fairly close proximity to each other. It is not much use if the two strands – the weft and the warp, so as to speak – are on different pages or are so far apart that they cannot be brought together in the act of reading. If the words are on one set of pages and the pictures elsewhere in the book, as is frequently the case in longer texts and illustrated novels, then it becomes difficult for the two forms of representation to enter into the construction of the story together. We now take the sophisticated combinations of word and image in books, magazines and advertising for granted but it is only relatively recently that printing technology has permitted this creative freedom.

Extract references

Moss, E. (1990) A certain particularity: An interview with Janet and Allan Ahlberg. *Signal*, 61, 20–6.

Nodelman, P. (1988) *Words About Pictures: The Narrative Art of Children's Picturebooks.* Athens, Georgia: University of Georgia Press.

Schwarcz, J.H. (1982) *Ways of the Illustrator: Visual Communication in Children's Literature.* Chicago: American Library Association.

Children's books in the extract

Burningham, J. (1977) *Come Away from the Water, Shirley.* London: Jonathan Cape.

Burningham, J. (1978) *Time to Get Out of the Bath, Shirley.* London: Jonathan Cape.

Cole, B. (1996) *Drop Dead.* London: Jonathan Cape.

Cooke, T. and Oxenbury, H. (illustrator) (1994) *So Much.* London: Walker Books.

McNaughton, C. (1991) *Have You Seen Who Has Just Moved in Next Door to Us?* London: Walker Books.

Comment

David Lewis builds his account on Allan Ahlberg's metaphor of the picturebook as a composite in which words and pictures, the verbal and the visual, are interwoven. The metaphor of the act of reading a picturebook as 'weaving' strikes Lewis as apt because the reader has to move back and forth between image and words to make meaning. Further, he points out that the word 'text' is 'etymologically and semantically close to *textile*' and this reinforces the notion of a weaving together, which creates something that becomes more than 'a mere accumulation of individual parts'. This analysis helps us to distinguish between illustrated books for children, whether novels or short stories, where sometimes for practical reasons the pictures are not necessarily alongside or even close to the written text to which they relate, and picturebooks where words and illustrations combine to make meaning. In the case study, six-year-old Jane moves spontaneously between words and pictures and shows us how her reading experience skilfully combines the two.

Questions to discuss with colleagues

It would be helpful for participants to bring some picturebooks for their chosen age group to the discussion.

1. With reference to a picturebook, suggest how recent developments in print technology have created new possibilities in linking words and images to make meaning.
2. Later on in the book from which the extract is taken, Lewis recognises the limitations of the 'weaving' metaphor when tested against some books. Sometimes, for example, an author will deploy words and pictures which are contradictory. Lewis points to Pat Hutchins' *Rosie's Walk* as an amusing example of this. Discuss what is powerful about *Rosie's Walk* and why it and books using a similar device seem to appeal to children.
3. Can some picturebooks have appeal for more than one age phase? Choose an example and suggest how you would use it with (a) children aged five and under, (b) children aged six and over.

Research inquiries

Either:

■ Choose a picturebook which you consider has potential appeal for children under six years. Read the book with one young learner or a small group. Note the children's spontaneous comments by recording the conversation or simply jotting down observations in a notebook. You might like to ask them about the books, tablet material and DVDs they have at home. Do they read picturebooks and stories online? Using these comments, write up a short analysis and include some thoughts on how the modern cultural context – for example the prevalence of digital technology or postmodern approaches to narrative – affects how children read/listen to and look at the pictures in the book.

Picturebook suggestions for younger children

Ahlberg, A. and Ahlberg, J. (illustrator) (2009, large format edn) *The Jolly Postman*. London: Puffin. This picturebook with its fairy tale characters and wonderful letters (including a letter of apology to the three bears from Goldilocks) was a landmark in the history of the genre. A classic? – certainly!

Almond, D. and Dunbar, P. (2014) *The Boy Who Climbed Into the Moon*. London: Walker Books. A bored little boy is helped to climb into the moon. Good for reading aloud and with great potential for children's discussion, writing and drawing.

Burningham, J. (2004) *The Magic Bed*. London: Jonathan Cape. Children and adults see the world differently. Young George is horrified when his beloved bed – where he has wonderful adventures in his imagination – has been replaced by a new one!

Daywait, D. and Jeffers, O. (illustrator) (2014) *The Day the Crayons Quit*. London: HarperCollins. The crayons are grumbling, for example the grey crayon is tired of colouring elephants and whales. How can Duncan get his mutinous crayons working together again? Some artwork by children.

Gravett, E. (2008) *The Little Mouse's Great Book of Fears*. London: Macmillan. The supreme example of the playful crossing of boundaries we expect from a delightfully postmodern book. Young children will empathise with the mouse – for example when he is sucked down a plughole.

Tullet, H. (2011) *Press here*. London: Chronicle Books. You can have an interactive experience without internet access or a battery.

Willis, J. and Ross, T. (illustrator) (2012) *Hippospotamus*. London: Andersen Press. About solving a conundrum.

Or:

■ If you are working with children at the older end of the primary age range, read and discuss with a small group a picturebook that you consider raises deep, human issues. Ask the children if they think the picturebook genre is a helpful one for exploring difficult experiences and feelings, for example to do with conflict, loneliness and sad events. Work with the class or group with a whiteboard or flip chart to capture the children's thoughts and conclusions.

Suggested books for older primary school children

Davies, N. and Carlin, L. (illustrator) (2013) *The Promise*. London: Walker Books. A thief reforms. Huge potential for philosophical discussion, not least about the importance of caring for the natural world.

Duffy, C.A. (2008) *The Lost Happy Endings*. London: Bloomsbury. Jub, the keeper of happy endings, has to find them after a witch with 'eyes like poisonous berries' has stolen them.

Jeffers, O. (2012) *The Heart in the Bottle*. London: HarperCollins. Profound story about love, loss and recovery.

Messenger, N. (2012) *The Land of Neverbelieve*. London and Somerville, MA: Candlewick Press. This great illustrator takes readers on a journey through an imaginary island with strange plants, creatures and doll-like beings. Pictures are detailed, lustrous and intensely coloured.

Smith, L. (2012) *It's a Book*. London: Macmillan. In a digital world, why is the print book still special?

Tan, S. (2007) *The Arrival*. London: Hodder Children's Books. A wordless, graphic picturebook with sepia illustrations that tells the story of a refugee's experiences in a new land. Older primary school children's visual literacy would be enriched by perusing and talking about these atmospheric and often moving drawings.

Ward, H. (2013) *Varmints*. Dorking, Surrey: Templar. With spare text and interesting artwork, this book makes the case powerfully for protecting the countryside.

N.B. As teachers know, picturebooks are multi-layered and the same book can be enjoyed by children of different ages, so the lists – which contain only a sample of the developing treasure store of superb creations – are offered to be used flexibly.

Further reading

Arizpe, E. and Styles, M. (2006, 2nd edn) *Children Reading Picturebooks: Interpreting Visual Text*. Abingdon: Routledge. This is an account of a valuable two-year study of children's responses to picturebooks created by Anthony Browne and Satoshi Kitamura. The children showed they were sophisticated readers of visual texts, able to understand feelings and to analyse different viewpoints.

Figure 6.2 Front cover of *The Promise* by Nicola Davies, illustrated by Laura Carlin. Cover illustration © 2013 Laura Carlin. Reproduced by permission of Walker Books Ltd., London SE11 5HU.

Burningham, J. (2012) *John Burningham Behind the Scenes*. London: Red Fox. The book begins with a foreword by Burningham's much revered contemporary, the US picturebook creator, Maurice Sendak, followed by an appreciation of Burningham's work by Brian Alderson. The rest of the book is John's account of his childhood, schooling and writing and illustrating career.

Graham, J. (2005) Reading contemporary picturebooks. In K. Reynolds (ed.) *Modern Children's Literature*. Basingstoke: Palgrave Macmillan, 209–26. Offers a careful analysis of different kinds of picturebook, including those that are wordless, with many examples and comments on how children read and make meaning from them.

Graham, J. (2008) Picturebooks, looking closely. In P. Goodwin (ed.) *Understanding Children's Books: A Guide for Professionals*, chapter 10. London: Sage Publications. Offers useful visual terminology and considers what different kinds of picturebook offer to children.

Nikolajeva, M. and Scott, C (2006, 2nd edn) *How Picturebooks Work*. Abingdon: Routledge. This interesting account explains much about word–image relationships in this genre of children's literature. The power of imagery in different categories of picturebook and how this relates to children's learning about the world is a strong theme in the book.

Van der Pol, C. (2012) Reading picturebooks as literature: Four- to six-year-old children and the development of literary competence. *Children's Literature in Education*, 1 January. A case study showing how young children learn to 'read' the genre.

Section 3: Traditional tales

Extract 47

Source

Cook, E. (1971) Myths, legends and fairy tales in the lives of children. In *The Ordinary and the Fabulous*. Cambridge: Cambridge University Press, 1–2, 6–9.

Traditional tales are ancient stories passed down the generations and include fairy and folk tales, myths, legends, fables and creation stories. They were first told and later on written down. They tell about enduring aspects of human nature, both at its best and its worst, and children learn from them about what is feared and what is valued in their own and other cultures. Young readers and listeners to the tales enter worlds that have their own logic and rules. The best can stretch young imaginations as curiosity is awakened: many of the stories seem to ask 'what if?' – what if I had three wishes or what if I had to escape from a giant? Theses puzzles are likely to nudge children towards independent and creative ponderings and these are a mark of critical thinking.

Elizabeth Cook, for many years a senior lecturer in English at Homerton College in Cambridge, was deeply interested in finding the best ways to introduce children to traditional tales. Much of the book from which the extract is taken is devoted to evaluating different 'tellings' by this pioneer in the development of critical approaches to children's literature. I have chosen two extracts from near the beginning of the book. The first gives a little background history, while the second illuminates those attributes of the best traditional tales which make them stories with special value and appeal for children under eleven. The extract concludes with a succinct set of ideas for encouraging children's creative response to their listening to or reading of the tales.

Past and present passions

… In rough and ready phrasing myths are about gods, legends are about heroes, and fairy tales are about woodcutters and princesses. A rather more respectable definition might run: myths are about the creation of all things, the origin of evil, and the salvation of man's soul; legends and sagas are about the doings of kings and peoples in the period before records were kept; fairy tales, folk tales and fables are about human behaviour in a world of magic, and often become incorporated in legends. Critics take an endless interest in the differences between them, but the common reader is more struck by the ways in which they all look rather like each other … They are not realistic; they are almost unlocalised in time and space; they are often supernatural or at least fantastic in character; and the human beings in them are not three-dimensional people with complex motives and temperaments. These stories do hold a mirror up to nature, but they do not reflect the world as we perceive it with our senses at the present moment. J.R.R. Tolkien, who has written fairy tales and legends, sees them as works of 'sub-creation': in reading them we live in a Secondary World which is internally consistent and intricate, and is related to the Primary World (in which we all live for most of the time) by the human prerogative of generalisation and abstraction. 'The mind that thought of *light, heavy, grey, yellow, still, swift,* also conceived of magic that would make heavy things light and able to fly, turn grey lead into gold, and the still rock into swift water.' Until the end of the eighteenth century traditional 'fairy tales' formed, almost by accident, the greater part of storytelling for very young children: uneducated nurses and servants told children the old stories they had been told themselves, because they were the only stories they knew. In the second half of the nineteenth century the work of men like Charles Kingsley and Andrew Lang was diverting the reading of eight- to twelve-year-olds away from drably realistic, moralising Victorian stories into the world of myth and 'faerie'. The Greek and Northern myths had become standard classroom reading by the 1920s … Since the last war many fresh versions of myths and legends have been made by accomplished and imaginative writers for children … Roger Lancelyn Green, Barbara Leonie Picard and Ian Seraillier. The original work of C.S. Lewis in the *Chronicles of Narnia* and J.R.R. Tolkien in *The Lord of the Rings* shows that the world of 'faerie' is not a dead world. The eight- to fourteen-year-olds who are never invited to enter it are, quite literally, deprived children.

Children's likes and dislikes

… Children under eleven are eager to know what happens next, and impatient with anything that stops them from getting on with the story. They want to listen to conversations only if direct speech is the quickest and clearest method of showing what was transacted between two people as a necessary preliminary to what these two people proceeded to *do*. At about nine or ten they are beginning to be interested in character, but in very straightforward and moral ways: they see people as marked by one particular attribute, cleverness, or kindness, or strictness, or being a good shot and they mind whether things are right or wrong. They are especially sensitive to the heroic view of justice, and they are beginning to notice why people are tempted to be unjust. They are not interested in the long processes of inner debate by which people make difficult decisions, and become very irritated with grown-ups who insist upon giving them not only the practical answer or information they have asked for but also all the reasons for it. They expect a story to be a good yarn, in which the action is swift and the characters are clearly and simply defined. And legends and fairy tales are just like that. Playground games show that children like catastrophes and exhibitions of speed and power, and a clear differentiation between cowboys, cops, and spacemen who are good, and Indians, robbers and space monsters who are bad.

Magic has a particular attraction for eight- to ten-year-olds, but not because it is pretty or 'innocent'. They delight, in more senses than the usual one, in seeing how far they can go. If some people are taller than others, how tall could anyone conceivably be. If some people are cleverer than others at making things, could someone alter what things are made of? … Such speculations carried *ad infinitum* are given concrete form in giants, and the enchantments of elves and dwarfs, and the magic of runes and spells. The 'if' kind of question always requires consistency in the answer, and children of this age are often fascinated by consistency for its own sake, looking at patterns because they are patterns, and working out for themselves intricate maps of imaginary islands and imaginary towns. The whole visual world of the Greek myths (or the Northern myths, or the Arthurian romances) satisfies this imaginatively, because of the consistent mood, form and colouring of its landscapes. So does the detail of most mythical conceptions. If the moon were a goddess, or if a goddess were the moon, where would she move, and what creatures would draw her chariot? …

Stories that lead to doing things are all the more attractive to children, who are active rather than passive creatures. Myths and fairy tales provide an unusually abundant choice of things to do. Largely because they are archetypal and anonymous (in quality, if not in provenance), they will stand reinterpretation in many forms without losing their character. They can be recreated by children not only in words but in drama, in mime, in dance and in painting. Action in them is not fussy, and lends itself to qualitative expression in the movements of the human body and the shapes and colours of non-figurative painting. I have seen two ten-year-olds playing at Theseus and the Minotaur in a solitary orchard with no grown-ups, as they thought, within sight or hearing.

Comment

Elizabeth Cook presents a convincing argument for giving traditional tales of all kinds a firm place in the literature programme for under-elevens. Narratives tend to be clear and there is usually dialogue that moves the action on. It is true that characters tend to be one dimensional – clever, brave, unkind and so on – but this suits the age group. Children will understand the characters' motives and enjoy speculating about what magic might make possible. Clues about what children will respond to are evident in their playground games and improvisations. Cook's book may no longer be at the top of lists of required reading on teaching courses, but her book contains much wisdom together with useful practical ideas for extending children's response.

Questions to discuss with colleagues

It would be helpful for you to bring examples of what you consider to be good retellings of traditional stories from different cultures to the discussion.

1. After reading the extract, consider the criteria you might use in selecting traditional tales for your age group.
2. Some comic strips and cartoons – *Wallace and Gromit* and *Thomas the Tank Engine* for example – seem to have some of the features of fables. Do you agree? If so, how might a teacher fruitfully link traditional fables with popular culture?
3. With reference to particular texts, share what you consider to be the advantages of talking with your class about traditional literature from different countries.
4. At the end of Extract 47 Elizabeth Cook sets out some ideas for children's activities. Perhaps with a particular traditional story in mind, how might you plan for children's creative activities to assimilate the meaning of the tale?

Research inquiries

Either:

■ Choose two or more retellings of the same traditional tale – be it fable, creation story, fairy tale, myth or legend – suitable for your age range and compare

　□ the language used (including the quality of the dialogue);
　□ the illustrations.

■ Read the different tellings to a group or class of children and ask their views, putting their points on a flip chart or whiteboard. Write a short account of your findings to present to the group.

Or:

- Read a modern fairy tale, or several tales, to a group or class and try out some activities to encourage a creative response from the children. Write an evaluation of your lesson or series of lessons.

Traditional tales for the under-elevens

Brocklehurst, R., Doherty, G. and Ligi, R. (illustrator) (2010) *Illustrated Grimm's Fairy Tales*. London: Usborne. Lively dialogue makes these retellings of the classic tales of the Grimm brothers appealing to the very young. Some of the more frightening episodes are omitted. 5+

Dickens, R. and Marks, A. (2009) *The Usborne Fairy Tale Treasury*. London: Usborne Children's Books. Classic retellings of tales by the Grimm brothers and Hans Andersen with evocative watercolour illustrations. 7+

Duffy, C.A. and Hyde, C. (illustrator) (2008) *The Princess Blankets*. Dorking, Surrey: Templar. A modern fairy tale with some traditional elements and an interesting vocabulary which might inspire drama, discussion and writing. 9+

Duffy, C.A. and Tomic, T. (illustrator) (2014, ornate cover edn) *Faery Tales*. London: Faber & Faber. Vigorous retellings in a visually appealing presentation of Grimm tales, tales from other countries and some new ones. Does not miss out some brutal events. 9+

Grifalconi, A. and Nelson, K. (illustrator) (2010) *The Village That Vanished*. Wincanton, Somerset: Ragged Bears. Moving story about how the Yao people of East Africa overcame the threat of violent people from the north. Communicates a tremendous sense of place and much suspense. 8+

Hoffman, M. and Downing, J. (illustrator) (2006) *A First Book of Fairy Tales*. London: Dorling Kindersley. A good introduction for the very young to some of the best known tales from the European tradition including 'Cinderella' and 'Jack and the Beanstalk'. Written in simple but not banal language and rich with charming illustrations. 3+

Hughes, T. (author and reader) (1996) *The Dreamfighter and Other Creation Tales*. London: Penguin Audio Books. Spell-binding tales brought together from previous collections. 8+

Hughes, T. and Morris, J. (illustrator) (2008 edn) *How the Whale Became and Other Stories*. London: Frances Lincoln. The skilful use of dialogue makes these tales good for reading aloud. 5+

McCaughrean, G. and Willey, B. (illustrator) (1995) *Myths and Legends of the World: The Golden Hoard*. London: Orion Children's Books. Fifty stories from many countries including Greece, China, Ethiopia and the West Indies. Benefits from the author's good ear for convincing dialogue. 7+

McCaughrean, G. and Ross, T. (illustrator) (1998) *The Wooden Horse*. (Orchard Myths). London: Orchard Books. One of a series of riveting tellings with the added bonus of Tony Ross's witty illustrations. 6+

Pinkney, J. (2000) *Aesop's Fables*. New York: SeaStar. This collection of straightforward tellings was placed thirty-fourth in Booktrust's survey of the best books of all time. 6+

Riorden J. (2000) *The Coming of the Night: A Yoruba Creation Myth from West Africa*. London: Frances Lincoln. Strong telling of this ancient tale and illustrations that show well the distinctive landscapes and characters. 5+

Soames, B. (reader) (2006) *More Tales from the Greek Legends*. Welwyn, Hertfordshire: Naxos Audiobooks. Legends can come alive in good audio recordings. This one includes 'Orpheus and Eurydice' and 'Narcissus and Echo'. 9+

Wilde, O. (1999 edn) *The Happy Prince and Other Stories*. London: Wordsworth. First published in 1886, there are now many editions. The title story tells of the remorse of a prince when he sees the distress of his people and tries, at last, to help. 9+

Wilde, O. *The Happy Prince*, read by Stephen Fry on YouTube at: https://www.youtube.com/watch?v=t33NWgOzjK8 (date of reading 1st July 2013, accessed 10th September 2015). A sensitive reading of a moving tale by a master story-teller. 9+.

Williams, M. (2006 edn) *Greek Myths*. London: Walker Books. These amusing tellings in cartoon format are likely to encourage children's own writing, drama and artwork. 8+

Further reading

Bettelheim, B. (1991) *The Uses of Enchantment: The Meaning and Importance of Fairy Tales*. Harmondsworth: Penguin. What do fairy tales 'mean' and what special benefits have they for children? This classic text suggests some answers and explains how fairy tales can nourish children's inner life and, among many other things, show that you can succeed against the odds: for example, as shown in 'Puss in Boots', 'Cinderella' and 'Jack and the Beanstalk'.

Bottigheimer, R.B. (2004) Fairy Tales and Folk Tales. In P. Hunt (ed.) *The International Companion Encyclopedia of Children's Literature*. London and New York: Routledge. The author helps

Figure 6.3 Front cover of *The Coming of Night* by James Riordan. Cover illustration © 2000 Jenny Stow. Reproduced by permission of the publishers Frances Lincoln, 74–77 White Lion Street, London N1 9PF.

readers distinguish between fairy tales and folk tales. With reference to fairy tales in the USA and different European countries, she believes that these 'depict the quests, tasks, trials and sufferings of usually royal heroes and heroines as well as intersections between their lives and fairyland inhabitants'. The folk tale, on the other hand, 'embraces a multitude of minor genres, like nonsense tales, jests, burlesques, animal tales and neverending tales'. Some derive from chapbook romances.

Dix, P. (2014) Ten of the best traditional tales retold. *Books for Keeps*, 209.

Halford, D.P. and Zaghoni, E. (2004) *Folk Tales and Fairy Tales: A Book Guide*. London: Booktrust. Provides annotated lists of the different categories of traditional tales.

Mallett, M. (2011, 4th edn) Traditional tales. In *The Primary English Encyclopedia: The Heart of the Curriculum*. London and New York: Routledge, 438–9. Looks at the overlapping of the different kinds of traditional tale: fairy and folk tales, myths and legends, creation stories and fables.

Saxby, M. (2004, 2nd edn) Myth and legend. In P. Hunt (ed.) *International Companion Encyclopedia of Children's Literature*. London and New York: Routledge. A scholarly analysis of the history and value of 'traditional literature', which ends with the observation that it is timeless and increasingly multicultural.

Section 4: Short stories

Extract 48

Source

Bearne, E. (4 October 2004) *Short Stories for Children*. Unpublished paper presented to students on the Children's Literature M.Ed. course, University of Cambridge Faculty of Education.

In recent years much critical attention has, justifiably, been given to a great flowering of the children's picture book and the children's novel, while short stories have received relatively little critical attention. Yet short stories can offer a distinctive reading and listening experience. Their economical form means that plot, characters and themes are established swiftly. This helps children develop an understanding of 'story structure' and narrative. They can help build the stamina of newly independent readers; and serve as bridging books, books which move from those that communicate through pictures and text equally to books in which print is the main conveyer of meaning. For older children, short stories can provide sophisticated reading material – material that can interest, challenge, intrigue and sometimes unsettle. Because the short story stable includes many different themes and forms, it can introduce children to what has been termed 'genre fiction': mysteries, science fiction, ghost and horror stories. In Extract 48, Eve Bearne provides some historical background and suggests that the short story reflects the views of childhood at a particular time.

I have excluded from this all forms of short story which began in the oral tradition – so folk tales, fairy tales, myths and legends are not included. The short story as defined here is essentially a print medium narrative. Early short stories for children were not always fictional, however, and many were meant to be recounts of genuine experiences, presented to children as moral lessons, so that in the early years of the form there was no necessarily clear dividing line between fiction and fact (or stories claiming to be factual). It is also worth noting that although the short story is a ubiquitous form of narrative, very little critical attention has been paid to it.

As Jan Mark's introduction to *The Oxford Book of Children's Short Stories* indicates, the short story for children pre-dates the short story for adults, particularly in the form of the 'frame novel' encapsulating a string of tales within one setting. It was for many years a form of instruction (1993, 2001). James Janeway was one of the very earliest writers of short stories for children, although he would not have considered himself as a fiction writer when he published *A Token for Children* in 1672. These were highly moralistic stories which often focused on deathbed scenes ...

Slightly later writers include Sarah Fielding (who wrote *The Governess* or *The History of the Fairfield Family*, one of the first frame novels) and Thomas Day (who began publishing *The History of Sandford and Merton* in 1783 – another frame novel). These were very much part of the reading experience of young middle-class readers. In *Good Wives*, we are told that Jo read Mrs Sherwood, Miss Edgworth and Hannah More as she tried to write a children's story but refused to bend to the formula of: '... naughty boys being eaten by bears or tossed by mad bulls, because they did not go to a particular Sabbath school, nor all the good infants who did go, of course, as rewarded by every kind of bliss, from gilded gingerbread to escorts of angels, when they departed this life with psalms or sermons on their lisping tongues' (L.M. Alcott *Good Wives*, 1869).

Similarly, Susan Coolidge in *What Katie Did at School* describes one of the children falling asleep while reading an 'improving' text by Mrs Hannah More and rolling off the sofa!

But the stories weren't always unrelieved didacticism and Mrs Sherwood did write in a more tolerant mode about young children's desires and feelings. Generally, however, the view of childhood represented in many of these early narratives for children was one of their imperfection and need for moral improvement. There was also a sense that these were 'guidelines to growing up, to learning by experience' (Mark, 1994, p. 23). Thomas Day reveals some enlightened attitudes where, in *The History of Sandford and Merton*, Tommy Merton's father realises that his son is a rather indulged and selfish child, engages a tutor for him and a companion who is the son of a neighbouring farmer. Harry Sandford is hard working and diligent – the opposite of Tommy Merton – and the book follows the development of their friendship as, with the guidance of their tutor, they learn humanity by experience. Similarly, in *Evenings at Home* by Anna Laetita Barbauld and John Aiken, containing stories to be read together by parents and children, there were some surprisingly 'modern' views ... 'Wars are very seldom to the real advantage of any nation' and 'a humane man will scarcely rejoice in them' (*Evenings at Home*, 1790) ...

One of the 'problems' of reading stories written for children so long ago is the necessary shift in attitudes which has happened in the intervening years. The content and high moral tone make it difficult to recognise the tales as having literary worth, although Jan Mark points out that modern authors may be held up to derision in future centuries: 'We all date. But whereas with adult fiction people are willing to read in context, we do not seem able to make that same effort for children's literature and to be fully appreciated, these stories have to be read in context, the context of an age with which we are not familiar' (Ibid. p. 25) …

At the beginning of the 20th century, many (short stories) would have been found in magazines and journals. Again, looking at compendiums of these stories, it can be quite surprising how enlightened (or open-minded) some of these stories were. The beginning of the 20th century saw some rather 'twee' stories for children, often involving fairies (and Christopher Robin!), as well as the inventive *Just So Stories* from Rudyard Kipling, but these were off-set by the healthy William stories by Richmal Crompton (from 1920 onwards). After the war of 1939–45 there was 'a new generation of skilled, innovative, witty and prolific writers' (Mark, 1994, p. 35): Joan Aiken, Philippa Pearce, William Mayne, Bill Naughton and Robert Leeson. More recently there have also been representatives of writers from other cultures – James Berry and Farrukh Dhondy, for example.

When considering short stories for children, it is not easy to escape the fact that every age tells stories intended to shape children into the adults that society wants. Children are constructed in and through the narratives. Where the earlier stories presented children as in need of moral instruction, later writers showed a more realistic (if at times idealistic) portrait of childhood. Echoing the kinds of developments in children's novels, there has been a proliferation of short stories for children and young readers in the last fifty years. One factor which does not seem to have changed much is the matter of setting. Most short stories for children, from the earliest to relatively recent narratives, occupy domestic settings. There are very few which stray from home. However, one significant development over the last thirty or so years has been the rise of a 'new' genre – the fantasy/horror/ghost story for children, but despite the rise of new content, many of these stories also take place in homes, with families.

Extract references

Mark, J. (1993/2001) Introduction. In *The Oxford Book of Children's Stories*. Oxford: Oxford University Press.

Mark, J. (1994) The Patrick Hardy Lecture. *Signal*, 75. Stroud: Thimble Press, 19–36.

Comment

Eve Bearne gives a succinct account of the history of the short story for children and how the form has developed. Many of the first short stories for children had, like the first poems written for children, a moralistic and improving tone and aimed to shape thinking and behaviour to conform with the societal norms of the time in which they were written. She points out that the indoctrinatory tone makes many of the stories difficult to appreciate as literature. There were exceptions to unrelieved didacticism, for example the stories of the writer Mrs Sherwood communicate children's feelings.

But, on the whole, we have to wait until the twentieth century to find writers whose short stories are of true literary merit. These writers, many of them writing after the Second World War, give a real sense of how a young person experiences their world and the people around them, and use wit and imagination to bring their stories alive. (A transcript of a group of children talking about a short story by one of the twentieth-century writers Bearne mentions, Philippa Pearce, is set out in Extract 9 in Chapter 2.)

While many short stories for children continue to be in domestic settings, there has been a broadening of the range of genres into ghost stories, science fiction, fantasy and even horror. One interesting thing I discovered when I first read this extract is the existence of the 'frame novel' associated with early short story writers like Sarah Fielding and Thomas Day. This is defined as a book of a string of stories within one setting and is still being written by contemporary writers of such collections as *My Naughty Little Sister* (Dorothy Edwards) and *Horrid Henry* (Francesca Simon).

Questions to discuss with colleagues

It would be helpful if you would do some preparation by reading some short stories from different genres.

1. Discuss how we might classify short stories.
2. Why do you think that many short stories are placed in domestic settings?
3. What do you consider is the reason for many children liking stories about aliens, ghosts and suchlike?
4. What are the things we look for in short stories for each of the following age groups: under fives; six to eight years; nine to eleven years?
5. How do short stories (as do children's novels) reflect changing constructions of childhood? What implications for choice of theme and style of writing might there be for short story writers living and writing today in our more diverse society?
6. Look at examples of children's stories written some time ago that are still in print. What qualities do those that endure over the years seem to have?

Suggestions for short story collections

Almond, D. (2007) *Counting Stars*. London: Hodder Children's Books. 'The Middle Earth', like many of Almond's other stories, communicates a sense of place powerfully and taps into the feelings of and experiences of children growing up in the north-east. 9+

Cabot, M. and Horowitz, A. (eds) (2011) *Midnight Feast*. London: HarperCollins. This is a treasure store of stories of different genres – many combining humour and magic. See, for example, 'The Unexpected Godmother' by Margaret Mahy about coping with change that may not be welcome. 10+

Cameron, A. and Smith, J (illustrator) (2013 edn) *The Julian Stories*. London: Tamarind. Amusing stories about a warm, lively African American family. 6+

Compton, R. (2006 edn) *Just William*. London: Macmillan Children's Books. One of a number of classic collections of stories about the adventures of William and the 'Outlaws' gang. 8+

Cooling, W. (compiler) (1996) *The Puffin Book of Stories for Eight Year Olds*. London: Puffin. Joan Aiken's story 'A Necklace of Raindrops' tells of the consequences of a little girl's gift from the North Wind. 'A Picnic with the Aunts' is riveting too – the boys' visit to an island in the middle of a lake does not go to plan! 7+

Crossley-Holland, K. (1998, 2011) *Short! A Book of Very Short Stories; Short Two! A Second Book of Very Short Stories*. Oxford: Oxford University Press. 8+ – but bear in mind that some of the stories are frightening.

Dahl, R. and Blake, Q. (illustrator) (2013 edn) *The Magic Finger and Other Stories*. London: Puffin. Delightfully brutal humour loved by children but not by all adults! 7+

Edwards, D. and Hughes, S. (illustrator) (2013) *My Naughty Little Sister Collection*. London: Egmont. Includes all five books. In my experience – liked by boys and girls first as listeners, then as readers. 4+

Gamble, N. (compiler) (2006) *Story Shop: Stories for Literacy*. London: Wayland Children's Books. Sixty short stories for seven- to eleven-year-olds in many different genres – historical fiction, fantasy, domestic stories and adventure – by such favourite writers as Robert Leeson, Malorie Blackman and Penelope Lively. 7+

Howker, J. (2007 edn) *Badger on the Barge and Other Stories*. London: Walker Books. The developing friendship between a school girl and an eccentric old woman she has been asked to visit is described movingly. 9+

Mark, J. (compiler) (2001 edn) *The Oxford Book of Children's Stories*. Oxford: Oxford University Press. As this collection covers more than 250 years, it helps understanding of the development of the form. 9+

Pearce, P. (2000 edn) *The Rope and Other Stories*. London: Puffin. A story about peer rivalry in which suspense builds. 9+

Van Allsburg, C. (2013) *The Chronicles of Harris Burdick*. London: Andersen Press. These fourteen stories came about in an interesting way: they were inspired by the intriguing paintings created by Chris Van Allsburg. Older primary children would enjoy weaving their own stories round the pictures. 9+

Wilde, O. (2009, reissued edn) *The Happy Prince and Other Stories*. London: Puffin Classics. The stories have a moral message, but a different one to that of earlier times. 8+

Research inquiries

Either:

■ Look over three or four short story collections and make an annotated list of the stories you think children in your specialist age group would enjoy. You might like to arrange your annotated list under headings following the discussion about classifying short stories.

And/Or:

■ Read some short stories with a class or group of children in your specialist age range over a week or so. Discuss which stories they like best and why. This might lead on to the children writing their own stories and arranging them in a class book. Older children might like to learn about how stories are anthologised and to appoint an editorial team to arrange the stories of members of the class and to write an introduction.

Further reading

Hollindale, P. (2001) Short stories for young readers: The neglected genre. *Books for Keeps*, 128. Considering that short stories can often be told in their entirety during a single lesson, it seems odd that they are not more favoured by teachers. This author considers their potential merits with reference to his own favourite collections.

Mills, C. and Webb, J. (2004) Selecting books for younger readers. In P. Hunt (ed.) *International Companion Encyclopedia of Children's Literature*. London and New York: Routledge. See page 775 for an account of 'bridging books' which suit newly independent readers who need books where pictures help with understanding, but where the written text becomes more central.

Section 5: Longer stories and novels – print, graphic, audio and film versions

Extract 49

Source

Mallett, M. (2010) Genre features of longer stories and novels. In M. Mallett (ed.) *Choosing and Using Fiction and Non-Fiction 3–11*. Abingdon and New York: Routledge, 99–100.

The novel, both classic and contemporary, is a huge and important category of children's literature and any discussion about it is bound to be selective. Most novels and longer stories could be flexibly placed in one of the following four categories: stories about animals; realistic stories (domestic, adventure and school); historical; fantasy. Novels for children, like those for adults, are sustained fictional narratives, long enough for the detailed development of character and plot. If we want children to become eager and critical readers of fiction, we need to provide within the school collection a range of different books by different writers whose experiences and viewpoints differ from one another. The children's novel now receives deserved critical attention in journals and scholarly books as well as in reviews in books, journals and online. Awards for the best new children's novels are well established and the selection of a Children's Laureate, very often an acclaimed writer or illustrator, to serve for three years in the United Kingdom helps to recognise the importance of children's literature.

The following extract has been chosen to examine some of the elements of novels identified by narratologists, for example story 'structure', 'shape' or 'grammar' and then goes on to identify some of the choices a writer makes.

> We owe it to our pupils to introduce them to exciting and imaginative writing; if you are sufficiently swept up by a long story to persevere with it, then you have made progress on the reading journey. In addition to the traditional print book we have audiobooks, stories in the form of film and electronic books. All offer a

distinctive experience and children can be enthralled by graphics and the moving image. However a print novel provides a unique and sustained reading experience.

Longer stories and novels for children have a story 'structure', 'shape' or 'grammar'. At its most basic a story structure has a beginning or 'orientation' in which the setting is established and the main characters introduced, a middle and an end, where conflicts are resolved or, at any rate, partially resolved. Some narratologists and linguists include a 'special event' after the 'orientation' stage which energises the tale and sets a series of events in motion (Gamble and Yates, 2008: 62). The point at which Tom accepts Willie into his care as an evacuee in *Goodnight Mister Tom* seems to be a 'special event' leading to all sorts of happenings. Robert Longacre calls this 'special event' an 'inciting moment'; he, along with others, also places a 'climax' just before the resolution of the story (Longacre, 1976).

'Story structure' may suggest that the events in a story are in chronological sequence. This is not always the case. For example, Nina Bawden's book *Carrie's War* starts with Carrie as an adult bringing her family to a place where she was evacuated as a child. All writers bring their own views and opinions to a story, consciously or not, which is one of the reasons we provide children with a rich variety of different authors and books. Children become increasingly able to detect intentions and bias.

Writers have important choices to make, for example whether to tell the story in the first or third person. A story written in the third person can offer several viewpoints about events, while writing in the first person shows everything from one perspective and can connect reader and writer in an inviting way. Quite a lot of stories for children are written entirely or partially in the form of letters between two or more characters. Michael Morpurgo's book *The Wreck of the Zanzibar* is written in letter and diary format, with some first-person narration. In other books using the 'letter' device, the reader has only one half of the correspondence and has to infer what the other character has written.

Are there particular themes we associate with longer stories? A common one is the tension between love of home and familiar surroundings and the need for independence and adventure. So there is often a home–away–home pattern (Nodelman, 1996; Gamble and Yates, 2008). Other themes often explored include friendship, loyalty, the tension between good and evil, fairness and unfairness and the human cost of war.

There are some language features associated with the story genre. For example, they are often written in an accessible style with much everyday sounding conversation. This does not mean that some young readers cannot cope with a more literary style, like that of Rosemary Sutcliff, for example.

Dialogue, including slang or dialect, is sometimes used to reveal a character's social group, personality and period. So Dickon's Yorkshire dialect is important in establishing character and period in Frances Hodgson Burnett's *The Secret Garden*.

Finally, like all texts, novels for children need cohesion to create what linguists call 'textuality' – the sense that we have a text rather than just a series of random sentences. The linguists who have contributed most to our understanding of cohesion are Michael Halliday and Ruqaiya Hasan, whose ground-breaking book *Cohesion in English* was published in 1976. It provides an analysis of the many kinds of connectives and cohesive ties and the ways they are used in particular kinds of text. The two main kinds, however, are grammatical and lexical. Grammatical cohesive ties include, at sentence level, the use of conjunctions (and, but) and adverbs (soon, there). And, at text level, pronouns (he, she, they) can help a reader make referential connections to an earlier part of the text. 'Lexical' cohesive ties are particularly important in story; lexical cohesion is achieved by the choice of vocabulary, often to create images linked to a particular theme. So in Philip Pullman's *The Firework-Maker's Daughter*, images of heat, flame and warm colours – 'red fire and flame licked and cackled' – pervade the book.

Where a story is communicated through film, cohesion will be partly achieved visually. So a film story set on the coast will include moving images of waves, boats and sea birds.

Extract references

Gamble, N. and Yates, S. (2008) *Exploring Children's Literature*. London: Paul Chapman/Sage.
Halliday, M.A.K. and Hasan, R. (1976) *Cohesion in English*. Harlow: Longman.
Longacre, R. (1976) *An Anatomy of Speech Notions*. Lisse: Peter de Riddes.
Nodelman, P. (1996) *The Pleasures of Children's Literature*. White Plains, NY: Longman.

Comment

The best novels and longer stories have the potential to help develop children's reading stamina because they require sustained attention and reflection. However, the books the teacher provides need to grab the imagination of the young readers, giving them the urge to read on. The extract draws attention to what narratologists and linguists have discovered about 'story structure' and to the choices the writer has to make. As they get older, children come to realise that every book has a point of view to exploit – even a bias – and this means that the whole school or class library collection should represent different viewpoints and share different human experiences. So every child, of every heritage, should have access to good books in which they can see and read about people like themselves. All children should also encounter, within the context of an interesting story, adults and children who have disabilities but who are not defined by these.

While an author's choice of vocabulary is a major part of achieving the 'lexical cohesion' which is so important in novels and longer stories, a film version of the story uses images to create cohesion.

Questions to discuss with colleagues

It would be helpful if each member of the discussion group brought an annotated list of some of the novels they have read, or would like to read, with children in their specialist age range, and some thoughts about their value and ideas for follow-up activities. The list of children's novels and books at the end of this section can only scratch the surface of what is available, but tries to include different kinds.

1. What do you consider to be the value of regular reading aloud to the whole class, even in cases where the children are capable of reading the text for themselves?

2. How far should children's preferences affect the literature programme and teachers' provision? Many children love the stories of Roald Dahl, while some adults express reservations. Which of the following appraisals match best your own views?

    a) Dahl's books appeal to 'the cruder end of childhood taste: to a rumbustious rudery ...' (Townsend, 1995: 249)
    b) 'Roald Dahl's chapter books are great for independent reading.' (Teacher)
    c) 'The BFG is one of the best and funniest books I have read.' (Christopher, age 9; available at www.lovereading4kids.co.uk/author/RoaldDahl)

3. Older children may both read a print novel and see a television or film version. How would you engage children in a discussion about how the setting, plot and characters are treated in each medium?

4. Do you find that children of all ages enjoy humour in stories? Share with the group the amusing elements in some of the stories and or novels you have read to children.

5. Some of the main genre features of longer stories and novels for children are explained in the extract. How would you help older children become aware of the importance of 'special events' in longer narratives and their significance for understanding characters' personalities and motivations? How do you consider this discussion would develop children's critical judgement of the longer stories and novels they read? (In *Skellig* one of the 'special events' – the boy's first sighting of the angel – happens on the first page of the story.)

6. Children need to see themselves and the people around them shown positively in the literature they see and view on-screen. Share your knowledge of quality novels and longer stories which reflect:

    a) our diverse society;
    b) adults and children with a disability in a way that does not define them by their disability.

Research inquiries

Either:

- Longer stories and novels come into the literature programme of older children, but some of the themes are recognisable in stories for younger children. Search out some stories with Nodelman's 'home-away-home' pattern that you think would appeal to children still at the Early Years stage and read them to a group or class.

Write a short paper or make an audio or video recording of the children's responses to share with colleagues.

Or:

■ Following the argument in the extract that every book embodies a different viewpoint and reveals the experiences of human beings in particular circumstances, select some novels and longer stories that reflect our diverse society. Work with a class or group of children on one of these, making notes on the children's responses in discussion, drama work and/or their own writing.

Children's books: longer stories and novels for under-elevens

See also the novels mentioned in Extract 49 and the list of short stories on pages 197–8, which includes 'bridging stories' – stories where the written text is becoming more dominant – for younger children.

Almond, D. and McKean, D. (illustrator) (1998, 2005) *Skellig*. London: Hodder. 'I found him in the garage': this is the first sentence (referring to when young Michael first encounters the strange creature of the title) in this moving and hugely imaginative story. Michael has a lot of worries: his family have just moved house with all the changes this brings and his little sister is ill. 9+

Farmer, P. (2013 edn) *Charlotte Sometimes*. London: Vintage Children's Classics. In this time travel story Charlotte, who has just started at boarding school, finds herself taken back to the times of the First World War. This is disturbing and she fears being stuck permanently in another place and time. Much food for thought here about friends, growing up and about the concept of time. 10+

Fine, A. (2009) *The Diary of a Killer Cat*. London: Puffin. A chapter book for younger readers who will enjoy the hilarious adventures of a very mischievous cat, whether they read it themselves or hear it read out loud. 6+

Horowitz, A. (2005) *Stormbreaker*. London: Walker Books. This spy thriller, arranged in chapters, has humour, pace and excitement – so it is no surprise that it appeals to older readers with a liking for adventure. And Alex Rider is a resilient and resourceful main character. Some sad and violent events, though. 10+

King-Smith, D. (1996) *Harriet's Hare*. London and New York: Yearling. Typical of this author's many magical animal books for young children, this one is about a wonderful hare that arrives on earth from a far-off planet and befriends a little girl. Ideal for children just beginning to enjoy chapter books. 7+

Le Guin, U. (reissued 1973) *The Wizard of Earthsea*. London: Puffin. In this first book of a quartet a young wizard from the island of Gont undertakes a quest. How can he redeem himself after undertaking spells which he was not able to control? Earthsea has been compared by some readers to the Narnia of C.S. Lewis and the Middle Earth of Tolkien. Exceptionally fine writing, appreciated by the young person with reading stamina. 10+

Lively, P. (2011) *A Stitch in Time*. London: HarperCollins. Maria often retreats into her own imaginative world. When she finds a Victorian embroidered picture she becomes intensely involved in the story of Harriet, the ten-year-old who made it. 9+

Magorian, M. (reissued 2014) *Goodnight Mr Tom*. London: Penguin. In this moving and well-loved story set during the Second World War, old Tom Oakley reluctantly takes on Willie, a young evacuee. They build a friendship and support each other through some harrowing events. Older readers will be able to read the book themselves and/or view the story on-screen. 9+

Morpurgo, M. (2010) *Kensuki's Kingdom*. London: Egmont. Written in the first person, this engrossing adventure novel follows Michael's fortunes after he is washed up in the Pacific after falling off the family yacht. Can he survive on his own? 9+

Morpurgo, M. and Birmingham I. (illustrator) (1996) *The Butterfly Lion*. London: HarperCollins. Bertie looks after an orphaned lion club from the African Veld. But what happens when he has to go away to boarding school? A hugely affecting animal story. 8+

Pearce, P. (2005) *The Battle of Bubble and Squeak*. London: Puffin. Family discord! Sid, Peggy and Amy love their gerbils, Bubble and Squeak, but their mother does not. There is more awareness now that stories should reflect the different kinds of family in our society. In this story, written some time ago, Philippa Peace brings in a stepfather in a natural way. Much liked longer story for children to read or listen to. 7+

Pullman, P. (1997) *Northern Lights*. London: Scholastic. This is the first book in *His Dark Materials* trilogy. Readers are taken into a parallel world where each person has a 'demon'. The other books are *The Subtle Knife*, in which Will meets Lyra, and *The Amber Spyglass*, in which further dangers are faced and overcome. Challenging, innovative and highly imaginative writing makes these books suitable for older, forward young readers. 10/11+

Sacher, L. (2009) *There's a Boy in the Girls' Bathroom*. London: Bloomsbury Press. Bradley's bullying ways make it difficult for him to make friends. Things change for the better when a new school counsellor arrives. Shows young readers that situations and people can change. 8+

Sullivan, J. (2014) *The Great Cake Bake*. Ceredigion, Wales: Pont Books. Aled has dyslexia but is not defined by it. He sets himself a baking challenge and deals admirably with the other issues he has to cope with. 8+

Whelan, G. (2008) *Homeless Birds*. London: Frances Lincoln. Koly lives with her family in India. She reaches a turning point when a marriage is arranged for her at the young age of thirteen years. A lucid text with convincing dialogue explains her predicament and the cultural reasons for it. An involving story about a thoughtful and resourceful young girl. 10+

Wilson, J. and Sharratt, N. (illustrator) (2006) *The Story of Tracy Beaker*. London and New York: Yearling Books. First published in 1991, this book has made a tremendous impact on many young readers. Written in the first person, the everyday thought, fears and triumphs of young Tracy shine out of the pages. She calls her children's home 'the dump' and adults do not find her easy to deal with, but she is a character of great resilience and courage and she discovers she has a talent. 7+.

Wilson, J. and Sharratt, N. (2008) *Sleepovers*. London: Young Corgi. How will young Daisy cope when it is her turn to have a sleepover for the members of the Aphabet Club – Amy, Bella, Chloe and Emily? How will they relate to Daisy's sister who has special needs? 8+

Further reading

Hahn, D. (2015, 2nd edn) *The Oxford Companion to Children's Literature*. Oxford: Oxford University Press. A classic book by Humphrey Carpenter and Mari Prichard first published in 1984 and updated by Daniel Hahn in 2015.

Hall, L. (2001) Time no longer – history, enchantment and the classic time-slip story. In F.M. Collins and J. Graham (eds) *Historical Fiction for Children: Capturing the Past*. London: David Fulton. An interesting account of how different novelists approached their 'time-slip' books, including Penelope Lively and Philippa Pearce.

Hordon, F. (2014) Editorial. *Books for Keeps*, 209. A review of difficulties in children's access to books – library closures, for example, and some promising signs – more books depicting our diverse society.

Lathey, G. (2011) A sense of time and place: Literature in the wider curriculum. In P. Goodwin (ed.) *The Literate Classroom*. London: David Fulton. See pages 98–100 for interesting suggestions for using historical stories and novels to link lessons in English and history.

Townsend, J.R. (1995) *Written for Children*. London: The Bodley Head. An insightful and sometimes witty account of children's literature through the ages. Chapter 22 explores books and novels in the category of fantasy by such imaginative authors as Clive King, Penelope Lively, Philippa Pearce, Penelope Farmer, Florence Parry Heide, Ian Mc Ewan, Roald Dahl and Anne Fine.

Wilson, A. and Scanlon, J. (2011) *Language Knowledge for Primary Teachers*. Abingdon and New York: Routledge. See pages 112–16 for ways of exploring a novel with special reference to an analysis of J.K. Rowling's story – *Harry Potter and the Philosopher's Stone*.

Extract 50

Source

Bearne, E. (2013) Seeing and hearing Dickens. In Bearne, E. (ed.) *Teaching Dickens in the Primary School*. Leicester: English Association Issues in English, No. 10, 22–5.

At what age do children become able to understand and appreciate classic texts? Eve Bearne – who has been actively involved in primary and secondary English work for many years as a teacher, lecturer, writer and researcher – illuminates this question with reference to the response she and her colleagues got from children introduced to the stories of Charles Dickens. In 2012, Dickens' bicentennial year, when one of the co-ordinators of the English Association's Children's Literature Special Interest Group, she helped organise the More Dickens Award in partnership with the Dickens Fellowship. Children from a number of participating primary schools explored Dickens' stories through adaptations, graphic novels, films and drama as well as tackling – with their teachers' help – parts of his original texts. Children made short films, wrote stories and drew the characters and settings. Drawing on the enthusiastic response of children and their teachers during the project, Eve Bearne argues that powerful classic stories can, with benefit, be included in the primary school literature programme.

> Many of us first met Dickens through hearing his stories read aloud at home or as dramatisations on the radio but also by seeing adaptations of his stories on television, film and on the stage. We may also have enjoyed the Boz illustrations and more recently we've been able to read Dickens in picturebook and graphic novel forms. All these different approaches to his intriguing stories and engaging characters would (I hope) have met with Dickens' approval as he was such a keen storyteller himself. But despite the approachability of his work in these forms, there are still challenges for young readers/viewers: many of his stories have chilling episodes with death,

cruelty and malice never far away. Can the brutal killing of Nancy in *Oliver Twist* or Wackford Squeers' beating of the boys in Dotheboys Hall be considered suitable for children? I believe they can, if approached with confidence in young people's ability to discriminate about moral dilemmas and the motivation of characters. And, importantly, if whole texts rather than melodramatic incidents are read/viewed, then children see how Dickens resolves the grim situations that many of his characters, particularly perhaps the child characters, find themselves in. Visual versions of Dickens make it rather easier to be sure that children experience the stories in their entirety.

Anyone who has listened to children discussing their favourite television programmes or films will know that they can be very astute critical audiences. They do not need to be fluent readers of verbal text before they can start on the road to analysis and comment about the structure, characters, themes and settings of narratives. They can also deal with rather more complex ideas of story structure than the traditional 'beginning, middle and end'; many of the programmes they watch – particularly soap operas – have several plots and sub-plots developing at the same time, all of which children can hold in their minds and talk about afterwards. Children can predict plot structures and talk about character when they have made the choice to watch or read something for their own interest. All this means that Dickens' often complex stories can be enjoyed through film as an addition to hearing or reading books. The teacher's expertise comes in using the children's critical abilities in the classroom to enhance their enjoyment and understanding of challenging texts.

Of course there will still be people who think that watching a film or DVD is somehow less praiseworthy than reading a book. But if we reflect on our own responses to watching a film or television drama we can quickly see that it provokes an emotional response but also a critical response. We may laugh or cry, be indignant about a character's actions, or hide our eyes, but most of all we talk about it. At home after (or even during) watching, at work the next day, with our friends, we express our opinions. In the case of Dickens we may find that the director has evoked the atmosphere well, or that an actor has created a compelling character. Two of my favourites are Gillian Anderson's massively controlled and suffering Lady Dedlock in Andrew Davies' television adaptation of *Bleak House* and Russell Tovey's poignantly honourable John Chivery in another Andrew Davies adaptation, this time *Little Dorrit*. What would your favourite interpretations be? Whatever they are, you have formed a critical opinion. Children do the same.

Following the plot – the living storyline

Through their knowledge of video and television texts, children have vast resources of information, not only about the stories themselves; they also have a wide experience of plot structure. They know, for example, about flashbacks and 'meanwhile'. They can predict complications in the plot and guess resolutions: *I know what's going to happen*. In doing this they are engaged in a kind of dialogue with the narrative, becoming involved, active and critical readers. In an increasingly visual environment, the encouragement and development of such discrimination is essential. Films and video won't go away.

If children are genuinely to be able to resist some of the alarming features of television and film depictions they need to be given credit for having some critical sense and encouraged to extend this through discussion in school about a wider range of texts. In Dickens' *Christmas Carol*, for example, there are some frightening moments (it is, after all, subtitled 'a ghost story') and potentially tragic situations, challenging perhaps for young readers/viewers, but as discussions have shown … young readers can not only handle some of the more grim aspects of Dickens' novels, in discussion they can also show balanced, thoughtful response to moral dilemmas and brutal actions.

Extract references

Davies, A. (2005) Television adaptation of *Bleak House* by Charles Dickens.
Davies, A. (2008) Television adaptation of *Little Dorrit* by Charles Dickens.
Dickens, C. (2012) *A Christmas Carol*; *Bleak House*; *Little Dorrit*; *Nicholas Nickleby*; *Oliver Twist*. See Penguin Classics Editions.

Comment

In this extract, the writer anticipates what might be the arguments for not exposing young pupils to the brutal events that are to be found in the stories of Charles Dickens. But she argues that the stories are so exciting and the characters so interesting that an early start to reading his books, preferably in their entirety, seems worthwhile. But how do we best do this? Eve Bearne recognises that children today are living in a very different cultural context to that experienced by children in Charles Dickens' time. We now make daily use of digital technology, and so film, television, graphic versions of the novels and audiovisual versions of Dickens' work are likely to be helpful in introducing and involving young learners in these powerful stories.

Eve Bearne draws attention to imaginative ways of bringing about this involvement. Beyond this extract, she suggests that children might compare one of the episodes from a film version of *A Christmas Carol* with the written story. Or the teacher might use a graphic version to help children focus on dialogue or character, and perhaps they might then share their ideas and opinions on the school website.

As other contributors to *Teaching Dickens in the Primary School* show – *Oliver Twist*, *David Copperfield* and *Great Expectations* also benefit from such exciting teaching approaches. The chart from page 25, 'Similarities and differences', which helps to structure younger primary children's analysis of how a film version of a Dickens story might differ from the book version, is reproduced on page 208, Figure 6.4.

Questions to discuss with colleagues

1. What qualities do you think a book we term a 'classic' should have? Share in discussion your 'top ten' list (see mine, Figure 6.5). Which more recent books do you think might deserve classic status in the future?

2. Do you agree with Eve Bearne that we underestimate the reading stamina of primary age pupils by not including stories often thought suitable only for older readers? Share your own experience of classic texts at a young age. Include examples where you read the text yourself, had it read to you or watched it in film form.

3. The extract suggests that it is the 'intriguing stories' and 'engaging characters' which capture children's imagination when they meet Dickens. Which characters in the work of Charles Dickens, William Shakespeare, Lewis Carroll or another classic writer are your favourites and why?

4. The extract writer comments that: 'Of course there will always be people who think that watching a film or DVD is somehow less praiseworthy than reading a book.' Do you agree or disagree with such a view?

5. It is argued in the extract that it is versions of these challenging texts – in film, on television and DVD – that help children with plot structure. Do you agree? Has any of your work in the classroom supported this?

- Were there any differences between what happened (the plot) in the film and the book?
- Were the characters any different? Choose one or two to compare.
- Do you think the setting shown in the film was what you had expected from the book? (or the other way round, depending on which was read first).
- How did the book and the film create atmosphere?
- What did you think about the ending in each version?
- Which version did you prefer? Why?

Talk about your ideas, then fill in the chart.

Different	The same
Plot	
Characters	
Atmosphere	
Ending	
Preferred version with reason	
Single attention grabbing sentence to start a review	

Figure 6.4 Similarities and differences between film and book versions. From *Teaching Dickens in the Primary School* by Eve Bearne (ed.). Reproduced with the permission of the English Association, c. 2013.

Research inquiries

Either:

■ In the same publication that the extract came from, Pam Dowson suggests that parts of two of Charles Dickens' stories could be made enjoyable for the five to seven age group as well as the seven to elevens. These are *Oliver Twist* and *David Copperfield*. Try out and record some of the ways you interested the children in parts of either of these stories, perhaps using some different media.

Or:

■ With a class or group of older primary school children, compare their response to print versions (conventional or graphic) of a novel by Dickens with their response to a film or television version. You may find Bearne's 'Similarities and differences' grid in Figure 6.4 helpful here.

Further reading

Bottoms, J. (2005) Shakespeare for Juniors: Introducing playworlds. *Primary English Magazine*, 10 (3).
Robins, G. (2009) Contemporary approaches to classic texts: H.G. Wells' *War of the Worlds*. *English 4–11*, 35. Contemporary media helped illuminate a classic text for a Year 6 class.

My top 10
Black Beauty, Anna Sewell
Alice in Wonderland, Lewis Carroll
The Secret Garden, Frances Hodgson Burnett
The Wind in the Willows, Kenneth Graham
The Tale of Peter Rabbit, Beatrix Potter
The Lion, the Witch and the Wardrobe, C.S. Lewis
Carrie's War, Nina Bawden
Tom's Midnight Garden, Philippa Pearce
Stig of the Dump, Clive King
Eagle of the Ninth, Rosemary Sutcliff

Figure 6.5 What makes a book a 'classic'?

Section 6: Multimodality and 'popular culture' texts – graphic books, magazines and comics

Multimodality, when applied to print texts, is to do with the combination of design, writing and images. Multimodal texts which are also multimedia may include speech and music in addition. While multimodality is not a new concept, increasing awareness of the importance of visual literacy has sharpened interest in its educational importance. As technological advances bring more and more kinds of text at a swifter rate than ever before, our concept of literacy has broadened and changed.

This greatly affects how teachers conceive of the literacy programme in school and these issues are taken up at many points in this book including, in this chapter, Section 2 on picturebooks and Section 5, where Eve Bearne draws attention to the potential of audiovisual material and 'popular culture' texts for enhancing children's enjoyment of reading the classics. Issues to do with the new literacies and developing a vocabulary to discuss visual texts are also addressed in Chapter 3 on reading, Chapter 4 on writing and Section 3 in Chapter 7 on children's non-fiction magazines and newspapers.

In this section, these developments are explored with particular reference to graphic texts and comics. These can helpfully link home and school reading and viewing and, as well as having great appeal for many children, being able to understand and use them is part of becoming literate.

Katia Pizzi, based at the University of London, is known for her research and writing on cultural identities and for a body of work on children's literature and illustration. In the first of the following two extracts, Extract 51, she argues that children's comics are an extremely resilient cultural form and likely, in both textual and non-textual form, to remain an important part of the cultural lives of children worldwide. In Extract 52, Hannah Sackett, a children's librarian, shares her experience of providing comics for children in the Primary Years and argues that comic and graphic books offer new and interesting forms of visual story-telling.

Extract 51

Source

Pizzi, K. (2004, 2nd edn) Contemporary comics. In P. Hunt (ed.) *International Companion Encyclopedia of Children's Literature*, vol. 1. Abingdon and New York: Routledge, (a) 385–6, (b) 393–4.

Part a

The crisis affecting post-war comics in the western hemisphere has been compensated, more recently, by 'enormous improvements in printing technology coupled with the emergence of a "direct sales" system of marketing to specialist comic shops' which not only improved the aesthetic and material quality of comic books, but also 'opened up new spaces for more complex and imaginative stories and artwork than ever before', ensuring the 'revival of the entire industry' (Sabin, 1996: 7). Comics evolved in parallel with the entertainment industry while the market at large adapted to young consumers' new competences and requirements. While television made the most significant impact on comics from the 1950s, and comics have similarly long been elaborating ideas later appropriated by both television and cinema, advances in and wider access to information technology have led to further changes, placing contemporary comics at the interface of a variety of complex communicative technologies. Communicative systems evolved in ways that occasionally forced traditional comics to metamorphose even radically in an effort to remain competitive. Comics, on the other hand, have not become obsolete, maintaining a capacity unknown to other media, to evolve and keep abreast of modern developments.

Comics from the Far East, rising steadily in numbers since the Second World War, have also penetrated western markets, feeding new ideas and technologies into what at times appeared to be a languishing industry. Though traditional comics have survived and continue to thrive, albeit in possibly less canonical areas, hybrid forms, which incorporate traditional forms of comics with more or less related forms of visual and textual communication, have also become the norm. Traditional characters have survived a number of metamorphoses, re-emerging later as parodied versions of their previous selves, at times in a number of different incarnations (see especially Superman, Spider-Man and Batman).

Contemporary comics have become increasingly parodical, relying on a substantive history of traditional narrative now reworked in meta-fictional form.

In short, contemporary comics have retained their specificity as well as reflecting both traditional media such as television, cinema and popular literature, and more advanced and increasingly cognate new technologies (Frezza, 1995: 143). Comics have progressively become a communicative system in themselves, speaking the language of our collective imagination at large …

Part b

The contemporary scene is characterised by more articulate and complex cross pollination between comics and television (including digital and satellite TV), cinema, literature, video-games, Internet and computer software, graphics and animation in general. While film continues to influence comics, comics continue to inspire the film industry, thanks to the development of computer graphics and continued to digital technologies …

The advent of global economics and global markets ensures the survival and dissemination of traditional characters throughout the developed world, from the recent Hollywood blockbuster movie *X-Men*, to text messaging in mobile phones, frequently accompanied by logos featuring characters such as Mickey Mouse,

Peanuts and the Simpsons, to phone cards bearing images of Disney and other characters (see the series 'Pippo olimpionico' or 'Olympic Goofy' in Italy, and also Tintin in Belgium and mangas in Japan) which have now become highly collectable items. In short, the daily activities, as well as the free time, of children and teenagers are saturated with comics and there are no signs of comics losing their powerful hold on the collective imagination of young consumers worldwide.

Extract references

Frezza, G. (1995) *La Macchina del Mito tra Film e Fumetti.* Florence: La Nuova Italia.
Sabin, R. (1996) *Comics, Comix & Graphic Novels: A History of Comic Art.* London: Phaidon.

Comment

This extract is taken mainly from the early part of a long analysis, rich with examples of comics in print and on-screen. In the part of the article reproduced here, Katia Pizzi examines some of the reasons why comics have survived well in global markets, not least because they have managed to change and develop in keeping with new technologies. Pizzi makes clear how print comics have impacted on screen cartoons and how television and film have, in turn, influenced the style and content of comics. She explains the tremendous commercial success of comics by pointing out that they speak 'the language of our collective imagination'. Pizzi's analysis gives support to teachers who are increasingly making comics and graphic texts – on-screen as well as in print – part of the literature programme for the under-elevens.

Extract 52

Source

Sackett, H. (2013) Children's comics for a new generation of readers. *Books for keeps*, 207 (2), 12–14.

Last Autumn I signed my school library up to a subscription with *The Phoenix* (published by David Fickling), interested to see if children would take to reading a weekly comic in the library. Six months later, and every Monday morning a boy in Year 3 puts his head around the library door and asks 'Is *The Phoenix* here yet?' *The Phoenix* is especially popular with Year 3, but is read by children across the Junior School. Some children read it from cover to cover, while others head straight to their favourite strips. Friends will often read the comic together, laughing at the jokes and sometimes drawing their favourite characters. Comic book artist Paul Duffield has argued that *The Phoenix*, with its great range of genres and styles and promotion of textual and visual literacy, may be one of the keys to unlocking a new generation of comic readers (and makers).

While weekly comics have declined, many children's graphic novels and comic books are available. Indeed, it seems that the range in style and content of these publications is expanding and offering new forms of visual storytelling.

Some mainstream publishers, including Walker Books and Hodder Children's Books, have pushed the trend for turning bestselling book series into graphic novels. The graphic versions of the Alex Rider books (by Anthony Horowitz) are amongst the most borrowed books in the school library. Other adaptations include Eoin Colfer's *Artemis Fowl* and Charlie Higson's *Young Bond* …

I have been surprised to find that the vivid pink and purple covers of the *Gum Girl* comics have not deterred boys from reading them! In America, Walker's sister company – Candlewick Press, have established *Toon Books*, an imprint that introduces comics (and beautiful art and design) to young children from the age of three, as well as producing *Toon Graphics* for the 8+ age range …

Some of the newer critically acclaimed comic books on the shelves have been deliberately designed to appeal to an All Ages audience. These include Garen Ewing's *The Rainbow Orchard*, with its ligne claire artwork appealing to fans of Herge's *Tintin*, and Luke Person's *Hildafolk* series which has a narrative depth and artistic flair that has drawn comparisons with Tove Jansson's *Moomins* and the Japanese anime films of Hayao Miyazaki. Meanwhile, the *Adventure Time* comic books (in spite of being television tie-ins) are written and illustrated with real flair and inventiveness … There are some excellent small press/independently published books out there too – notably Philippa Rice's *My Cardboard Life* comics.

The educational possibilities of comics are also being explored. Comics have the potential to become a key component in reading for pleasure in school (now officially approved by the National Curriculum). The UK is fortunate in being home to a large number of talented comic artists. To this end, Jamie Smart (creator of *Bunny vs Monkey* and *Fish-head Steve*) has created an online comic to showcase the range of talent available in the UK … My experience in the school library shows that there is a ready audience for the next generation of comics.

Comment

Hannah Sackett brings the perspective of a children's librarian to appraising the huge number of comics and graphic books now on the market, and provides a useful guide to the ever-changing scene of what is available. She points out their potential for encouraging reading for pleasure in and out of school and their contribution to developing visual kinds of literacy. Further, she believes the range in style and content leads to new kinds of visual story-telling. This, perhaps, accounts for the popularity of print comics today in spite of competition from computer games, film, television and online worlds. Might the availability of such beguiling reading material make it less likely that children will persevere with more sustained written text in longer books and novels? This need not be the case if teachers make sure both kinds of reading are encouraged and children are helped to take up a critical approach to each kind.

Questions to discuss with colleagues (Extracts 51 and 52)

It would be helpful to bring to the discussion some examples of comics/graphic books you consider would appeal to your age range.

1. The writer of Extract 51 points out the two-way connection between films and comics – film influences comics and 'comics continue to inspire the film industry'. Share with the group an example of this in your own reading and viewing.
2. Katia Pizzi (Extract 51) believes that comics 'speak the language of our collective imagination'. Bearing this insight in mind, which comics or graphic texts have you found children in your specialist age range enjoy?
3. How far do you agree that with those who, like Hannah Sackett, argue that comics and graphic books are the key, or at least the partial key, to reading for pleasure?
4. How would you agree or disagree with my concern that if comics and graphic books became too great a part of children's reading diet, children may be less likely to persevere with the sustained attention needed for longer stories and novels?
5. Hannah Sackett observes in Extract 52 that she was surprised that the vivid pink covers of the *Gum Girl* comic has not deterred boys from reading them. Have you noticed differences in the choices girls and boys make:

    a) in their reading of fiction in general;
    b) in their reading of comics and graphic books?

Research inquiries

Either:

■   With a group or class, carry out a survey of their favourite comics and books in cartoon format. Older children would be able to fill in a short questionnaire you have designed, while interviews might be the best way to proceed with younger ones. Show the children the results, perhaps by producing a graph, and discuss the reasons for their preferences. Share your findings with the discussion group. Some children might like to create their own cartoon strip, perhaps in pairs.

And/Or:

■   Carry out a similar survey, but this time ask the children which television or film cartoons they watch at home. Share the results with the children and, perhaps, show the favourite cartoon in school. Ask the children why they like the characters in their favourite cartoon. Older children could be asked to write short, illustrated reviews for a display.

You might find it interesting to examine the results of either of these surveys and judge how far gender seems to influence children's choices.

Children's texts using graphics and comic strips

Aardman (2005) *Good Night, Gromit*. London: Simon & Schuster. In this board book version, Gromit cannot get to sleep because Wallace has the television turned up. 5+

Alley, Z.B. (writer) and Alley, R.W. (artist) (2008) *There's a Wolf at the Door*. New York: Roaring Book Press. Five traditional tales including 'The Three Little Pigs' and 'Little Red Riding Hood' are told through this big book comic. 5+

Almond, D. and McKean, D. (2009) *The Savage*. London: Walker Books. The narrator in the story, a boy called Blue who has lost his father, writes about his encounter with a wild boy. The illustrations are full of energy, and sometimes menace with their distinctive green palette. 8+

Bestall, A. (2008, facsimile edn) *Rupert Annual 1963*. London: Egmont. Beautifully reproduced classic Bestall annual, transporting readers to the magic of Nutwood. 7+

Briggs, R. (2001) *Ug, Boy Genius of the Stone Age*. London: Jonathan Cape. A graphic text likely to appeal to both adults and children because of the quality of the pictures, the interesting combinations of print and illustration and the interesting discussion the plot and characters are likely to inspire. 8+

Brown, K. (illustrator), Appignanesi, R. (text adapter) and de Somogyi, N. (text consultant) (2008) *Manga Shakespeare: A Midsummer Night's Dream*. London: SelfMadeHero. The artwork is stunning and this is the kind of book likely to inspire a creative response. 9+

Child, L. (2000) *I Will Not Ever Never Eat a Tomato*. London: Orchard Books. The Charlie and Lola series of picturebooks, about an endearing sibling relationship, are among the many picturebooks which are by definition, multimodal. 4+

Grey, M. (2006) *Traction Man* series. London: Random House. This miniature superhero has extraordinary adventures in the bath and on 'planet duvet'. 3+

Kerwin, B. (2010) *Wallace and Gromit in the Wrong Trousers: A Graphic Novel*. London: Egmont. Hugely amusing antics by the famous pair. 8+

Kinney, J. (2008) *Diary of a Wimpy Kid*. London: Puffin. The first in a series that, at the time of writing, is now into the ninth story, *The Long Haul* (2014). The stories began as online comic strips and were so well liked that they were published in book form. It is about the struggles of the main character, Greg Heffley, to be 'cool' and involves the kind of excitements and adventures that children love. The stories are available on CD, on-screen and in print. 8+

Park, M. (director) and Gibson, M. (narrator) (2000) *Chicken Run*. DVD. Hilarious film showing the adventures of feisty chickens trying to escape from a farm. 9+

Schulz, C.M. (2014) *Charlie Brown and Friends: A Peanut Collection*. USA: Andrew McMeel Publishing (AMP Publishing for Kids). *Peanuts* cartoon stories are published in film and print. This book introduces Charlie Brown's friends to young readers – not least his faithful dog, Snoopy, well known for his observations and reflections on life. 8+

Slade, C. (2007) *Korgi, Book 1. Sprouting Wings!* (2007); *The Comic Collector* (2008). Marietta, GA: Top Shelf Productions. These wordless comic books are about the adventures of a small girl and her dog in a make-believe world. 6+

Smith, J. (2009) *Little Mouse Gets Ready*. New York: Toon Books. This is a helpful introduction to comic narratives for very young children. 5+

Tan, S. (2007) *The Arrival*. London: Hodder Children's Books. Imaginative and moving wordless picture book telling of a man's experiences on coming to a new country. 9+

Thomas, V. and Paul, K. (illustrator) (2006) *Winnie's Magic Wand*. Oxford: Oxford University Press. One of the graphic books in the Winnie the Witch and her cat Wilbur series which amuses with a lovely text and cartoon-like illustrations. In this story, Winnie puts her wand into the washing machine – the combination of the everyday with magic is what appeals. 4+

Watson, D. and Wallis, K. (2004) *Wonderland*. Orange, CA: Image Comics. This dark tale set in the future has a strong female main character, Sarah, who sets out on a quest to find her father. 9+

Williams, M. (2008) *My Secret War Diary by Flossie Albright*. London: Walker Books. This hand-written account of a child's daily life during the Second World War makes its impact by the creation of imaginatively designed pages with contemporary photographs, letters, extracts from magazines and newspapers. 9+

Williams, M. (2009 edns) *Mr. William Shakespeare's Plays; Bravo, Mr. William Shakespeare!* London: Walker Books. Using distinctive and detailed comic strip, this author–illustrator introduces young readers to some of the stories of the bard's plays. The sombre palette, language and facial expressions in the retelling of *King Lear*, in the second of these books, shows that stories told in comic strip are not only capable of making us laugh, but can also move and sadden us. 8+

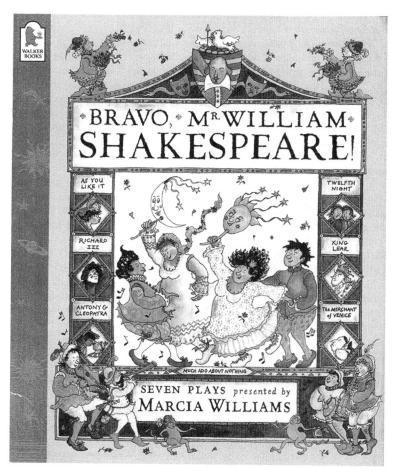

Figure 6.6 Front cover of *Bravo, Mr. William Shakespeare!* by Marcia Williams. Cover Illustration © 2009 Marcia Williams. Reproduced by permission of Walker Books Ltd., London SE11 5HJ.

Further reading

Bearne, E., Ellis, S., Graham, L., Hulme, P., Meiner, J. and Wolstencroft, H. (2005) *More Than Words 2: Creating Stories on Page and Screen*. London: QCA, and Leicester: UKLA. Considers how children's page designs and illustrations can complement their writing of fiction.

Bearne, E. and Wolstencroft, H. (2007) *Visual Approaches to Teaching Writing: Multimodal Literacy 5–11*. London: Sage, with Leicester: UKLA. How do we help children to 'read' images and to recognise the relationship between writing and image in multimodal texts? This publication includes a CD with examples of children's multimodal work.

Bearne, E. (2009) Multimodality, literacy and texts: Developing a discourse. *Journal of Early Years Literacy*, summer, 2–65. A scholarly and detailed analysis of the contribution being able to combine different ways of communicating makes to children's literacy development.

Cremin, T. and Arthur, J. (eds) (2014, 3rd edn) Gender and reading. In *Learning to Teach in the Primary School*. Abingdon and New York: Routledge. In this summary of research into gender and reading, these authors note that girls tend to favour reading narratives and topics about life experiences more than do boys.

Etherington, R. and Etherington, L. (2013) The comic art of imagination: Visual literacy in the classroom. *English 4–11*, 49. Leicester: English Association. These creators of comics argue that reading comic and graphic novels deserves to be a stepping stone towards literacy.

Millard, E. (2005) Writing of heroes and villains: Fusing children's knowledge about popular fantasy texts with school-based literacy requirements. In J. Evans (ed.) *Literacy Moves On*. Portsmouth, NH: Heinemann. Explores the educational implications of a tendency for boys to be influenced by film narratives and action-packed stories and girls' preferences for traditional narratives.

Stafford, T. (2010) *Teaching Visual Literacy in the Primary School*. Abingdon and New York: Routledge. This book provides a theoretical underpinning to visual literacy and practical approaches to helping children understand innovative texts.

Wilson, A. and Scanlon, J. (2011, 4th edn) *Language Knowledge for Primary Teachers*. London and New York: Routledge. See chapter 11 for a discussion of non-book and electronic texts, and how to help teachers develop their ability to appraise these.

Wyse, D. *et al.* (2013, 3rd edn) Multimodality and ICTs. In D. Wyse (ed.) *Teaching English, Language and Literacy*. Abingdon and New York: Routledge. Examines how ICTs can enhance children's learning and literacy.

Other useful resources

N.B. This chapter has explored the main kinds of fiction for children in all its many forms and media. Not everything of value can be discussed or even listed. And there is, of course, a constant stream of new literature for children. Here are just some of the print magazines and websites which help teachers and others to keep informed.

Books for Keeps. An online journal with reviews of and articles about all kinds of children's books.

Booktrust. Reports on research studies to do with all kinds of reading and recommends books for all ages from 3–11. See www.booktrust.org.uk/programmes/primary.

English 4–11. The English Association's print journal on Primary English includes in each of its three issues each year several pages of reviews of children's books. See books.engassoc@le.ac.uk.

Loves Reading 4 Kids recommends new books for all age groups from babies to early secondary. See www.lovesreading4kids.co.uk.

Many quality newspapers, for example the *Sunday Times* and *The Guardian* review children's books. See www.theguardian.com/childrens-books-site. The *Sunday Times* has a list of the best 100 children's books. See www.thesundaytimes.co.uk.

Teaching English. This journal of the National Association for the Teaching of English includes a 'Book Box' section with book reviews of books for both primary and secondary school children. See info at nate.org.uk.

The Centre for Literacy in Primary Education has regularly updated booklists online. See www. clpe.org.uk.

The School Librarian. Each issue of this quarterly journal includes a large review section commenting on new books for children from the pre-school to sixth-form years. See www.sla.org.uk.

Seven Stories, National Centre for Children's books. It is known for its exhibitions of the work of children's authors and illustrators and for its ever increasing archive of modern and contemporary children's books. Information and book suggestions are available on their website: www.sevenstories.org.uk.

United Kingdom Literacy Association. Carries out research into all aspects of reading and gives an award to what children and their teachers consider are the best children's books each year. See www.ukla.org.

Non-fiction literature in English lessons

Introduction

English lessons are the special home of fiction and this is reflected in the length and depth of analysis of a range of genres in Chapter 6. However, some kinds of non-fiction have an important place in the English curriculum and have, perhaps, not always received the attention they deserve. And yet the best writing of this kind has qualities which help develop critical literacy and accelerate children's progress in reading and writing. What are the genres of non-fiction of value in English lessons? I include here autobiography and biography, 'lyrical' texts and those texts in print or on-screen which set out arguments to inform and nourish the debates that are a feature of lively English lessons.

The extracts in Section 1 are concerned with diaries, autobiography and biography. Extract 53 takes up a broad canvass and confirms the place of literary kinds of non-fiction including diaries, letters, autobiography and biography – in the English programme. Extract 54 sets out Sue Unstead's review of Michael Rosen's biography of Roald Dahl and indicates what she values in his innovative approach to informing and involving his young readers about a gifted writer and sometimes eccentric human being.

In Section 2, Extract 55, from Mallett's Bookmark publication on the lyrical voice in non-fiction, attention turns to a poetic non-fiction text which describes the life cycle of the eel in such a way that text and pictures combine to draw upon and develop the imagination and feelings as well thinking and understanding. Calling such creations 'information picturebooks' hardly does them justice; children who have shared this book with me have commented that it is a 'sort of poem in words and pictures'.

Section 3 turns to some of the texts that support and inspire that part of an English programme which allows children to reflect on all the many issues that concern human beings as they live their lives. Extract 56, from an article by Rob Sanderson and Jo Bowers, considers the variety of magazines, print and online, available for children in the four to eleven age range and their potential for encouraging thinking and debate.

Section 1: Autobiography and biography

Extract 53

Source

Mallett, M. (2010) Logbooks, diaries, letters, autobiography and biography. In M. Mallett (ed.) *Choosing and Using Fiction and Non-Fiction 3–11*. London and New York: Routledge, 255–6.

The best autobiography and biography for adults is often regarded as non-fiction writing with the status of 'literature'. Do texts of this genre for children deserve this recognition? Mallett comments on what might be some of their most desirable features and on their potential for use, and that of other recounts, in English lessons.

The appointment diary or calendar on the wall helps us manage our time. A 'diary' can be something much more personal, a journal which can record the writer's actions, inner thoughts and preoccupations. Some 'information stories' use the diary format as a device to help young readers understand the lives of people in history or those who live in different parts of the world. *Castle Diary: The Journal of Tobias Burgess, Page* by Richard Platt is about the life of a medieval page and takes in feasting, jousting and hunting. Above all we learn about the page's private opinions of those living and working alongside him. Using the diary device in a similar way in his book *Charles Darwin*, Alan Gibbons charts the events through Darwin's journey to collect scientific specimens through the eyes of a ship boy. To be clear about where factual information is accompanied by invention he writes in an author's note that: 'James and his pet are fictional characters that I have created. They were not on the *Beagle's* voyage, but the people in James' diary did exist, and the events described are based on what actually happened.' Autobiographies are more sustained first-person accounts, often drawing on diaries, telling of the events of a life from the person's point of view. The writer may seek to justify, explain or excuse particular actions and attitudes. And of course the author is inevitably, and for their own reasons, selective about what is included, what is left out, what is skimmed over and what is emphasized. No reader whether child or adult is going to be entertained by the banal or self promoting sort of autobiography. We want to be intrigued, puzzled perhaps or led to review our attitudes and opinions.

Authors of biographies usually write life stories in the third person. Over the last 30 years biographies written for children have become more varied and more care has been taken over accuracy. But when judging whether to bring a biography into the classroom, we consider more than how well 'the facts' are recorded. A good biography for children needs to encourage reflection and this is achieved partly by not hiding the puzzles and inconsistencies that are so often a part of an honest account of someone's life. Margaret Meek comments that we look for 'an encounter with a life and ideas' (1969: 60). In the UK, publishers have brought out quite a number of books, very often in series, about great lives with an eye on the English and history programs of the National Curriculum. As is the case in autobiographies, many of these add interest by including remembered snippets of conversation, letters, diary entries, photographs, timelines, maps, posters and theatre programmes. Printed out email and text messages now join this list. Children can be helped to see all these as identifying features of the genre and will, with encouragement, learn to use them in their own attempts at biographical writing. Teachers and children will find television programmes and DVDs helpful. Biographies in this medium can show location, historical context and dramatic recreations. For more recent figures children will be able to see and hear from the biographer's subject. It is worth checking what is available to complement print accounts. The motivational aspect of electronic biographies should not be underestimated. But print biographies may also draw in children who are not normally avid readers. Linnea Hendrickson recommends for these young learners 'well-illustrated small biographies of sports heroes and entertainers' (Hendrickson in Watson, 2001: 83). Biographies (as well as autobiographies) can help young readers understand the choices a writer makes and these insights help when they attempt their own writing.

Extract references

Hendrickson, L. (2000) Biography and autobiography. In V. Watson (ed.) *The Cambridge Guide to Children's Books in English*. Cambridge: Cambridge University Press.

Meek, M. (1969) *Information and Book Learning*. Stroud: Thimble Press.

Platt, R. (2014, 2nd edn) *Castle Diary: The Journal of Tobias Burgess, Page*. London: Walker Books.

Comment

It is argued here that the best autobiographies for children, as for adults, manage to be honest and, if possible, intriguing or at least interesting. Roald Dahl makes this point in a typically blunt manner in introducing his book – *Boy: Tales of Childhood*: 'Autobiography is a book a person writes about his own life and it is usually full of all sorts of boring details. This book is not an autobiography.' He means of course it is not a run-of-the-mill autobiography. *Boy* does not just set out 'the facts', but rather is an opportunity to share adventures and experiences and to explain why particular views are held. One danger is that the writer of an autobiography may be tempted to select what shows them in a good light and to justify behaviours they do not want to be subject to too much scrutiny. It is also possible for biographies to be too flattering. Every life has some puzzles and inconsistencies and discussion of these makes us speculate and wonder.

Visual material often complements and extends the written text: photographs of people, buildings and landscapes, drawings and diagrams like family trees and timelines. Such material can enrich our understanding of someone's circumstances and life experiences and open up more issues to explore. Finally, while print autobiographies and biographies continue to be important, it is suggested here that these can be supplemented by material on-screen.

Before discussing the questions following this extract and Extract 54 it would be helpful to track down a selection of autobiographies and biographies for children and to bring them to the discussion group. Access to the internet would make it possible to review material online, for example the BBC Primary History website. Suggestions include the following.

Autobiography

Dahl, R. and Blake, Q. (illustrator) (reissued 2013) *Boy: Tales of Childhood*. London: Puffin. Roald Dahl's absorbing, sometimes startling, account of his interesting life.

Frank, A. (2007, definitive edn) *The Diary of a Young Girl*. London: Puffin. This edition is suitable for children aged ten or more.

Wassiljewa, T. (1999) *A Hostage to War*. London: Scholastic. Tatjana keeps a diary during the Holocaust, telling of hardship and friendships, suitable for over-tens.

Biography

BBC Primary History. Available at: www.bbc.co.uk/schools/primary/history/onlinebiog. Offers a long list of the lives of historical figures, for example Winston Churchill, Mary Seacole and literary figures, for example William Shakespeare, C.S. Lewis.

Famous Victorians. See www.channel4learning.net for a list of DVDs for children on this topic from about five years upwards.

Fox, G. and Foreman, M. (illustrator) (2004) *Dear Mr Morpingo: Inside the World of Michael Morpurgo*. London: Wizard Books. Links are made between childhood events – in school days for example, and what happens in later life.

French, V. (2007) *Chocolate: The Bean that Conquered the World – A 'Biography of Chocolate'*. London: Walker Books. This is a beautifully designed and original book. It covers the history of chocolate from the Aztecs to modern times with a lively text and interesting illustrations and recipes.

Hunt, R. (2003) *Alex Brychta: The Story of an Illustrator*. Oxford: Oxford University Press. One of the books in the Oxford Reading Tree True Stories series. A nice touch that will appeal to children at about age seven and older is the inclusion of pictures of the artist's childhood drawings of insects.

Manning, M. and Granström, B. (2009) *Tail-end Charlie: Taff in the WAAF* (2013). London: Frances Lincoln. The effective and interesting design of the pages – the medley of text and illustration – enliven these two biographies about people living active, dedicated lives during the Second World War.

Manning, M. and Granström, B. (2014) *The Beatles*. London: Frances Lincoln. The story is well told for young readers and the illustrations showing clothes, furnishings and street and concert hall scenes give a splendid flavour of the 1960s.

Orion Books *Brilliant Brits* series. Strip cartoon, speech bubbles and subjects associated with popular culture – for example *The Beatles* and *David Beckham* – make these biographies appealing to many young readers from about age 8.

Poole, J. and Barrett, A. (illustrator) (1998) *Joan of Arc*. London: Hutchinson. Poole's story-telling skill and Barrett's visionary illustrations combine to make their interpretation of a true story accessible to children about seven years and above.

Williams, M. (2008) *My Secret Diary By Flossie Albright, 1939–45*. London: Walker Books. Nine-year-old Flossie writes a diary full of pictures as well as interesting writing during the years of the Second World War. This is an example of the diary as a device to show the sort of things that happened to many people at this time rather than being based on an actual person.

Figure 7.1 Front cover of *The Beatles* by Mick Manning and Brita Granström. Cover illustration ©
2014 Mick Manning and Brita Granström. Reproduced by permission of publishers Frances
Lincoln, 74–77 White Lion Street, London N1 9PF.

Extract 54

Source

Unstead, S. (2013) Review of 'Fantastic Mr Dahl' by Michael Rosen and Quentin
Blake (illustrator). *Books for Keeps*, 198 (2), 25.

The main aim of an information text is to inform or instruct about a topic, an event
or ideas. But some, as well as doing that, are written with the sensitivity, imaginative
insight and empathy of good fiction, and may also be poetic in the nature of the feelings
they evoke through the combination of text and illustration. Sue Unstead in her review
of Michael Rosen's biography of Roald Dahl shows a biographer approaching his task
informed by a foundation of information from research but also with imaginative insight.

Remarkably this is described as 'the first authorised biography of Roald Dahl written
especially for children'. It opens with a description of an interview in which Dahl was
asked the ingredients of a good story for children. 'Above all it must be FUNNY.'
So who better to tell the story of the dreamer, prankster, fighter pilot, spy and hugely

popular storyteller than Michael Rosen, whose own award-winning books always put humour at the top of the agenda, and who describes himself (albeit in modestly small lettering on the front cover) as 'Roald Dahl's biggest fan'. Rosen explores how the events of Dahl's life influenced and found their way into his writing, from the beating and the bullying of boarding school days (think of Miss Trunchbull), to the myths and Norse legends his mother told him of wicked trolls and monstrous giants (think of the BFG). He recounts idyllic summers spent in the Norwegian fjords, fishing, boating, collecting birds' eggs, with a clamour of noisy family and friends but always with time to think, wonder and dream. Rosen gets right under the skin of Dahl the writer, analysing just how he builds up suspense and captures the reader's attention. He includes plenty of examples from the books, and even storylines that were discarded. Matilda, it seems, was originally to be the wickedest child in the world with kind, long suffering parents. The pages are enlivened by Quentin Blake's wonderfully inventive characters, Twits, Willie Wonka and Witches amongst them, but there are also drawings of family trees and favourite foods, in addition to reproductions of boyhood letters home, passports, family photographs and of course Dahl writing in his little brick hut. Roald Dahl's life may have been, like his books, nothing short of extraordinary, but this biography belongs in the same category – fantastic.

Comment

Sue Unstead identifies what makes a biography for children absorbing and exciting. She believes that Rosen has shown how things that happened in Dahl's life seem to have found a path into his stories in interesting ways. Illustrations are important, too, in bringing a life and work alive for young readers; and in this biography there is a huge variety, including Blake's quirky drawings of the characters and letters and family photographs. Humour helps attract young readers and, above all – like good biographies for people of any age – this gets right under the skin of an extraordinary children's writer. Sue Unstead's review helps us to understand that Rosen has brought a novelist's empathetic eye to the life and work of another writer.

Questions to discuss with colleagues (Extracts 53 and 54)

If possible, a copy of Rosen's biography of Dahl would be a useful resource for the discussion group as well as some other biographies written for children. (See the suggestions for children's books in the list following Extract 53.)

1. From Sue Unstead's analysis, does this biography seem different from other biographies for children you have read and used in school?
2. Can a biography or autobiography be a creative achievement? Or, to put it differently, can a biography or autobiography for children deserve to be classed as 'children's literature'? What qualities would be needed?
3. How far does the particular subject of a biography call for a particular approach to text and illustration?

4. Biography and autobiography can successfully link history and English work. What might a biography of or an autobiography by an historical figure offer that a conventional information book might not?
5. How would you use Rosen's biography of Roald Dahl, or one of your choice about another writer, to enhance the enjoyment and insight that children may have already gained from reading their books or seeing their stories in other media – film, musical or play?
6. When we read a story in an English class we think about the characters' motives, feelings and behaviour. How might you help children apply insights of this kind to their reading of a biography of an historical figure, perhaps one whose achievements have been studied in a history lesson?

Research inquiries

Either:

■ Choose a biography, either the one by Michael Rosen, reviewed by Sue Unstead, or another one written for children that you think has merit. Read it over several lessons with a group or class of children in your specialist age phase. (See the suggestions for biographies for children in the list following Extract 53.) Discuss with the children what they think makes a biography interesting and how far they think the biography you have read to them succeeds. Ask if there is anything they would change or add to improve it. Have they, for example, found that the questions they had about the person have been adequately answered?

   Write and present a short paper to colleagues on what you consider to be good biographical writing for children, referring to the children's opinions and insights.

Or:

■ Read a selection of autobiographies for children and write a short paper to present to colleagues about their merits and/or shortcomings. You might wish to assess how particular writers invite young readers into their life story, how successfully or otherwise they communicate their ideas and feelings about events and people important to them and how you consider illustrations contribute to young readers' enjoyment.

Further reading

Collins, M. and Graham, J. (2001) *Historical Fiction for Children: Capturing the Past*. London: David Fulton. What is the contribution of historical stories to children's understanding of the past? How do 'facts' and imaginative speculation combine in the best books? The distinguished authors and scholars contributing to this book – for example Rosemary Sutcliff, Philip Pullman and Judith Graham – explain the issues. In 'The historical picturebook', chapter 6, Graham looks at how far particular picturebooks succeed by providing visual markers – clothing, transport – of an era.

Meek, M. (1996) *Information and Book Learning*. Stroud: Thimble Press. See pages 59–61: writing about history for children is discussed, including biographical writing.

Section 2: Lyrical non-fiction

Extract 55

Source

Mallett, M. (2008) *The Lyrical Voice in Non-Fiction: 'Think of an Eel', by Karen Wallace and Mike Bostock*. English Association Bookmark 3. Leicester: English Association, 3–6.

The writers of Walker's pioneering series 'Read and Wonder' brought imaginative power to non-fiction books by using language and illustration with a poetic quality. Books in the series include feelings about a topic as well as information, thoughts and ideas. So, for example, *Spider Watching* by Vivian French tells of a child's dislike of the creatures as well as giving much information about webs and prey. After all, one aspect of knowing about spiders is that some people are arachnophobes and the book suggests this condition can be reversed by promoting knowledge and understanding. To regard books like this as 'transitional genre' seems to underestimate their qualities, although I have seen them used successfully in many Early Years classrooms alongside more conventional information books. *Spider Watching* and *Think of an Eel* might well enrich English work with any age within the 4–11 span, perhaps on an animal theme that included poems and drama. In Extract 55 Margaret Mallett sets out the qualities of what she terms 'lyrical non-fiction' and explains why she considers it has considerable appeal for children.

Three qualities would seem to allow us to describe a non-fiction book as lyrical. First, it should appeal passionately and directly to hearts as well as to minds. Second, it needs to communicate thoughts and feelings by employing poetic devices which are more often associated with stories and poems. Thirdly, the illustrations should embody the distinctive 'line', 'hue' and 'tone' to be found in paintings or picture-book illustrations. Where these three qualities combine, young learners are energised and encouraged to imagine and reflect. *Think of an Eel* seems to embody these lyrical features in particularly good measure.

The appeal to heart and mind

The appeal to heart and mind, and what Margaret Meek calls the 'poetic riches' of *Think of an Eel*, are evident as soon as a child explores the cover. Here the picture of the eel's long body and huge round eyes, swimming in luminous blue and green waters, grabs the attention. And then the reader is drawn to a poetic invitation written in waving hand lettering:

Listen to the story of a long long journey …
Imagine you could find your way
To a place you'd never been before …
Learn about an underwater world …

The lettering and the words beguile and give a personality to the facts soon to be introduced. The words offer a powerful invitation to share in a special journey: a journey from the Sargasso sea where eels are born, across thousands of miles of ocean to the very rivers from which their parents came. So the cover has both aesthetic appeal and the promise of a book that will give much more than a formulaic recital of 'the facts'. The book's narrative organisation – round a journey and a life cycle – will involve and sustain the interest of young readers …

Lyrical writers and illustrators also aim to nourish young readers' understanding by passionate attention to the accuracy and depth of information they offer. In *Think of an Eel* the authorial voice invites rather than commands; young readers are invited to share in what has been discovered and there is a willingness to admit there are still some mysteries. In the case of eels these mysteries are about egg laying and egg hatching.

Poetic devices

As in other books in the 'Read and Wonder' series, the main narrative is undoubtedly poetic, but the hand lettered facts also offer something personal and intimate. The hand lettered 'fact' '*Eels feed mostly at night*' (page 18) – swirls round an atmospheric picture of an eel emerging from the water onto a moonlit riverbank.

Eels feed mostly at night (in waving writing)

The rhythmic language of the main text matches the relentless drive of the eel's life cycle from egg to elver to eel to egg. The choice of vocabulary helps too. Words associated with water spill through the text 'weedy', 'soupy', 'warm weedy sea' – as do those communicating the character of the eels' movements – 'navigating', 'wriggling through the water' and sometimes 'sinking through the sea'. There are onomatopoeic words like 'ooze' and a wonderfully alliterative abstract simile: silver eel 'squirms like a secret from seabird and sailor'. Exciting images are another hallmark of a lyrical writer: here there are verbal images that appeal to the senses of sight, touch, taste and smell which dance with the pictures: the young eel is like 'a shoelace made out of glass'. But the image long remembered by a particular group of eight-year-olds who had enjoyed hearing the book read aloud is of the dying eel sinking into the sea 'like a used silver wrapper', its purpose now fulfilled (page 26). In lyrical non-fiction writers draw on their linguistic resources to ignite the reader's senses and to entice them to bring to bear on the narrative all their knowledge, experience and intuition …

Lyrical illustrations

The 'line', 'hue' and 'tone' of the pictures in *Think of an Eel* come together to show the very spirit of the eel as it is transformed from something like a tiny transparent leaf to a creature that is thick, green and brown. A light but crisp line is used to communicate energy and purpose as the creatures 'navigate by instinct' but always seem to know where they are going (pages 14/15) …

The use of colour or 'hue' is used to reveal the sheer beauty and luminosity during their elver and silver stages. The restricted palette on the double spread (pages 22 and 23) shows maturing eels tangled in a ball in shades of blue, grey and silver, and this appeals to young children's aesthetic sense. These lyrical illustrations tell about the appearance of the eels, the way they move and the changes in environment they encounter in the course of their journey. More conventional information books use diagrams and, as such, the end pages in *Think of an Eel* summarise the changing appearance of the creature in illustrations that function as diagrams while retaining the lyrical quality of the illustrations in the body of the book.

Extract reference

Wallace, K. and Bostock, M. (illustrator) *Think of an Eel*, 'Read and Wonder' series. London: Walker Books.

Figure 7.2 Front cover of *Think of an Eel* by Karen Wallace, illustrated by Mike Bostock. Cover illustration © Mike Bostock. Reproduced by permission of Walker Books Ltd., London SE11 6HJ.

Comment

The argument in this extract centres on the nature and status of what the author terms 'lyrical non-fiction'. The main purpose of this kind of information or fact book, like that of more traditional non-fiction texts, is to inform and communicate knowledge and to encourage understanding. However, in doing so, lyrical non-fiction texts use some of the devices normally associated with fiction – appeal to the feelings, imagery and lyrical illustration. This makes them a good resource for children's writing, including poetry. I have seen this particular book used to inspire children's poems about animals. Some believe that the best of such books deserve to be acknowledged as a distinct genre of children's literature.

Questions to discuss with colleagues

If possible, bring to the discussion some of the books in the 'Read and Wonder' series (Walker) or in *Wonderwise* (Franklin Watts) or other books on information topics that you consider to have lyrical qualities.

1. Do you consider that, as seems to be the case with some of the best autobiographies and biographies for children, lyrical non-fiction deserves to be regarded as a genre within 'children's literature'? Whatever you believe, how would you defend your view?
2. With reference to a 'lyrical' non-fiction text you have brought to the discussion, consider if it has some of the qualities identified by Mallett in the extract. Comment on: any literary devices used, its attention to feelings as well as thoughts and information, and the style and nature of the illustrations. What might be the advantages of using 'lyrical' books alongside more conventional information books in topic work?
3. If you work with the zero to five age group, share some books you have brought to the discussion that you consider have lyrical features and comment on what their value to very young children might be.
4. How far do you consider that 'lyrical' information books, while often read with younger children, are a genre which can be enjoyed by any age group?
5. Genre confusion or imaginative insight? Would you find it acceptable for a children's science, history or geography book to include poetry?

Research inquiry

Choose two books on the same topic, one which you feel has lyrical qualities and one which is a conventional non-fiction text. Read the books to a group or class of children in your specialist age range. Ask the children what they think are the good points about each book and any possible limitations.

Write some notes on the children's responses and use them to make a short presentation to colleagues. If the children have responded with interest to the topic and the books, you may wish to extend the work by inviting the children to do their own writing and drawing.

Further reading

Meek, M. (1996) *Information and Book Learning*. Stroud: Thimble Press. Margaret Meek explains what she considers to be the 'poetic riches' of the books in Walker's 'Read and Wonder' series (see pages 100–2).

Section 3: Texts to support conversation and debate

Extract 56

Source

Sanderson, R. and Bowers, J. (2013) It's not always about books. *English 4–11*, 49 (autumn 2013), 2–4.

As well as choosing and using fiction of all kinds, teachers seek to enrich the English programme with non-fiction texts that encourage thinking and debate about all manner of issues. Print non-fiction texts and websites provide information to inspire thinking and debate: for example about endangered species, problems of war and famine across the world. Magazines and newspapers for children, in print and on-screen, which include articles on current affairs and issues that affect us all are also well worth considering for use in the classroom, as the authors of Extract 56 argue.

Jo Bowers is a Senior Lecturer in Education at Cardiff Metropolitan University and editor of the English Association's primary journal *English 4–11*. Rob Sanderson is Children's Librarian at Wigan Library Service. Both write and research about children's books of all kinds and turn their attention here to the variety of magazines available for readers aged from four to eleven and suggest how they can be used in the classroom to support work in English and in other lessons.

Recent research shows that a significant number of boys and girls number comics and magazines amongst their favoured reading material (Clark, Osborn and Akerman, 2008; Swain, 2009). There is an argument, then, that this type of reading material should be included in the classroom repertoire. Not only so that the classroom reflects the readers' interests but also to develop a critical response to reading comics and magazines in a multimodal age with an ever-changing range of new kinds of texts.

There are now various magazines developed for primary age children – an excellent option for children who prefer non-fiction over fiction or who might find reading a full book a daunting prospect. With magazines, the reader is encouraged to dip in and out of articles, try out quizzes and puzzles, solve problems, ask and answer questions, read short stories, all of which require different skills, knowledge and understanding.

In this article we explore some magazines and newspapers available for young readers and test some of them out on the intended audience ...

Aquila

This magazine, for readers aged 8–12 years old, has a full colour page layout design that is similar to some current non-fiction books. The magazine favours non-fiction although there are occasionally stories. Topics vary; in the October 2012 edition there is a large article on earthquakes and volcanoes, also featured on the front cover, pieces on wheelchair basketball, the discovery of Tutankhamun's tomb in 1922 and interesting practical features showing how to make a lava lamp. Don't worry, no electrics are needed!

Written in an accessible style, *Aquila* offers something for everyone. The tone is lively and never patronising and the pages are packed with information: 'Did you know?' panels, maps, photographs and illustrations with different page layouts for each feature. The magazine focuses on English, Maths and Science subjects, and encourages questioning making it suitable to enhance classroom learning or encourage curious minds to seek out more about subjects of interest.

Molly (aged 7) liked lots of sections of the issue of the magazine on the theme of Canada: 'I love the cover, it looks interesting' and reading it 'helped me to know things about Canada'. The quiz page was a 'just pick it up and do it' page, which she also liked. Overall the non-fiction parts of the magazine were Molly's favourites as the story looked a bit too long and the colours did not attract her.

Discovery Box

From the same stable as Story Box and Adventure Box, this has a similar layout, but is aimed at readers aged 9 or over. Regular features include: an historical event being retold as a picture story; information about animals; scientific topics with instructions for simple experiments and a feature looking at how other people around the world live. The reading – and learning – experience is further enhanced by quizzes, fun facts, games, recipes and things to make and do.

In the issue reviewed here, Mozart's life story provides the basis for the picture story and the cover illustration, focusing on him as a child star, with fact boxes giving details of his life and some of his amazing achievements ... The graphic novel format is used to explore blood circulation ... and there is a fascinating look at some of the world's tallest skyscrapers, showing them in comparison to each other. London's Shard at 305 m tall looks positively tiny next to the 828 metre tall Burj Khalifa in Dubai!

First News

This weekly full colour newspaper in tabloid format is designed for readers between 7 and 14 years. The stories are short and easy to read and illustrated by large, clear photographs. Advertising is kept to a minimum, and there is a heavy focus on puzzles, competitions and reviews. For older readers this may seem lightweight, but it would work well for reluctant readers and is a good introduction to the world of newspapers. Running to 24 pages, it is a manageable read, and the news stories are punchy. At times, it feels a little low on facts, or a little too localised, but there is a good variety of news articles from across the UK.

The Loop

'The magazine that thinks it is a newspaper' is the strapline on the front of this magazine. Or is it a newspaper? It's certainly in newspaper format printed on the same kind of paper stock as a newspaper. The layout is contemporary with a consciously designed grown-up feel. The pages are minimal, with a style that feels more akin to a broadsheet than to a children's publication. It's printed in full colour and much of the text is green, rather than the traditional black for newsprint which may not be easy to read for some children. The approach seems more suited to 'gifted and talented' readers.

The Loop is beautifully designed with some illustrations evocative of the style of the 1950s, with comic strips – 'Belka and Strelka' and 'Molly's Mystery' – which reflect that era too. The articles are interesting and varied and in the edition reviewed here, there is everything from nanotechnology to quantitative easing, and from suggestions for what to read to a recipe for tangy tamarind cupcakes (yum!).

The first issue suggests that this is a strong product, and certainly worth considering if you are keen to ensure your school library or classroom has something to engage children who may be turned off by the more traditional children's magazine publishing.

Extract references

Clark, C., Osborn, S. and Akerman, R. (2008) *Young People's Self-perception as Readers: An Investigation Including Family, Peer and School Influences*. National Literacy Trust.

Swain, C. (2009) *Reading Magazines with a Critical Eye in the Primary School*. Leicester: United Kingdom Literacy Association (UKLA).

Website references

Aquila. Available at: www.aquila.co.uk.

Discovery Box. Available at: www.bayardmagazines.co.uk.

First News. Available at: www.firstnews.co.uk.

The Loop. Available at: http://theloop-news.com.

Comment

Magazines and newspapers like those reviewed in this extract have content suitable for use in many lessons – particularly in science, art, geography and history as well as English. And, of course, the material could also support interesting cross-curricular projects. Some of the articles, news stories and photographs would inspire the sort of critical and creative thinking that invigorates debate and discussions in English lessons, not least the material on issues of the day, the environment, reviews of children's books and websites and topics to do with school. Practise in talking about issues gives children confidence in their ability to organise and express their opinions on many topics – the sooner they broaden their view of the world in all its complexity the better!

Many of these publications are interactive and encourage children to write in with their opinions about both the content and about the quality of the publication. *The Loop*, for example, presents children's writing and drawing following an article on a recent 'Save the Bee' theme (http://theloop-news.com, accessed 20 November 2014). Sanderson and Bowers believe that for some children, magazines and newspapers are a route into reading enjoyment because of their attractive artwork and pithy articles. And reading the best children's newspapers and magazines is likely to help children see the possibilities of different formats when creating their own class or school magazines.

Questions to discuss with colleagues

A selection of magazines and newspapers for children and access to the internet would be helpful to have at hand during the discussion.

1. How far do you consider that reading magazines and newspapers and accessing information from internet sites on school topics can help link, in a beneficial way, school and home reading? What would you do in the classroom to support this?
2. How might reading magazines and newspapers link English with topics in other lessons?
3. The extract includes comments by seven-year-old Molly on the magazine she has been reading. How would you encourage children in your age range to become confident about the expression of informed critical opinions? The following research inquiry suggestion may help here.

Research inquiry

Sanderson and Bowers suggest, later in the article from which the extract is taken, the following task to encourage debate and discussion:

'Many of these magazines open up new facts and ideas that create opportunities for children to ask questions. Choose an article to read with your class or group and ask the children to respond to it with questions or opinions as a starting point for critical enquiry.'

Write up your findings in note form and present them to your student group.

Further reading

Bearne, E., Clark, C., Johnson, A., Manford, P., Mottram, M. and Wolstencroft, H. (2007) *Reading on Screen*. Leicester: United Kingdom Literacy Association (UKLA). What are the processes of teaching and learning involved in on-screen learning at home and at school? These researchers – with evidence gathered from teachers in Birmingham, Croydon, Essex and Sunderland – examine on-screen reading in different curriculum areas with children aged five to sixteen years.

Kress, G. (2003) *Literacy in the New Media*. London and New York: Routledge. What are the implications for teaching and learning of the move from page to screen? Kress argues that literacy is not just a matter of language but also of 'motivated multimedia design'.

Mallett, M. (2010) *Choosing and Using Fiction and Non-Fiction in the Early and Primary School Years*. London and New York: Routledge. In chapter 32 ,'Argument: Discussion and persuasion texts', Mallett suggests that we help children to want genuinely and passionately to find out if we seek out 'the controversial, mind-stretching issues that lie at the heart of so many topics and then explore them through reading, talk and writing'.

Swain, C. (2009) *Reading Magazines with a Critical Eye in the Primary School*. Leicester: UKLA. Explores how we can support children as they learn to assess information in the magazines and children's newspapers they read.

Online resources

BBC. Journalist writing – 'Writing a newspaper'. Available at: www.bbc.co.uk/bitesize/ks2/english/writing/newspapers. Offers guidance on the structure of newspaper reports (accessed 30 November 2014).

BBC. Newsround. Available at: www.bbc.co.uk/newsround. Items on this online resource (accessed 30 November 2014) included 'New threat to humpback whales?' and 'What should be Britain's national symbol?'

Channel 4 Learning. Available at: www.channel4learning.com. Resources for lessons across the curriculum are listed. The 'What's so good about …' DVD for older primary/younger secondary children sets out what is known about five authors' lives and work as a basis for discussion (accessed 30 November 2014).

Scholastic magazines. 'News for your classroom'. Available at: www.magazines.scholastic.com. Items on this online resource (accessed 30 November 2014) included 'Is chocolate disappearing?' and 'An historic climate agreement'.

United Kingdom Literacy Association (UKLA). Materials on the critical reading of magazines for the over-eights can be downloaded at www.ukla.org.

Planning, assessing and recording progress in English
The learning cycle

Introduction

There are different views, often passionately held, about how teachers can best assess and record children's progress in English and other lessons across the curriculum. There is more than one view, too, about how assessment and record keeping relate to planning what is to be taught and how it is taught. 'Assessment' is, of course, an umbrella term, a term for all the ways in which we evaluate children's learning; the method of assessment used at a particular time depends on its purpose. So, for example, 'diagnostic' tests are used by educational psychologists to identify particular kinds of learning difficulty. But in school the two main types of assessment are 'summative' and 'formative'.

In a summative assessment children complete specially designed tests and tasks. The standardised assessment tests (SATs) carried out in schools in parts of the United Kingdom are an example of this kind of testing. Scores from summative tests are used to inform teachers, parents and sometimes outside agencies about a child's progress. This means their progress can be compared with that of large cohorts of children of a similar age. Summative tests provide a snapshot of a child's achievements at a particular time. One criticism of those who rely too heavily on the results of summative tests is that government agencies and the world in general receive an incomplete picture of the achievements of individual children and of a school. Moreover, too fierce an emphasis on summative testing risks narrowing the teaching and learning programme so that it may focus on those things that will be tested, leaving less time for other activities of value.

Formative approaches to assessment give a richer picture of a child's progress. These require careful observation of everyday work and activities and the recognition and recording of significant achievements. This approach is particularly appropriate for assessing progress in important parts of the English curriculum. Notes about speaking and listening, reading and writing in different classroom contexts can form a core of evidence for an assessment. Even in the case of the youngest children, whose language moves flexibly from helping organise practical activities to talking about the real world and about the worlds of their imagination fed by stories and poems, we can identify the beginnings of what we might call an 'English' perspective.

In English lessons, assessment is best concerned with charting the development of all those uses of language, and of thinking and feeling, which have been at the heart of each chapter of this book. Reading and talking about fiction is central of course. Children become increasingly able to make links between what they read or have heard read aloud and their experience as human beings living their lives in the real world (text to life) and links between what happens in the real world and what has been read (life to text). When it comes to writing in English lessons, we want children to find their own 'voice' and to gain control over a number of genres, particularly those to do with writing stories, poems and personal accounts. All this needs to be communicated using the conventions of grammar, spelling and punctuation and progress here has a place in assessment.

Progress in speaking and listening is hugely important. It makes possible fruitful collaboration with others and can move children on considerably in their reading and their writing. Formative assessment is helpful here as it recognises that we are looking for processes rather than just products and that teachers can fruitfully assess children's achievements through the day. The chapters on children's speaking and listening, reading and writing aim to point to what is worth learning and therefore deserving of careful assessment and recording. Let me give one example, to suggest the sort of progress that is worth recording. Chapter 3 on reading and responding to texts includes an extract of children talking together about a short story by Philippa Pearce. The children's growing ability to share the enthusiasms, puzzles and understanding of patterns (explained in Aidan Chambers 'The three sharings') is well worth a place in a teacher's records (Chambers, 2011).

Teachers have to take account of the statutory requirements for assessment in the country they work in. These are often changed or modified and need to be checked on relevant government websites. However, this chapter concentrates on formative kinds of assessing and recording children's progress, the kind which feeds readily into planning for successive rounds of teaching and learning. In Extract 58, Mary Drummond sets out a powerful argument proclaiming the value of an approach to formative assessment – known as 'learning stories' or 'learning journeys' – which supports a child's developing sense of identity as a learner. Here, teachers observe children throughout the school day as they learn, and record significant steps in their development and progress. The curriculum for young children is fluid and flexible, and so the records kept will cover all manner of activities from, say, constructing dens or 'building a space ship' to early writing, artwork and music. And of great importance – teachers jot down children's significant talk, questions and observations. Rather than just taking account of products, like some other kinds of assessment, this one homes in on the processes involved in becoming a language user.

The 'learning story' is an appropriate way of charting young children's development in the kinds of thinking, feeling and use of language that is the meat and substance of English lessons. I am thinking, of course, about children's story-telling, their reading, their talk about books and their early attempts at writing. This 'English' perspective has to do with what was referred to in Chapter 1 of this book as language use in the 'spectator role'. In English lessons children find a time within the school day when they can bring to bear all their experience of the real world as well as the world of their imaginations. It is where all the experience, including social and cultural experience, and all the kinds of thinking and all the feelings human beings are capable of, is integrated. It is this richness that a 'learning story' approach and other kinds of formative assessment can capture.

Although the 'learning story' was developed for use in Early Years settings, formative approaches to evaluating children's progress, those based on a philosophy that sees planning, assessment and record keeping in a dynamic relationship, are of continuing importance in the Primary Years. Rather than view assessment as something just to be done at the end of a phase of learning, formative assessment is fully integrated into daily teaching and learning. The notes, writing samples and transcripts that teachers collect provide a rich evidence base from which to select information for developing a profile of each child.

Are there benefits if children are helped to assess their own progress in writing? The researchers in the National Literacy Trust's 'Transforming writing' team believe that both self-assessment and assessment of peers, with some guidance from the teacher, leads to a young writer's maturing ability to review their own work and progress. Part of progress here is the development of a metalanguage to talk about their writing (see Extract 59).

There are a number of published formats for record keeping, but teachers in some schools devise their own framework and constantly adjust and enrich it. One of the best known frameworks for keeping a record of developing language abilities is *The Primary Language Record* prepared by Myra Barrs and her colleagues at the Centre for Literacy in Primary Education. Although the record was created and published decades ago it is still an inspirational starting point for planning formative kinds of assessment and record keeping for Language and English. In Section 4, Extract 60, Godwin and Perkins set out some of the valuable features of this way of recording formative assessments of children's English and language work. Their argument concentrates particularly on the collaborative feature of the record – the inclusion in the record of the evaluative comments of parents and children. The home school collaboration needs, increasingly, to take account of the use of electronic sources and new technologies in both settings as the range and nature of reading and writing changes.

But the first extract, Extract 57, in this final chapter presents a framework for thinking about planning units and lessons. Wyse and Jones and associates present ideas and strategies broad enough to have relevance in English and lessons in every other part of the primary curriculum.

Section 1: Planning the English programme

Extract 57

Source

Wyse, D., Jones, R., Bradford, H. and Wolpert, M.A. (2013, 3rd edn) Planning. In *Teaching English, Language and Literacy*. Abingdon and New York: Routledge, (a) 275–6, (b) 278–9.

What do student teachers and teachers at the beginning of their classroom career need to understand about planning? This account offers a helpful starting point by providing some pertinent questions and practical ideas. These writers believe teaching that is interesting and creative nearly always draws inspiration for classroom activities from many sources. Providing a coherent structure to a programme and building in progression are thought important – but this team also believes that flexibility is desirable and taking account of the needs, interests and questions of the young learners is crucial if we seek truly involved learning.

Part a

Planning is commonly described in three levels: long-term, medium-term and short-term. Long-term planning tends to mean planning for a year or more and provides a broad framework of curricular provision for each year of each primary school year, to ensure progression, balance, coherence and continuity. Medium-term planning refers to planning for terms and half-terms. Short-term planning is usually weekly or daily and includes detailed lesson plans, including objectives, procedures, differentiation, resources and assessment considerations. Within this overall structure, teachers need to provide high-quality, responsive literacy experiences for the pupils in their class. Key questions to be asked include:

> Does the planning take account of prior knowledge of the pupils?
> Are you clear about what you intend the children to learn?
> Is the planning underpinned by secure subject knowledge and secure pedagogy?
> Does the planning take account of potential barriers to learning?
> Does the planning encourage creative and innovative responses to the task?
> Are the children likely to be motivated by the suggested activities?
> Across a sequence of lessons, does the planning demonstrate progression?
> A critical question you should ask about any planning is to what extent are children's choices taken into account?

There are many ways to find ideas for activities. The best way is for you to think about what you want your children to learn and then create a suitable activity. When you create activities and resources yourself, you go through a process of development which includes having teaching objectives that are closely matched with the needs of your class. The creative process can, of course, involve you using ideas from all kinds of sources: colleagues; the internet; published materials, etc. While it can be tempting to use published schemes and material, these must always be tailored for the specific learning needs of your class ...

Part b

Long-term and medium-term planning leads to lesson planning. New teachers often need to devise individual lesson plans. These provide structure and security but should not be seen as completely inflexible; it is important to be responsive to the children during the session. Elements of a lesson plan are likely to include:

> administrative details (date and length of session, number and age of children, supporting adults, etc.);
> curriculum links;
> learning objectives;
> success criteria;
> assessment opportunities;
> key vocabulary;
> resources;
> phases of the lesson (introduction, activities, plenary);
> roles of others.

Lesson plans should be annotated after teaching with evaluation and comments about children's learning.

Comment

In Extract 57, Wyse and co-workers take up a systematic approach to planning, whether long-term or medium-term, and give detailed advice about what might be included in a lesson plan. They consider that teachers need to achieve a balance between working within a structure and having 'objectives' and building in 'progression', and showing flexibility. What do they mean by 'showing flexibility'? This has to do with taking account of children's interests, choices and needs and welcoming their creative and innovative responses as lessons progress.

Questions to discuss with colleagues

1. What potential problems might 'long-term' planning of English lessons or units present and how are these best avoided?
2. The authors of the book from which Extract 57 is taken stress the importance of a teacher having 'secure subject knowledge' to inform planning. What have the chapters in this *Guided Reader* led you to consider are the most important elements of this knowledge? How do you think this would inform and enrich your planning for:

   a) children's developing knowledge about language;
   b) children's enjoyment of the texts which have their natural home in English lessons – picturebooks, short stories, novels and poems;
   c) children's progress as speakers and listeners, readers and writers?

3. The extract also refers to the importance of 'secure pedagogy'. How might your understanding of how children develop and learn as they progress through the Primary Years inform your planning for talk and collaboration in English lessons?

Research inquiry

Choose either an English lesson you have carried out or one you have observed; after the lesson, return to your lessons plan, add an evaluation and comment and share what you have learnt with colleagues.

Further reading

Bearne, E. (1998) *Making Progress in English*. London: Routledge. Practical, timeless and well thought out suggestions are given for planning for talk, reading and writing.

Chambers, A. (2011, 2nd edn) *Tell Me: Children, Reading and Talk* with *The Reading Environment*. Stroud: Thimble Press.

Cremin, T. and Barnes, J. (2014, 3rd edn) Planning for creativity. In T. Cremin and J. Arthur (eds) *Learning to Teach in the Primary School*. Abingdon and New York: Routledge, 476–9. There are some research-informed suggestions here; for example, planning opportunities for open-ended learning opportunities and collaboration, framing work round children's questions and interests and taking account of children's emotional links to topics.

Drummond, M.J. (2012, classic edn) *Assessing Children's Learning*. London and New York: Routledge. See pages 129–31 for a convincing argument that planning, particularly for the youngest children, should be 'tied to a rigorous process of review'. Drummond believes that 'too frequent use of the future tense can lead us to neglect the present tense, the reality of the moment, the only curriculum that our pupils ever experience'.

Medwell, J. (2014, 3rd edn) 'Approaching long- and medium-term planning' and 'Approaching short-term planning'. In T. Cremin and J. Arthur (eds) *Learning to Teach in the Primary School*. Abingdon and New York: Routledge.

Section 2: Learning stories – a formative approach to assessing the progress of young children

Extract 58

Source

Drummond, M.J. (2012, classic edn) 'Learning Stories' and 'Returning to Jason'. In *Assessing Children's Learning*. London: David Fulton, (a) 163–4, (b) 171–2.

Mary Jane Drummond has been a primary school teacher, head teacher and university lecturer. She has had a research interest in assessing children's learning for many years and her books on this subject are valued by all those concerned with the education of young children. In the first of two extracts she defines what she considers assessment to be: 'the ways in which, in our everyday practice, we observe children's learning, strive to understand it, and then put our understanding to good use'.

She evaluates and recommends an approach known as 'Learning Stories', which has been adopted for Early Years classrooms in New Zealand and which has a holistic perspective towards learning and assessment. Drummond's thinking is also considerably influenced by the beliefs and work of early childhood educators in the region of Emilia Romagna in Italy. At the centre of what is known as the 'Reggio' approach is the belief that children are powerful learners and that the expressive arts should be at the centre of the learning programme.

The second extract follows an explanation of the difficulties that summative kinds of testing can present to young learners. Seven-year-old Jason has been confused and unable to understand what is required of him in a spelling test. Drummond goes on to imagine how he might have responded to an approach that offered rich opportunities for meaningful activities.

Learning Stories

Learning Stories are about children's identities as learners; they are written by their educators, with contributions from children, parents, and extended family. They are public documents, much handled, much appreciated; they are favourite reading material in early childhood settings, by both children and their families. *Learning Stories* take a credit, not a deficit approach to learning; their perspective is holistic, not atomistic. Learning is not subdivided and fragmented into areas, skills or aspects of knowledge; the *Learning Stories* record children's enterprises and enquiries over several days, ranging over every aspect of their experience. Perhaps most significantly, *Learning Stories* embody a coherent understanding of progression: over time. Carr demonstrates (2001, pp. 159–61) the *Learning Stories* become longer, deeper, broader and more frequent. The interests and dispositions they document become more complex; they appear in different activities in the programme; they extend over longer periods of time.

The New Zealand model of learning and assessment, and the narrative method at its core, have, I believe, enormous potential for educators in other places. In adopting the dominant metaphor of story, in the place of the tape measure (or long jump), educators are committing themselves to taking each child's learning seriously as a process, with its own life and living landmarks. They are rejecting the whole set of product-based metaphors with which, in this country we have grown familiar over the years, in which learning is described in terms of targets, levels, outcomes, goals … All these product-based metaphors suggest that learning is time-bound, momentary, and discontinuous; they suggest that learning is what children *have* (measured in terms of scores, grades, marks or levels) rather than something they *do*. The New Zealand approach emphasises learning as a moving event, dynamic and changeful, practically synonymous with living, a perspective with which I wholeheartedly agree. I will also note, with a certain pride, but I hope without arrogance, that Carr's book (2001) is structured round my own definition of assessment, as it appeared in the first edition of this book and still stands:

'The ways in which in our everyday practice, we observe children's learning, strive to understand it, and then put our understanding to good use.' (Quoted in Carr (2001, p. 19)

Extract reference

Carr, M. (2001) *Assessment in Early Childhood Settings*. London: Paul Chapman.

The following extract continues Drummond's account of seven-year-old Jason's poor performance in a classroom spelling test. The humiliating mark has been made public.

Returning to Jason

This will not be the first time Jason has received such a low mark for his performance as a pupil: his teacher is unlikely to be surprised by it, and we can feel fairly confident in assuming that she or he will use it to predict Jason's unsatisfactory and undistinguished career as a learner.

Now let us imagine a different scenario, where Jason's future is shaped in a different way. In this imaginary but not impossible classroom. Jason is educated by teachers who are committed to the ideas I have been exploring in these pages, by teachers who reject the long-jump model of testing, who reject ability labelling, who believe that assessment must work for children by promoting their learning. Suppose Jason to be educated by teachers who put their trust in him as a learner, who are committed to the Reggio construction of children as 'rich, strong and powerful' because they trust Jason's power to learn, these teachers give Jason the opportunities to exercise and strengthen his powers in ways that make human sense. They give him, for example, mathematical experiences that have meaning for him as a person, where his hitherto untapped capacity to think mathematically has relevance and impact. Jason's mathematics learning now takes place in real-world contexts of shops, money, building materials, big blocks and planks of wood.

In this imagined classroom, Jason's teachers are equally convinced that Jason has emerging powers as a writer: again he is offered literary experiences that have real-world significance. He is given opportunities to write important notices, lists, letters, invitations, poems, secret messages, recipes, stories and magic spells, under his own direction. His teachers recognise the relationship between writing and other forms of communication that the Reggio educators call the hundred symbolic languages of children (99 of which, they claim, are ignored in school). Jason's teachers do not ignore them: they give him opportunities to sing and dance and make music, to represent his thought in sound, paint, clay and, above all, in sustained purposeful talk.

Now Jason is daily engaged in many kinds of classroom talk that are a far more nourishing diet for his learning than any number of spelling tests. He joins in talk that sets the world to rights or solves a pressing social problem (in the playground or the toilets); talk that plans an adventure or relishes an old one; talk that imagines the future and all the impossible things that might never happen; talk that remembers the past and all the amazing things that happened there. With this programme and more, Jason flourishes as a learner. From trusting him as a learner and giving him the freedom to act as a learner, setting off on his own inimitable journey. Jason's teachers take up their next responsibility: to document, in their assessment practices, Jason's unique and impressive learning story. I persist in my optimism for all the Jasons of the future.

Comment

Drummond explains the complexity of children's learning, and of assessing that learning, particularly in the Early Years. She argues that some formal methods of assessing children's progress simply fail to show the richness of their potential as learners and achievers. Further, failure to meet the expectations of the 'long-jump' approach to assessment can reduce a child's confidence as a learner. In the second of the two extracts she provides a case study which, while imaginary, shows the typical imaginative teaching and learning which many would regard as good Early Years practice. Jason's ideal curriculum is built round activities that make 'human sense' and which are highly adventurous and motivating as they are tailored to his interests and abilities. So it follows that the assessment of his achievements in all areas, and not least as a language user, are useful and encouraging and, above all, work for him. This approach supports the view of seeing learning, assessing and planning as circular, as what is observed and achieved forms the next phase of planning.

Questions to discuss with colleagues

1. Thinking of your own early or primary school days and your development as a speaker, listener, reader and writer, what do you consider was most worth assessing and recording?
2. Has the 'learning story' approach to learning, assessment and record keeping a place in the upper primary school classroom, alongside other kinds of assessment? How might a teacher adapt it for children beyond the Early Years?
3. Particularly as children move towards the later Primary Years, teachers have the challenge of preparing them for whatever summative tests and assessments are required. How would you enrich summative assessments of a young learner's achievements in English with formative assessment?

Research inquiries

Either:

- In a series of English lessons where you are the teacher, or you are observing a colleague, note what you consider to be a significant achievement for one young learner. The achievement might be to do with insightful talk about a book in a small group setting or to do with writing that shows progress in controlling a particular genre. Write a short comment on this achievement and discuss it with colleagues.

Or:

- Observe a teacher of young children at work and then discuss with him or her the values they bring to their approach to assessment and record keeping.

Further reading

Blenkin, G. and Kelly, A.V. (1992) *Assessment in Early Childhood Education*. London: Paul Chapman Publishing. The essential features of those kinds of assessment most likely to be supportive of the learning and progress of young children are set out.

Paley, V.G. (1987) *Wally's Stories: Conversations in the Kindergarten*. MA: Harvard University Press. An American kindergarten teacher shares her developing understanding of what the told and 'acted out' stories of young children tell us about their thinking and progress. These insights are hard won, as Paley learns to tap into the children's imaginings about such things as robbers and secret squirrels. Mary Jane Drummond, author of Extract 58, drew inspiration from these classroom examples in developing her 'learning stories' approach to assessment.

Section 3: Children's self and peer assessment

Extract 59

Source

Rooke, J. (2013) Teachers used a variety of marking techniques to engage children in assessment. In *Transforming Writing: Final Evaluation Report*, Appendix 2. London: National Literacy Trust, 46–8.

What might be the benefits of involving children in self and peer assessments in their writing and what marking techniques seem most effective? These issues are illuminated in the extract below taken from the first part of Appendix 2 of the final report of a two-year action research project. This project developed an approach to the 'teaching and learning of writing' embedding formative assessment. Children and teachers of twelve schools participated, and the project was sponsored by the Esmee Fairbairn Foundation. Jonathan Rooke – a researcher, writer and a Senior Lecturer in Education (English for Primary ITE) at the University of Winchester – led the research team. Research results suggested that 'the focused use of formative assessment by teachers with children and by children with peers can make a major difference to children's writing progress in terms of attainment, engagement and confidence'. (See Chapter 2, Extract 13, for an analysis of the benefits of involving children in discussion about the merits of their own and their peers' writing, using a visualiser, from the same report.) The comments after the extract are those of the author and not necessarily the opinions of the authors of the report or of the National Literacy Trust.

Appendix 2, Section 1

Teachers used a variety of marking techniques to engage children in assessment.

Teachers used a range of techniques to engage children in collaborative assessment of their own and each other's writing. The techniques described here supported children's active response to assessment as well as initiation of assessment. The teachers' intention was that these in turn would empower children to develop their own capacity and skills to formatively assess their own writing.

1. Children initiating the teacher assessment of their own writing

Children wrote assessments at the end of their own passage of writing identifying which parts they felt worked best and which parts they felt needed further work. Teachers then responded to this. Such an approach offers children a 'critical point of communication' with the teacher. It inverts the practice of the teacher evaluating writing and doing something to the writing that the child must respond to. Here, children evaluate their own writing first, identify an aspect which they feel needs addressing and the teacher then responds. This supports teachers' formative assessment processes because it reveals the child's priorities, and the level of complexity in writing that the children believe they can work. Teachers felt that requiring children to provide a written response to their own writing can elicit a higher quality response than a verbal response.

> 'Some occasions we expect just written responses to their writing. These tend to be better quality than talking partner discussions. Writing it seems to focus the quality of the response.'

Source: teacher.

2. Peer marking

During peer marking, children gave a written response to their partner's writing. Teachers believed this helped them to overcome the challenge of teachers having to monitor and respond to many simultaneous peer assessment exchanges, and it required the children to be focused on the assessment of their peer's writing. It lent some permanence to the impermanent assessment of conversations children have together ...

3. Teacher writing a personal written response to children's composition

Teachers said it was important to sometimes write a personal response to the children's composition. In order to focus children on compositional skills and the impact they might have on the reader, one school included as part of marking response, a written comment by the teacher describing the way the writing made the teacher feel and identifying for them how they had achieved that effect.

> 'This part makes me want to focus on what happens next.
> This part is scary because you have used this word.'

Source: teacher.

Teachers said their written assessment was best when it subsequently included a next steps 'moving on' comment and required the child to respond before continuing. Detailed written marking of assessment was identified as 'extremely' time consuming and in some ways disheartening, because children did not always respond to the marking in subsequent pieces of writing.

4. Building in sufficient time for children to actively respond to marking

Teachers thought that written feedback was most effective when children had time at the end or beginning of a lesson in which to respond and act on the written feedback. Schools used extended plenaries at the beginning of the lesson the day after marking during which the children could respond. One school ensured children had a response task to their writing to do at the start of the day.

5. Children using highlighters

Highlighters used within a collaboratively constructed two- or three-colour-code supported formative assessment. They were used by children to locate and identify aspects of writing that had the intended effect or needed improvement. These were used collaboratively by peer partners, with teachers or by children independently for self assessment. Teachers said highlighting motivates children because they see their own good writing explicitly identified. It clearly identifies sites for revision and focuses children on analysing segments of their own writing which is at the heart of the revision process. It supported peer and collaborative talk and reduced teachers' marking load.

6. Arrows to focus assessment talk

Teachers said it was effective when children used stick-on arrows in their writing to identify their use of collaboratively agreed writing goals (the toolkits) for the genre they were writing. The arrows helped the children to assess their own and their peers' writing. The arrows indicated the focus for the peer talk and helped them to talk at length. Using arrows and talking around them is a skill that has to be explicitly taught …

7. Immediate teaching in response to precise assessment

Prioritising assessment and immediately acting upon it were regarded by teachers as essential qualities of an effective Transforming Writing teacher. Teachers need to identify the single most important piece of feedback and be very focused on one feature of writing that children can tackle and will lead to an immediate improvement. Assessment done by teachers needs to be addressed in the next lesson. The teacher needs to know exactly what it is s/he wants the children to respond to as a result of the assessment.

Comment

The close involvement of classroom teachers in this research led to a realistic appreciation of the time likely to be available for written assessments. 'Detailed written marking of assessment was identified as "extremely" time consuming' and did not always lead to children responding to it in subsequent pieces of work. So, rather than teachers composing long assessments, the team recommend shorter ones which, importantly, include a next steps 'moving on' comment.

Some of the findings and recommendations seem consistent with other studies and the everyday good practice of some teachers. In this category I would place: reinforcing the value of teachers giving their own personal written response to children's writing, mentioning how the writing made them feel; using highlighting to identify both those parts of written accounts that were successful and those that needed working on; using a 'response partner' approach. Other findings identified successful practice less frequently found in classrooms. I found it interesting that participating teachers felt that 'requiring children to provide a written response to their own writing can elicit a higher quality assessment response than a verbal response'. However, it is made clear that talk about their writing is valuable, particularly when carefully focused on specific aspects.

Questions to discuss with colleagues

1. How would you help children to acquire a vocabulary, a metalanguage, to talk about and assess their own writing progress? What terminology would you include?
2. Rooke and colleagues comment in the extract that some teachers found that children's 'written response to their own writing can elicit a higher quality assessment response than a verbal response'. Does this result surprise you? And if so, why?
3. Younger children would not be able to write the assessment comments suggested in the extract. How would you encourage them to use spoken language to make a start in evaluating their own work? What kind of language and ideas would you introduce them to?
4. This study considered writing across the curriculum and in all genres. Do you consider that the analytic approach suggested in the extract is more appropriate for improving some kinds of writing than others? Some teachers might argue that writing a good story sometimes involves flouting the 'rules', and that following suggestions for improvement might risk inhibiting the creative energy which builds up a writing momentum.

Research inquiries

Either:

■ Work with two children on writing stories over a week or so. The sessions might proceed as follows.

   ☐ Talk together about the genre and about what often makes a story interesting. You might arrive at a 'genre list' – a written list of some things to guide writing a story: perhaps include the importance of creating a strong setting, introducing convincing characters, working to a strong plot and using the best words to convey atmosphere and meaning.

   ☐ Invite the children each to write their own story during a session in which you can provide advice.

    ☐ Make copies of both stories and ask each child to read their story out loud while you and the other child follow it in the copies.

    ☐ Look at each story, assessing it against the 'genre list'.

    ☐ Highlight one good feature with a felt-tip pen and one 'aspect to work on next time' in a different colour.

    ☐ Ask each child to write another story, reminding them of the 'aspect to work on' identified last time.

Or:

■ Work with two children or a small group of children on writing stories. After each child has finished their story, in the spirit of subsection 3 in the extract, 'Teacher writing a personal written response to children's composition', write a personal response to each of the children's stories. When the stories are returned to the children, ask them to read them and the written comment, to the group and then encourage a discussion about how helpful or otherwise the written personal response was.

Further reading

Hargreaves, E., Gipps, C. and Pickering, A. (2014, 3rd edn) Peer and self assessment. In T. Cremin and J. Arthur (eds) *Learning to Teach in the Primary School*. London and New York: Routledge, 318–20. This section of the book argues that self and peer assessment can be motivating but children need clear guidelines for it to be effective.

Laycock, L. (2009, 3rd edn) Monitoring and assessing writing. In J. Graham and A. Kelly (eds) *Writing Under Control*. London: Routledge. See chapter 7 for an analysis of ways of assessing writing with examples of children's work across the Primary Years.

Section 4: Recording progress

Extract 60

Source

Godwin, D. and Perkins, M. (2002, 2nd edn) Planning, assessment and recording. In *Teaching Language and Literacy in the Early Years*. London: David Fulton, 126–7.

A little research will show that there is more than one way to design a format in which to record the planning and assessment of teaching and learning in English lessons. Most promising are those formats that recognise a cycle of learning. In other words, an approach which allows practitioners to build on a child's achievements when shaping the next round of teaching. One of the best known and most influential recording formats is the Centre for Literacy in Primary Education's *Primary Language Record*.

The principles of this format have informed other frameworks, for example the National Assessment Agency (NAA), *Building a Picture of What Children Can Do* (2004), and Croydon LEA's *Writing Development Framework* (Graham, 1995). Godwin and Perkins, both experienced Early Years teachers and teacher trainers, pinpoint some of those features of the Centre for Literacy in Primary Education's formative evidence-based kind of assessment and record keeping that make it valuable in the Early Years as well as during the primary school years.

We would like to return to *The Primary Language Record* (Barrs *et al.*, 1998), a package produced for primary schools which sets out a comprehensive list of procedures for recording children's progress in oracy and literacy. It also includes detailed descriptions of ways of undertaking regular conferences with children and parents. The handbook is accessible and the chapter regarding the discussion between the parent and the teacher is particularly helpful here, despite its being designed for children of statutory school age. *The Primary Language Record* has several features which could reasonably be adopted by the early years practitioner.

1. It uses evidence of achievement as a vehicle for discussion. This means that the discussion uses examples of what the child does or says as a vehicle for assessing development and progress. This has the potential to be a powerful source of dialogue regarding what we see as progress. Simply comparing a drawing done on entry to the setting with one done several months later can be a very useful strategy for assessing the success of teaching and learning. The same applies for other samples you might keep. Of course you need the agreement of the child that a particular picture or model can be kept rather than sent home immediately, but I have found most children are amenable to the idea that they have a special folder or container which is being saved so that it can be shown to their parents later.
2. It records parents' comments in collaboration with the teacher. This enables progression from one meeting to the next. This means that parents can feel genuinely included in their child's learning, and that their contributions are valued and listened to. We ought to make it clear that this is undertaken in a shared situation where comments are negotiated and views from both parties are given equal weight. The end point of one discussion can become the beginning of the next, thereby making it possible to gain a sense of continuity and forward movement rather than a summing up of the past.
3. It gives parents the opportunity to comment on the child's progress in talking, reading and writing. This means that you have access to information which can inform your future plans and response to that child. What you know about a child affects what you say to the child. *The Primary Language Record* has a useful list of topics for discussion during a conference, which they envisage lasting approximately 20 minutes.

In addition to indicating the above as a source of useful information, we would like to add a few of our own thoughts. Remember that your formative assessments will be in direct relationship to your plans, in particular to your learning intentions for that child. When you talk to parents about their child's performance remember to put it in the context of what you wanted her to learn and how you went about it.

You should practise confidentiality and not record or repeat detailed discussions with parents which they would not like made public. What you record should be with the complete understanding of the parent concerning its use. You should exercise discretion at all times and be sensitive to parents' needs. Be aware that some parents may need support, for example, when their first language is not English.

The context of discussion with parents should be seen as an opportunity for both parties to learn from one each other and as a result make a positive contribution to the child's development.

Extract reference

Barrs, M., Ellis, S., Hester, H. and Thomas, A. (1998) *The Primary Language Record*. London: Centre for Language in Primary Education. (Now named Centre for Literacy in Primary Education.)

Comment

Godwin and Perkins pinpoint the advantages of a format for assessment that keeps planning, assessment and recording together, recognising the part each plays in the cycle of learning. Their analysis concentrates on one published format for observing and recording the developing abilities of children in speaking and listening and reading and writing. They emphasise that the format is evidence-based and arises out of the Centre team's rich background of knowledge, research in schools and their careful reflection on that research.

Earlier in the book from which the extract is taken Goodwin and Perkins remind us that the Centre's language record was developed with the help of many teachers in multilingual inner London primary schools and draws on understandings about learning English as a second or additional language. A main argument in the extract is that helping children make progress, and recording that progress, is best achieved by a collaboration between teachers, parents and the children themselves – all of whom have the chance to have their comments recorded.

The Centre staff have also done much work in schools which has confirmed their belief in the power of the best books of all kinds – not least fiction – to nurture young readers and writers. They have shown in many of their publications that sharing with children the more shaped kinds of oral story-tellings and poems develop their reading and writing.

Younger children in the Nursery or Reception classroom change their activities and interests constantly and, for them, teaching and learning is fluid and flexible. Nevertheless, we can detect what we might term 'an English perspective' early on; *The Primary Language Record*, and similar formats, enable teachers to observe and show evidence of progress in telling and listening to personal anecdotes, in appreciating the more shaped kind of language of story-telling and of becoming confident readers and writers.

Since the publication of *The Primary Language Record*, and the book by Godwin and Perkins from which the extract was taken, children's reading and writing repertoire has been extended by the relentless innovations brought by new technology. This means that the ability to read on-screen and to read and create multimodal and multimedia texts need to be part of records of children's progress in language literacy and understanding literature.

Questions to discuss with colleagues

1. What do you consider are the benefits of treating planning, teaching, assessment and record keeping as a cycle? What are the practical implications of this for teachers?
2. Increasingly, teachers need to assess and record children's reading and understanding of on-screen texts. How would you involve parents in linking home and school experiences of on-screen reading and writing in this digital age?
3. Talk, and particularly 'booktalk', has been shown to be important in helping children think about and respond to what they have read and may sometimes enrich their writing. Is there a case on occasion for assessing children's progress in all the areas of language together – speaking and listening, reading and writing?
4. How far does knowledge of children's social lives and cultural contexts affect how we make meaningful judgements on their progress?

Research inquiry

Observe a young learner reading a story online and discuss with them the impact of sound effects, animation of text and images. Make some notes and share with colleagues what you have learnt about the child's understanding as a reader and assessor of on-screen texts. You would find *Reading on Screen* helpful in structuring your analysis (Bearne *et al.*, 2007).

Further reading

Barrs, M., Ellis, S., Hester, H. and Thomas, A. (1988) *The Primary Language Record: Handbook for Teachers*. London: Centre for Language in Primary Education. A resource to use alongside *The Primary Language Record*.

Bearne, E., Clark, C., Johnson, A., Manford, P., Mottram, M. and Wolstencroft, H. (2007) *Reading on Screen*. Leicester: United Kingdom Literacy Association (UKLA). Reading increasingly involves the use of electronic sources and new technologies and this book supports teachers in gaining skills to assess these. This research team examined the on-screen reading of children from five to sixteen in school and out-of-school settings 'in order to understand the implications for how schools can bridge home and school learning'.

Drummond, M.J. (2012) *Assessing Children's Learning*. Abingdon and New York. See pages 148–51 for a discussion of the role of parents in assessing and recording their children's progress. Drummond recognises the contribution of *The Primary Language Record* and the *All About Me* booklet developed by Wolfendale in 1990 which, like 'Learning Stories', encourage collaboration between teachers and parents.

Faragher, S. (2014) *Assessment in Primary Education*. London: Sage. A very thorough account of the different kinds of assessment and record keeping used in the primary school years. Covers the gathering of the kinds of evidence to help show what pupils can do.

Graham, J. (1995) *Writing Development Framework*. Croydon: LEA. Gives advice on questions to ask about progress and examples of helpful annotations on children's written work.

Graham, J. and Kelly, A. (2010, 3rd edn) *Writing Under Control*. London: David Fulton. See pages 198–9 for advice on record keeping.

Grugeon, E. (2005, 3rd edn) *Teaching Speaking and Listening in the Primary School*. London: David Fulton. Chapter 6 sets out how to plan for, assess and record progress in speaking and listening.

Hall, K. and Sheehy, K. (2014, 3rd edn) Assessment for learning: Summative approaches. In T. Cremin and J. Arthur (eds) *Learning to Teach in the Primary School*, Unit 5.2. Abingdon and New York: Routledge, 324–38. This text sets out the purposes of summative kinds of assessment and covers the SATs carried out in schools in England. Issues to do with the impact of 'high stakes' testing on young learners and on the curriculum are clearly explained.

Johnson, S. (2011) *Assessing Learning in the Primary Classroom*. Abingdon and New York: Routledge. This book attends to assessment and record keeping across the primary curriculum. Sections on assessment of language – oracy, reading and writing – are pertinent to the English lesson.

Jones, D. (2012) Speaking and listening in the primary classroom. In D. Jones and P. Hodson (eds) *Unlocking Speaking and Listening*. Abingdon: Routledge. Chapter 2 gives advice about how teachers can embed planning, teaching and assessment of speaking and listening (oracy) in everyday classroom contexts.

National Assessment Agency (NAA) (2004) *Building a Picture of What Children Can Do*. London: NAA. See www.naa.org.uk for the full account, which looks at useful contexts for assessing and recording children's progress across the curriculum as well as in reading and writing.

Wyse, D., Jones, R., Bradford, H. and Wolpert, M.A. (2013) Multimodality and ICTs. In *Teaching English, Language and Literacy*. Abingdon and New York: Routledge, 289–95.

Index